professionalphotography **location**portraits

A **RotoVision Book** Published and Distributed by RotoVision SA, Rue Du Bugnon 7, CH-1299 Crans-Près-Céligny, Switzerland. RotoVision SA, Sales & Production Office, Sheridan House, 112/116A Western Road, Hove BN3 1DD, England. Telephone: +44 (0) 1273 72 72 68 Facsimile: +44 (0) 1273 72 72 69 ISBN 2-88046-514-1 **Book design** by Brenda Dermody & Austin Carey, Dublin. **Illustrations** by Austin Carey. **Cover Photograph** courtesy of Dennis Cox. **Production & separations** in Singapore by ProVision Pte. Ltd. Telephone: +65 334 7720 Facsimile: +65 334 7721

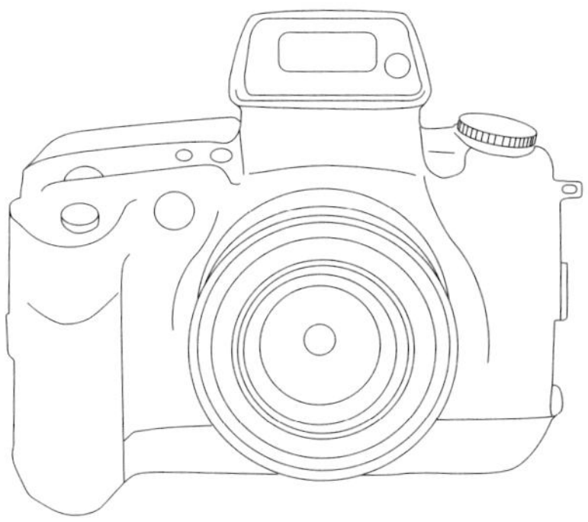

professionalphotography locationportraits cathyjoseph

RotoVision

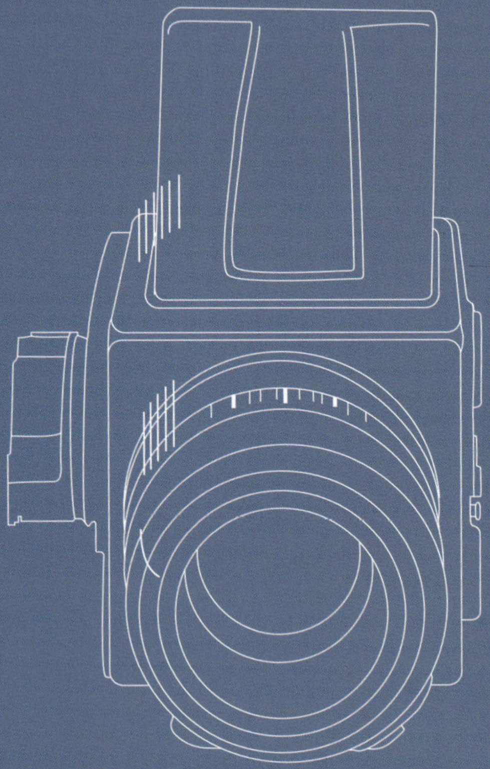

contents

introduction & gallery

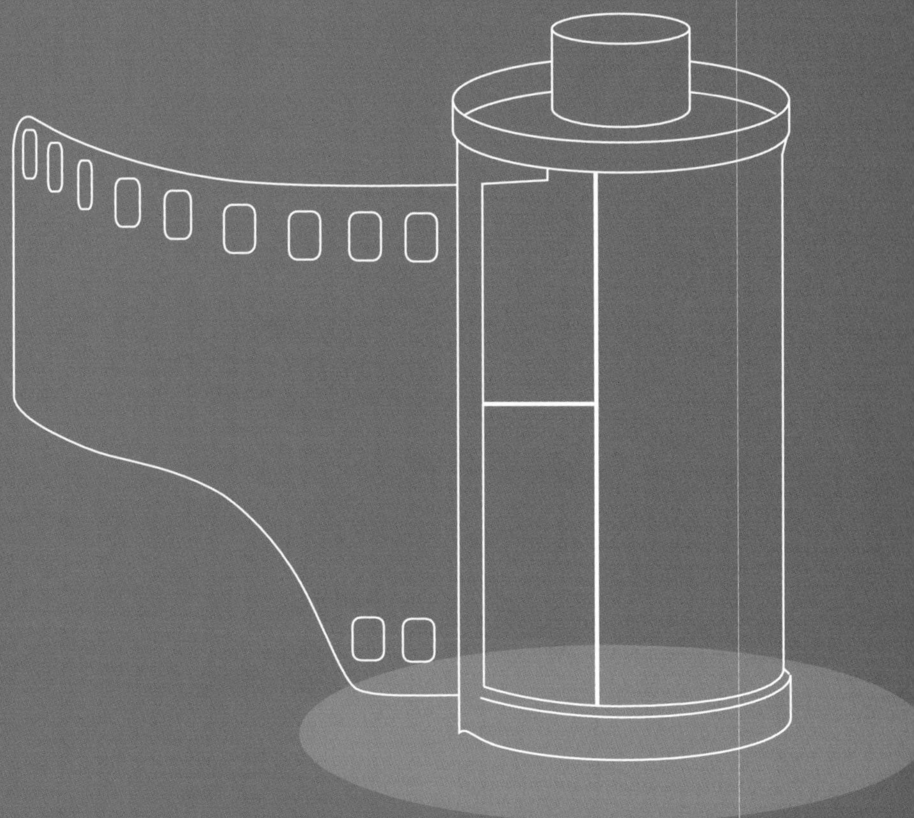

In advertising, fashion and editorial photography, the trend in the last few years has been to get out of the studio and into real life settings. The loss of complete control over lighting is amply made up for by the more natural, reportage feel of the images.
The success of an outdoor location shoot may, to some extent, be at the whim of the weather, but forward planning can minimise this – forecasts offer no guarantees but can at least increase your chances of a dry day.
In fact, advance preparation in all areas will pay dividends, from researching suitable locations, noting the direction and quality of the light at certain times of day and considering additional props that may be needed.

Location photographers also need the ability to think on their feet. If, for example, you're taking a portrait of a company executive in an office environment, you will need to take a creative approach to the lighting, pose and props to make up for, what may be, an uninspiring setting. You'll also need to work quickly because your time will often be limited by the client's schedule.

Travel photography very often involves portraits of local people within the landscape or in their urban environment. The possibilities of capturing different characters and cultures are virtually limitless and there is a broad range of commercial possibilities for successful images.

This book brings together fine examples of the many different aspects of location portraiture. They serve to illustrate the variety of styles and techniques that can be used in this exciting and accessible area of photography.

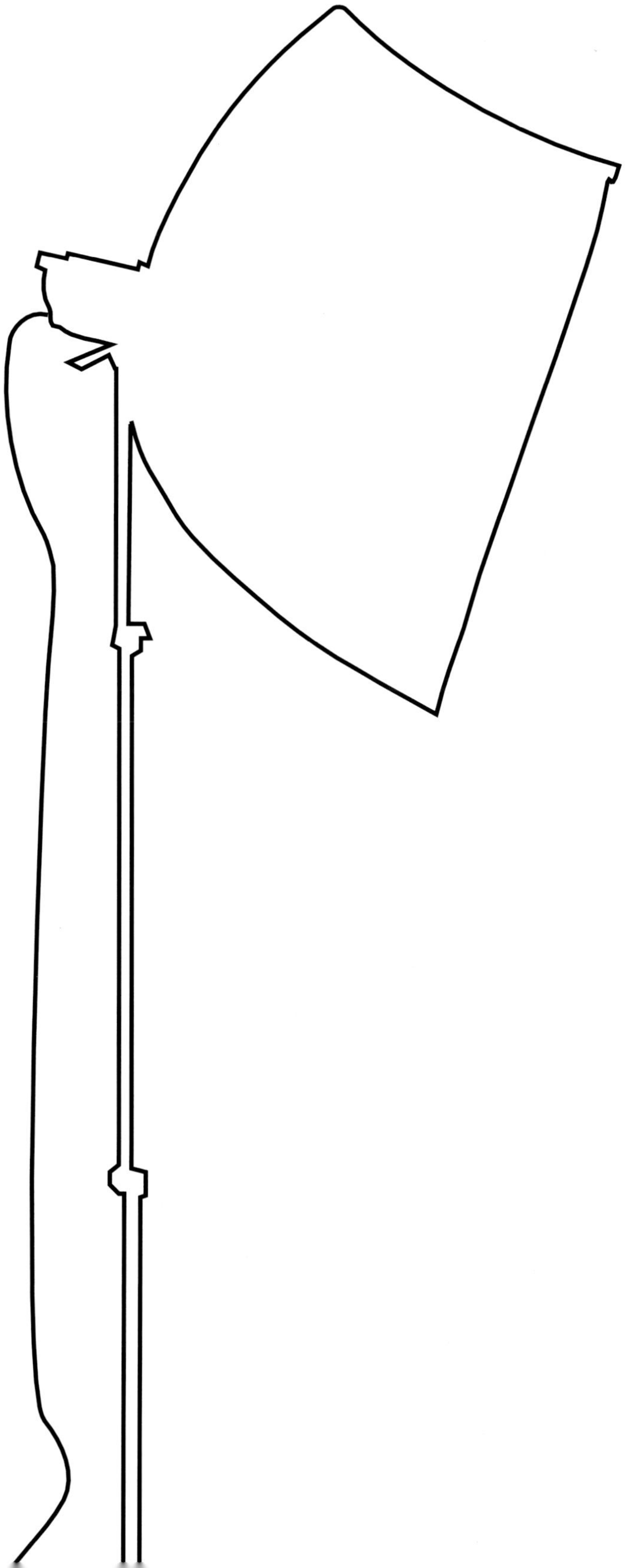

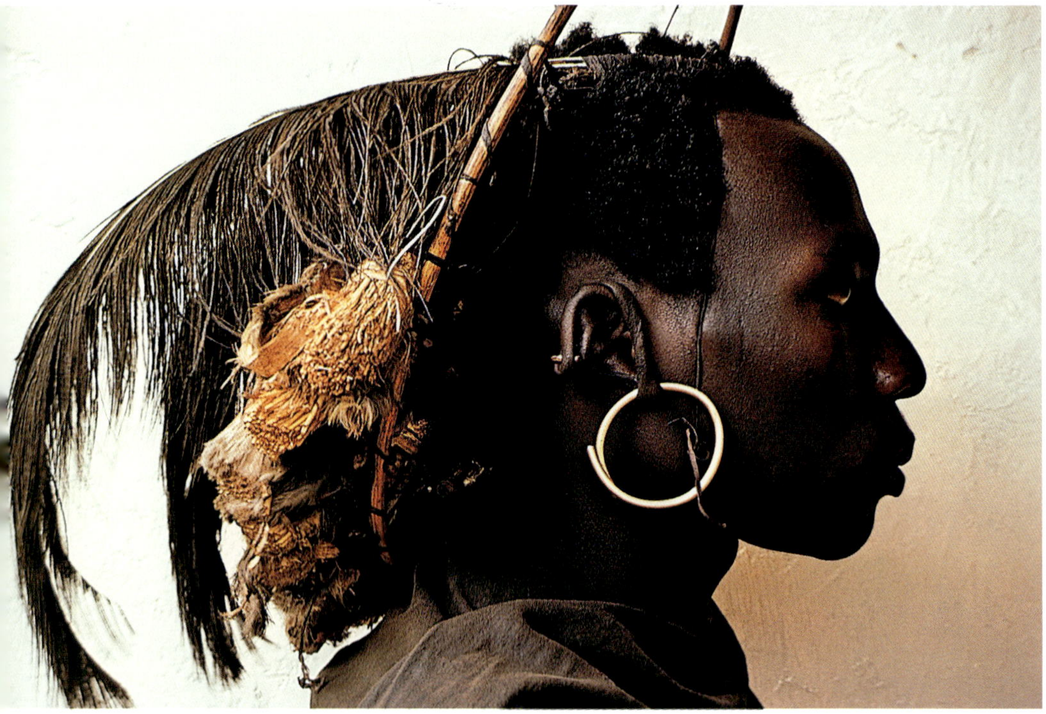

Pete Turner's striking images are called Electric Earring (above) and Pineapple Can Earring (right). Taken in 1970 in the porch of a hotel in Kenya, they show the custom of the Masai people to stretch their ears with all sorts of objects. For more portraits which show cultural differences, turn to page 88.

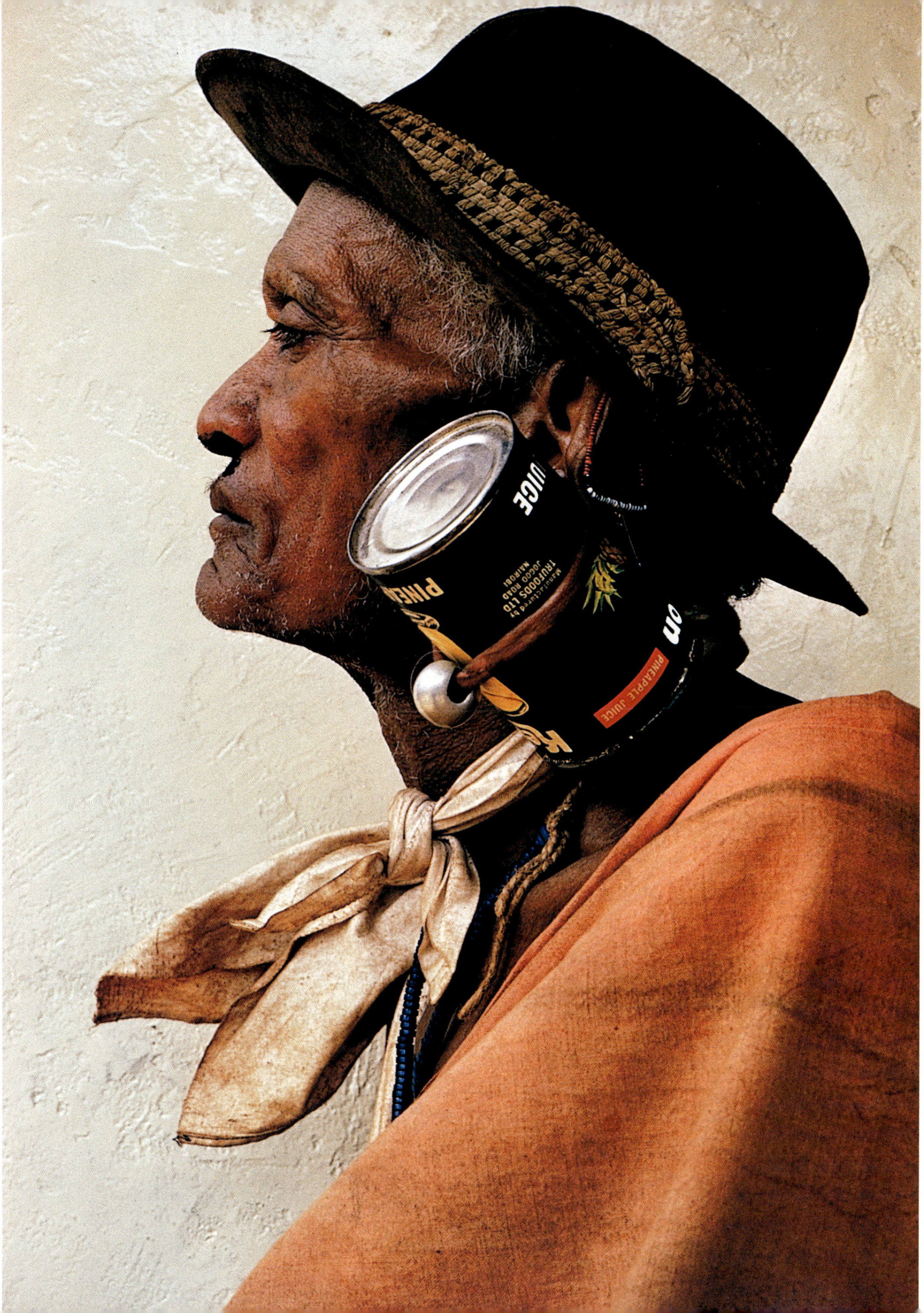
PINEAPPLE JUICE

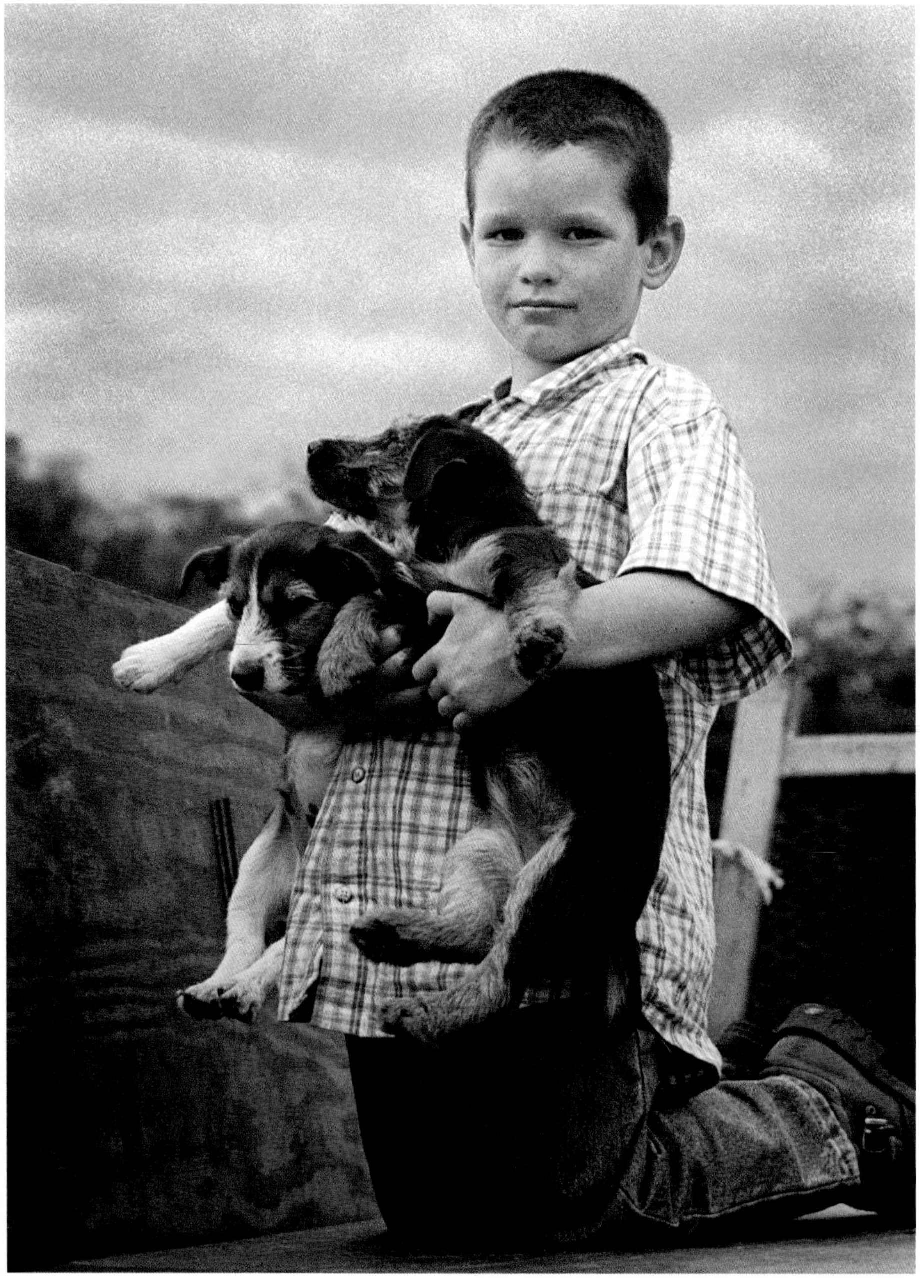

Philip Sprague's portrait of a gypsy boy was taken at a festival in Staffordshire. See chapter 5 for more examples of photo-journalism.

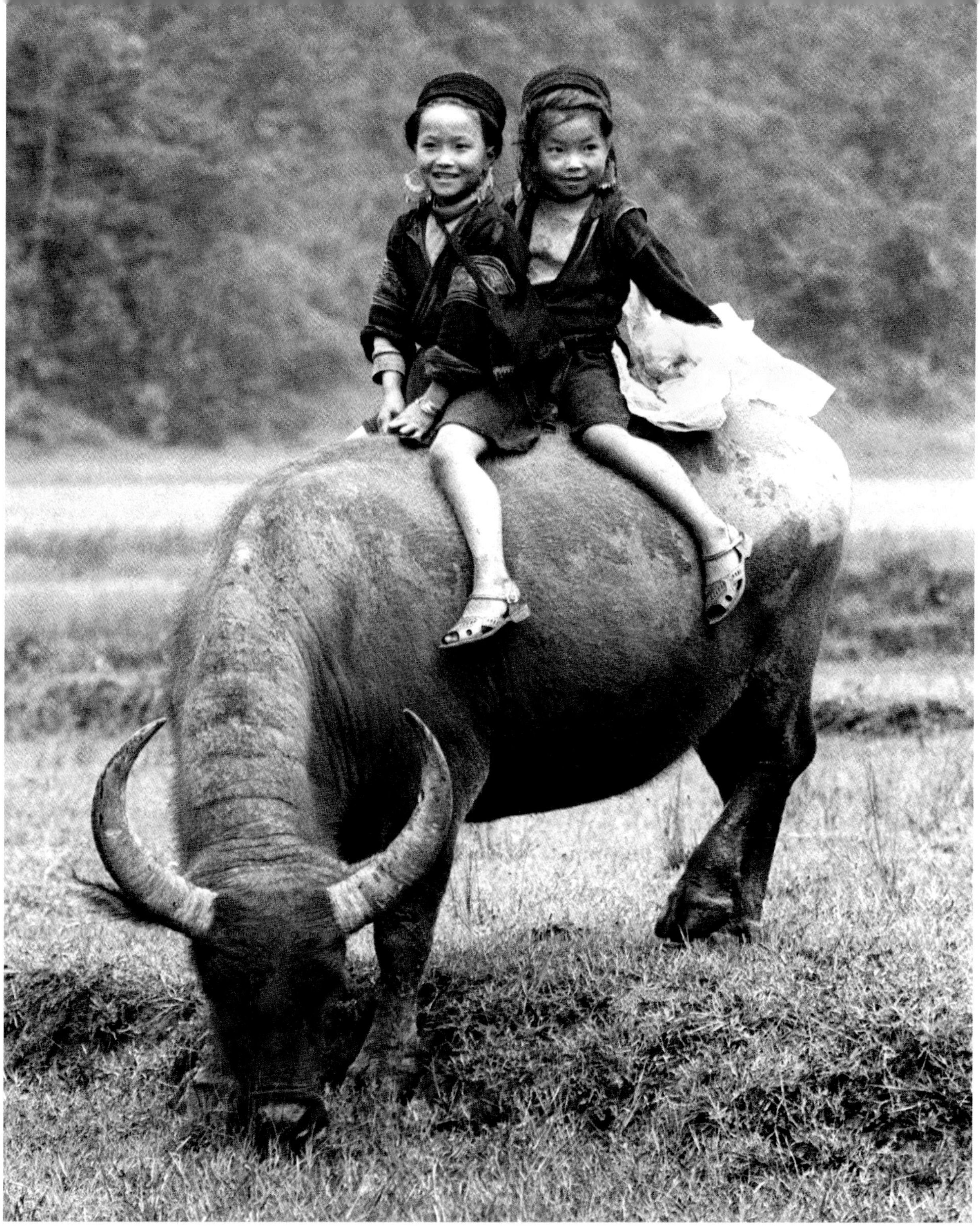

In a remote village of North Vietnam, Philip Sprague was amazed to see these girls riding a buffalo. Turn to page 108 for more black and white travel portraits.

A moving and eye-catching portrait of a Somalian child by Angelo Cavalli. See page 100 for more close-up portraits.

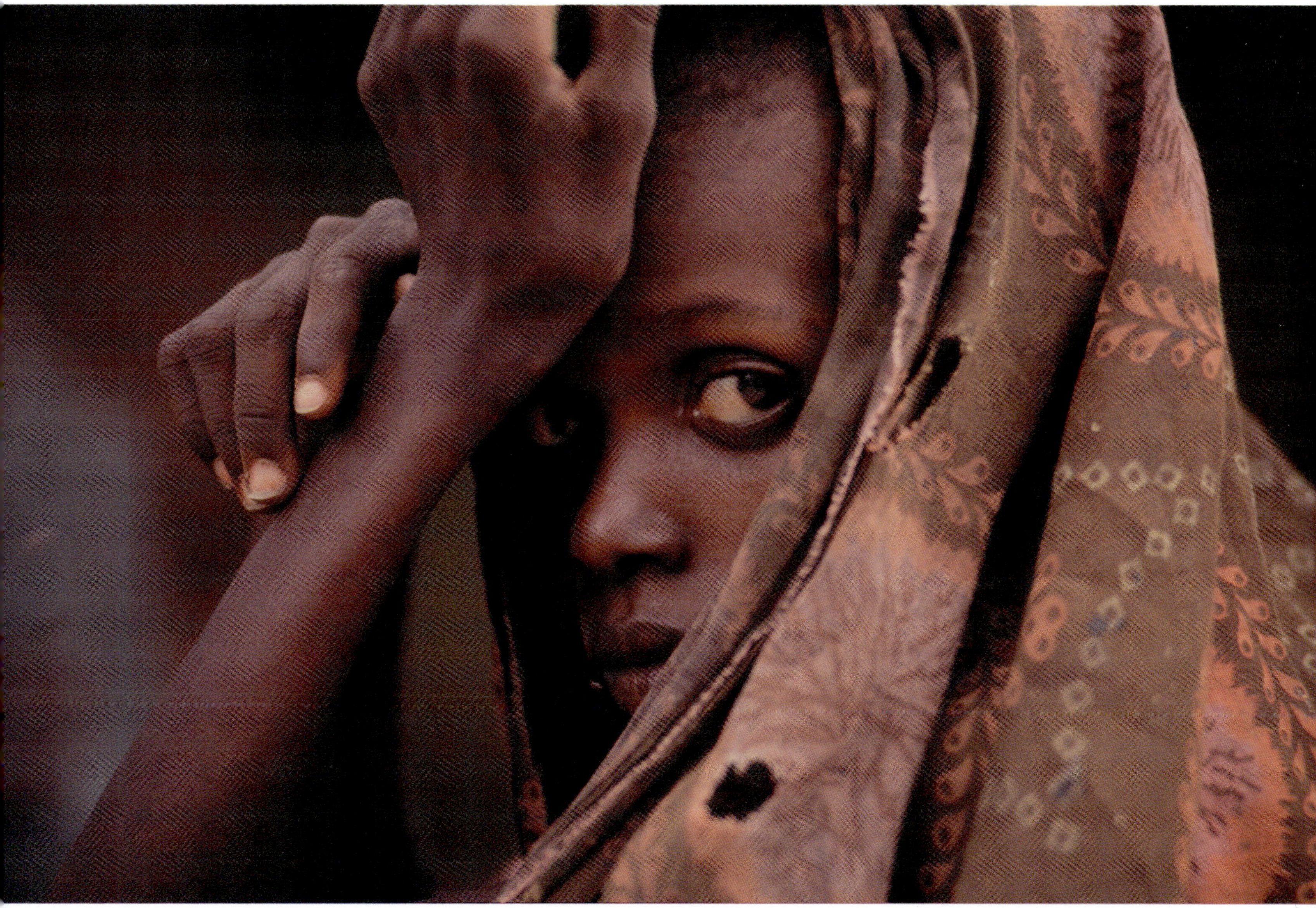

1

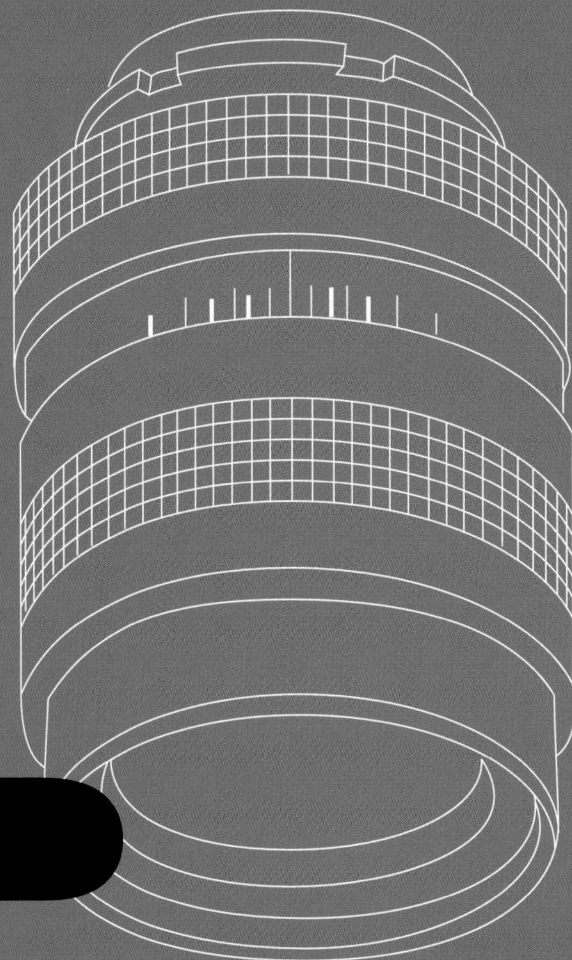

going on location

Unlike studio portraiture where you have all your equipment, props and backgrounds readily to hand, location work requires you to take it all with you – or make the most of the situation as you find it. Getting the best out of any photographic trip or outdoor shoot requires careful planning. Check all of your equipment before you go and make sure you have spare batteries, a second camera body, tripod, adequate lenses and, above all, more film than you think you may need. You may feel more like a cart-horse than a photographer, but it's far better to put up with the extra weight than miss a crucial opportunity because you were ill prepared.

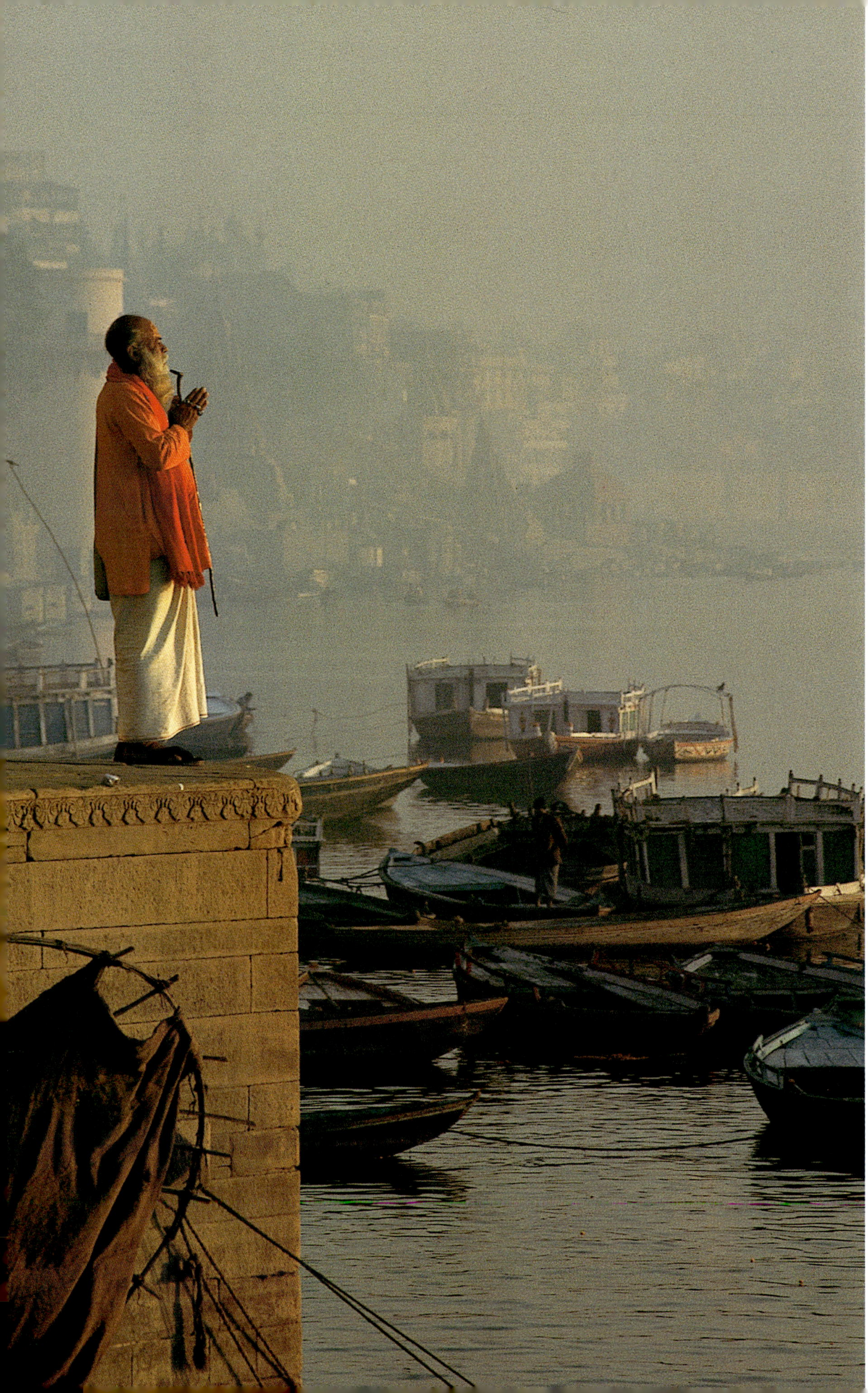

Composition
Jon Hicks was walking along by the river Ganges in Varanasi, India, when he spotted this man standing on a ghat. He wanted to show the peaceful solitude of the subject in his environment without disturbing him and so took the shot from a distance. The hazy background worked to his advantage allowing the man to stand out – particularly as he was clothed in a red shirt. The wheel-like structure below the ghat adds interest to this area while the boats fill the rest of the bottom half of the frame.

Technique
Jon used a polarising filter to cut down on some of the early morning haze to allow the colour to come through. A tripod helped him to compose the picture accurately and eliminated the possibility of camera shake.

Lighting
A 5am start reaped benefits for this and other shots by the Ganges. Early morning is when most people come to bathe in the river and the magical, warm light just after the sun comes up is the best time to capture atmospheric portraits there.

Technical details
Nikon FA camera with 70–210mm lens. Film was Fujichrome 100 with an exposure of 1/125sec at f/5.6.

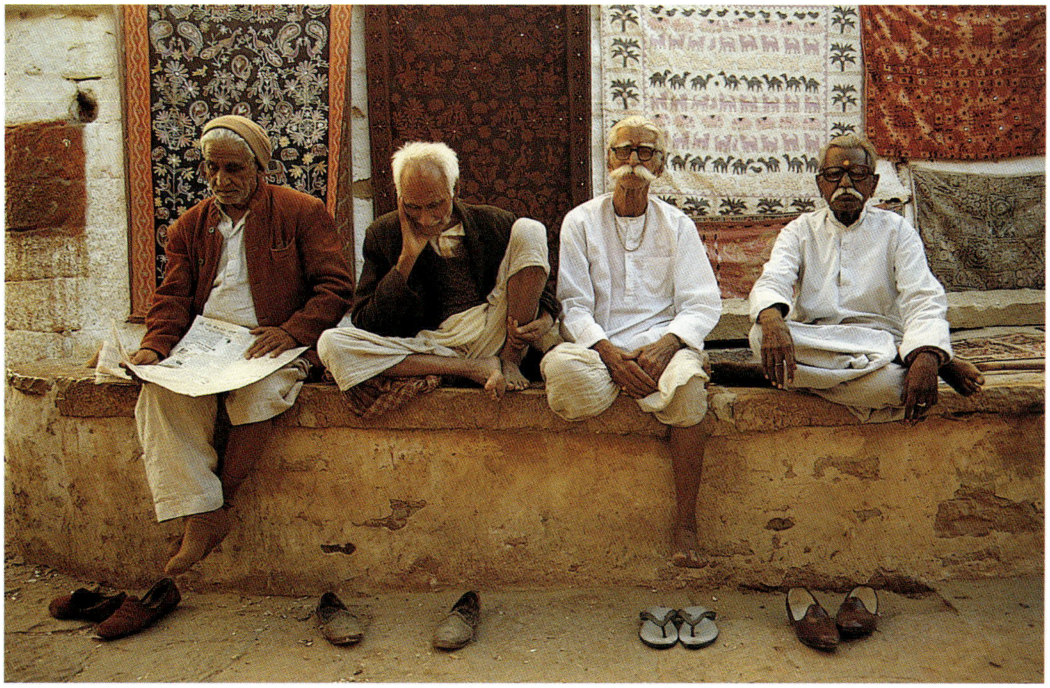

This is the kind of image you're likely to see in a travel brochure, a row of men sitting in their accustomed place in Jaisalmer, Rajasthan unperturbed at being photographed. The subjects, echoed by the row of wall hangings and their shoes lined up on the ground, make a great composition.

Technical details
Nikon FA camera with 35mm lens. Film was Fujichrome 100 with an exposure of 1/125sec at f/5.6.

'I always do as much research about a place as possible before I go, using reliable guide books to hotels and hostels. You don't want to start looking for places when you arrive. I'm never afraid to return to the same locations. I often find I get better results the second time because I know exactly what I'm looking for – although luck always plays a part.'
Jon Hicks

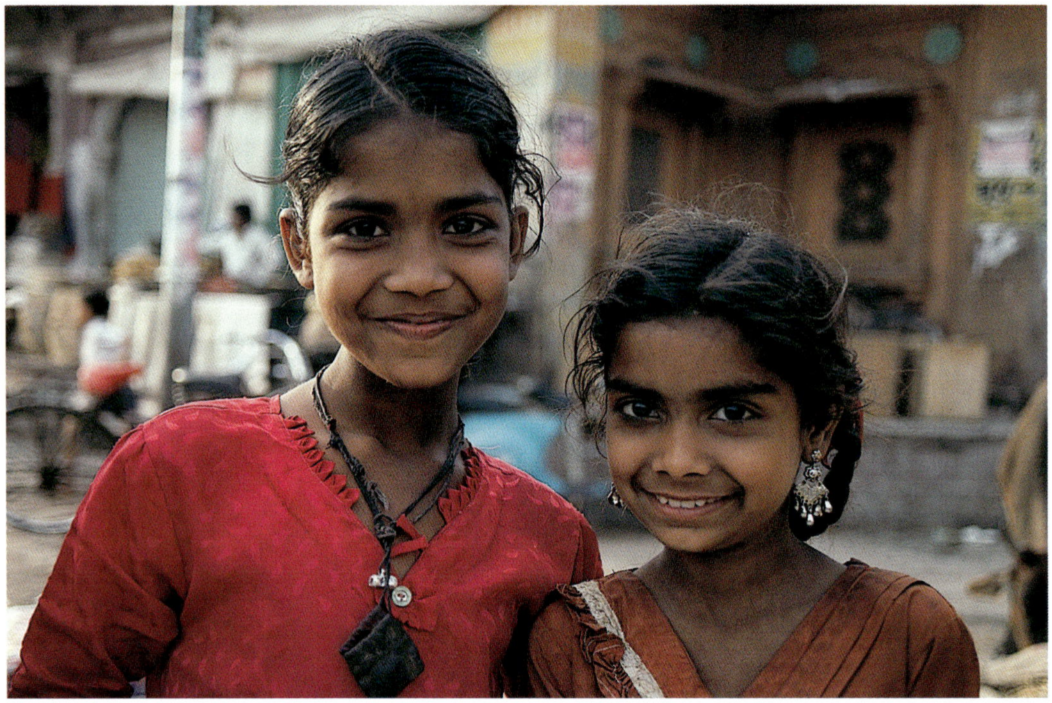

These pretty young girls were delighted to pose for pictures in the marketplace of Jhodpur, Rajasthan, and Jon Hicks took several shots, varying his composition. The soft overcast light is flattering to the girls and brings out the colours and textures in the image.

Technical details
Nikon FA camera with 35mm lens. Film was Kodachrome 64 with an exposure of 1/125sec at f/5.6.

‘I always carry two camera bodies, three lenses, a tripod and selection of filters in a photographic rucksack. I keep film in a separate bag and always ask for used film to be checked by hand at airports, rather than pass through an X-ray. A lot of people have film and equipment stolen while travelling. If I’m on a train, I’ll chain the bag to the luggage rack.’

Jon Hicks

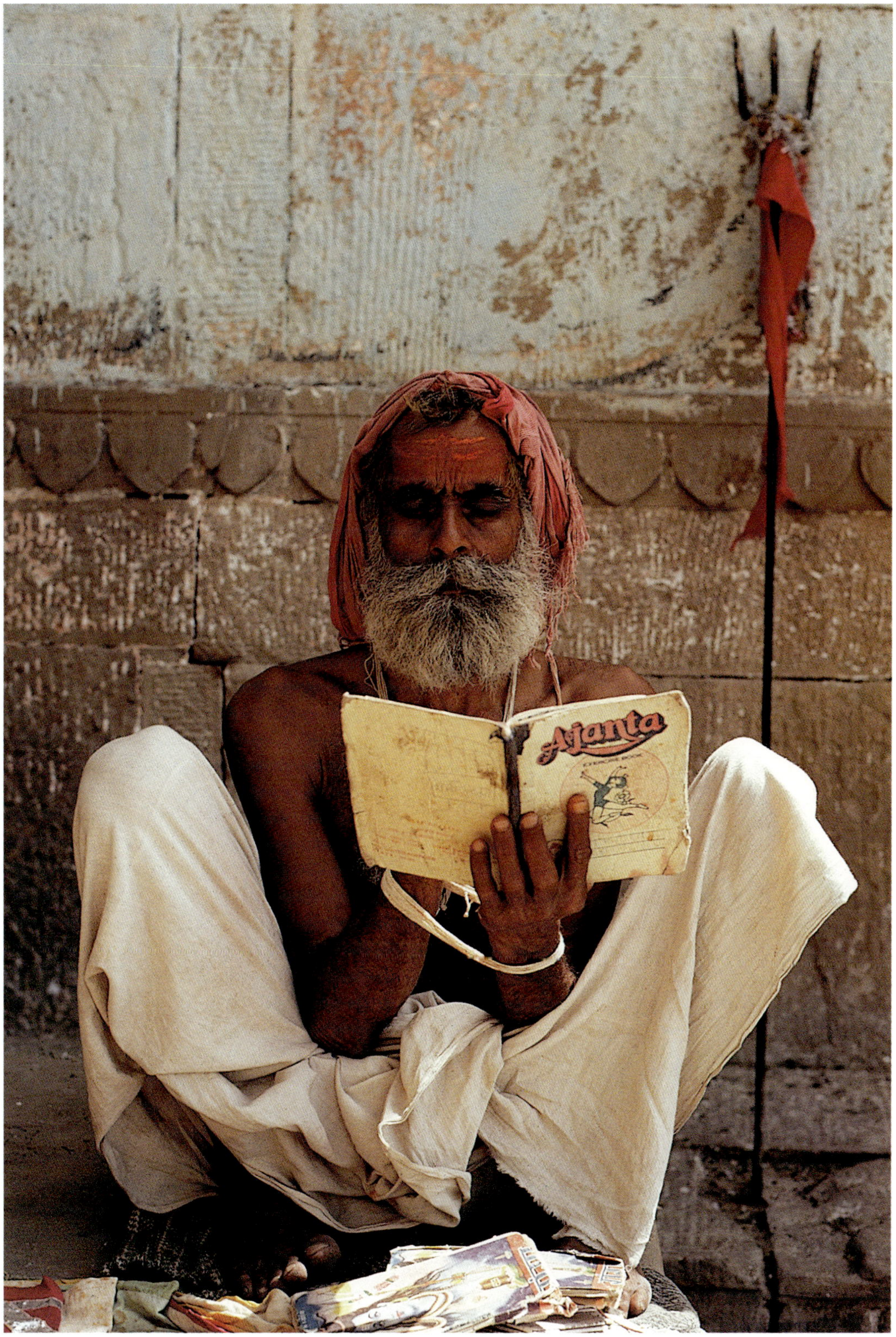

Composition

This seated holy man in Varanasi was almost crying out to have his picture taken, although in this case not literally. 'He wasn't bothered about me at all, in fact he totally ignored me,' says Jon Hicks. He opted for a fairly tight composition, leaving space for the trident, propped up against the beautifully textured wall.

Technique

Jon took this picture late in the day as he was wondering around the city, getting his bearings and looking for potential pictures. As well as early morning, this is his favourite time for photography because the light is softer and warmer than in the harsh heat of earlier in the day. He uses a tripod whenever possible, 'because I have shaky hands', and this can often attract attention in India. 'I've stopped the traffic before,' he says. 'I believe it's much better to be open about what you're doing and make friends with people than to snatch pictures. You have to accept people's interest in you and go along with it.'

Technical details

Nikon FA camera with 70–210mm lens. Film was Kodachrome 64 with an exposure of 1/125sec at f/5.6.

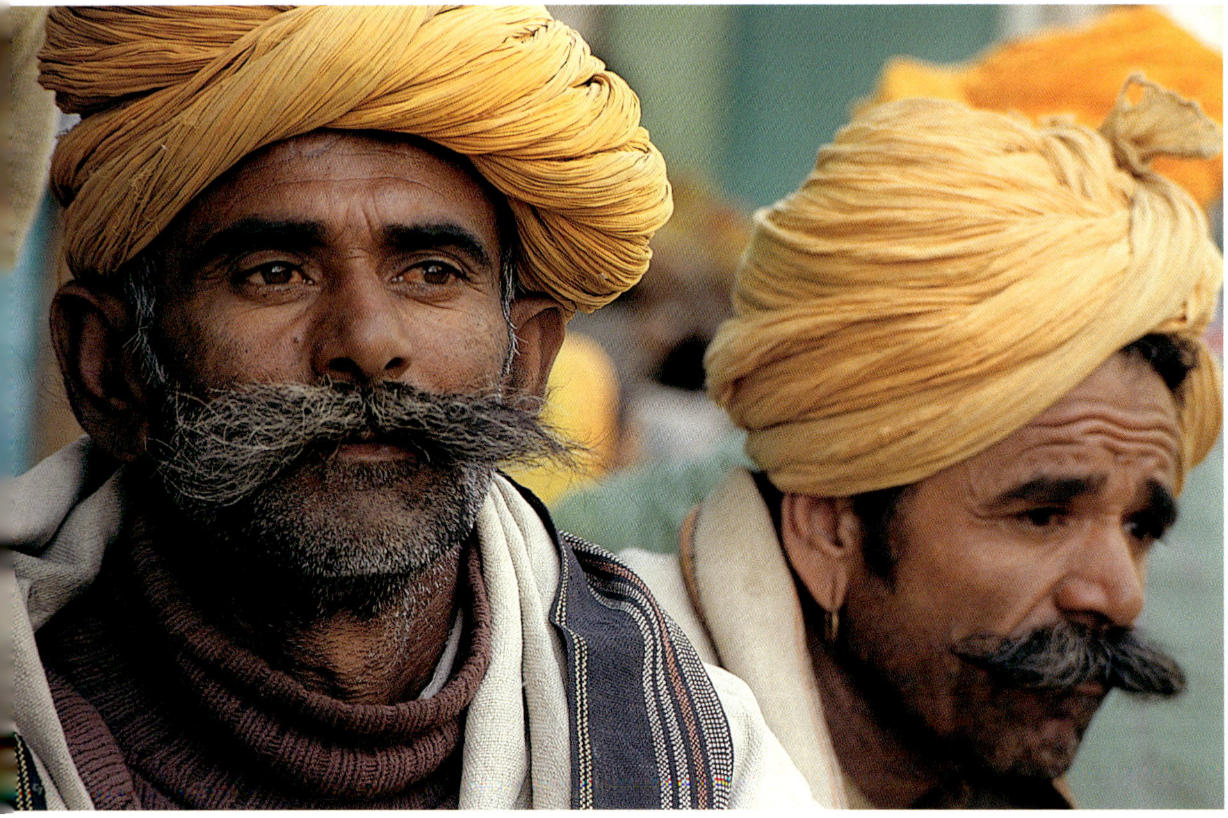

Composition

Jon Hicks likes using this technique of a close-up double portrait where the foreground figure is sharp and the second one, slightly further behind is just out of focus. 'It's easy to do in India because you find so many people sitting in rows,' he says. 'This was at a tea shop in Jaisalmer and I was sitting at an adjacent table. I like the orange turbans and the character in the faces of the men. India is a great place for faces.'

Technique

A telephoto lens is perfect for this technique because it has the effect of flattening perspective, making people or objects appear closer together than they really are. A wide aperture of around f/4 or f/5.6 provides the necessary narrow depth of field, so the background is out of focus.

Lighting

Jon avoids taking portraits in direct sun where high contrast and deep shadows can be difficult to deal with. People living in hot countries also tend to seek shade wherever possible, which makes candid portraits of people relaxing in cafés and on street corners perfectly possible.

Technical details

Nikon FA camera with 70–210mm lens. Film was Fujichrome 100 with an exposure of 1/125sec at f/5.6.

Technical details
Nikon FA camera with 70–210mm lens. Film was Fujichrome 100 with an exposure of 1/125sec at f/5.6.

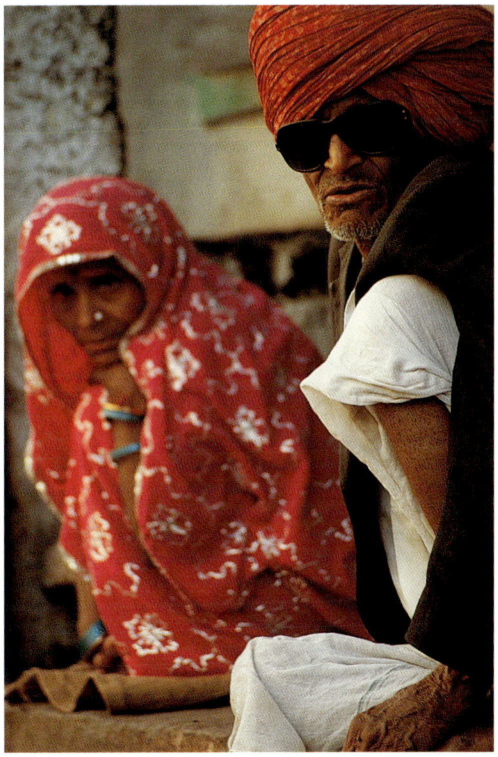

Another example of Jon's double portrait technique. He was attracted by the man wearing sunglasses here, and the colour of the woman's dress in the background. Again, he focused on the foreground figure, letting the wide aperture render the woman slightly blurred.

'When I arrive at a new location, I walk around first, checking the position of the sun and finding points of interest. I use the hottest part of the day to look for possible locations and then return early in the morning or late afternoon when the light is more suitable for pictures.'
Jon Hicks

2

Corporate brochures, in-house publications, business magazines and newspaper editorial – all these printed media regularly require portraits taken in the work environment. It's a broad and challenging area of photography. During the working day, people have little time to stop and pose for a portrait sitting and so speed and efficiency are essential. Boardrooms and offices do not always offer inspiring backdrops – it's up to you to find creative solutions. Do as much research in advance as possible to ensure you have the correct lighting and equipment on hand which will enable you to maximise the time you have with the subject.

at work

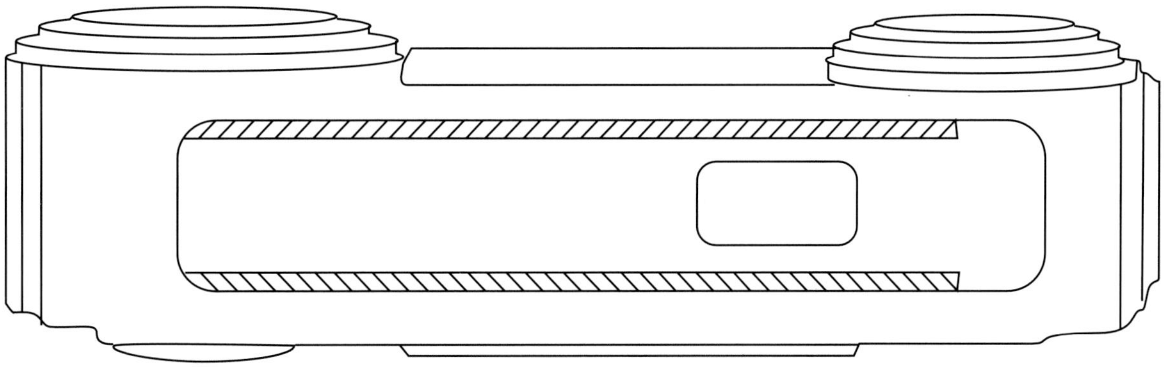

Composition
Dennis Cox took this for the brochure of an office design company. The aim was to show the office environment, as well as members of staff working within it looking as natural as possible. It was essential to plan the shot carefully, however, to ensure correct lighting and prevent the composition becoming haphazard and messy. Dennis arranged the two main figures centrally, using the paperwork on the table as a point of interest between them and also to put across the corporate message. Three other subjects were asked to pose in the background, neatly filling these areas and giving the viewer the impression of a busy working environment. It was important to ensure there was adequate interest in the image without attempting to include too much.

Technique
With a 35mm camera, Dennis used a 24–35mm zoom, set at its shortest focal length to include a wide angle of view in the frame. A small aperture of f/11 ensured maximum depth of field for all the subjects from foreground to background. Non-professional models who are not used to posing may feel and look awkward with a camera pointing at them. Take your time to put them at their ease by talking to them, taking several shots if necessary before they feel more comfortable.

Lighting
'In order to cover a fairly large area with the minimum of lighting equipment, I lit each area in the shot selectively,' says Dennis. 'The foreground and background subjects were each lit with a Lumedyne 400 W flash in small Chimera (rectangular diffusion) light boxes.'

'The art directors for corporate publications tend to be fairly conservative and will often be on the shoot to supervise.'
Dennis Cox

Technical details
Minolta X-700 camera with 24–35mm lens. Film was Kodachrome 64 with an exposure of f/11.

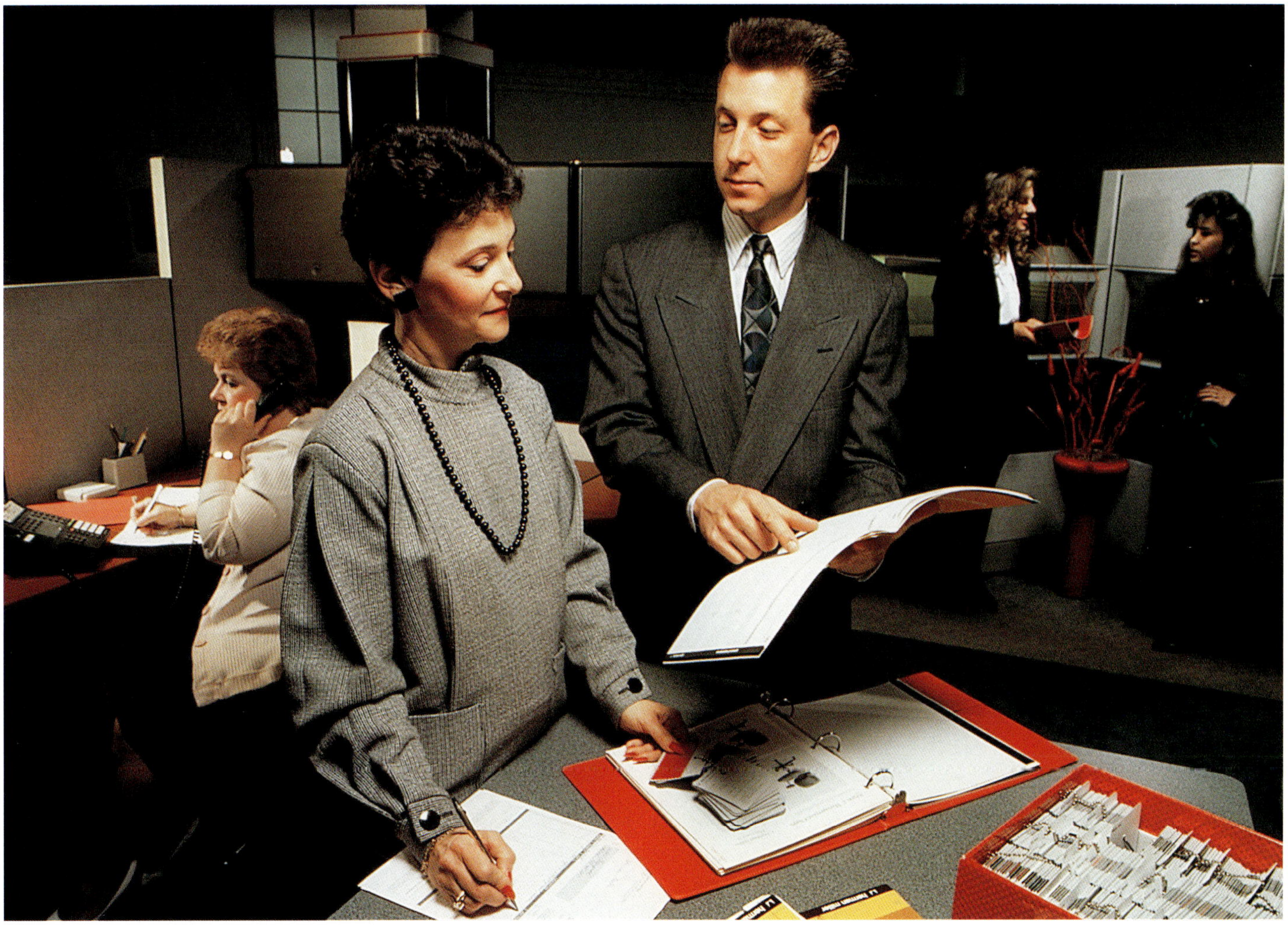

Technical details
Bronica ETRS camera with 75mm lens. Film was Fujifilm Neopan 400 with an exposure of 1/15sec at f/5.6.

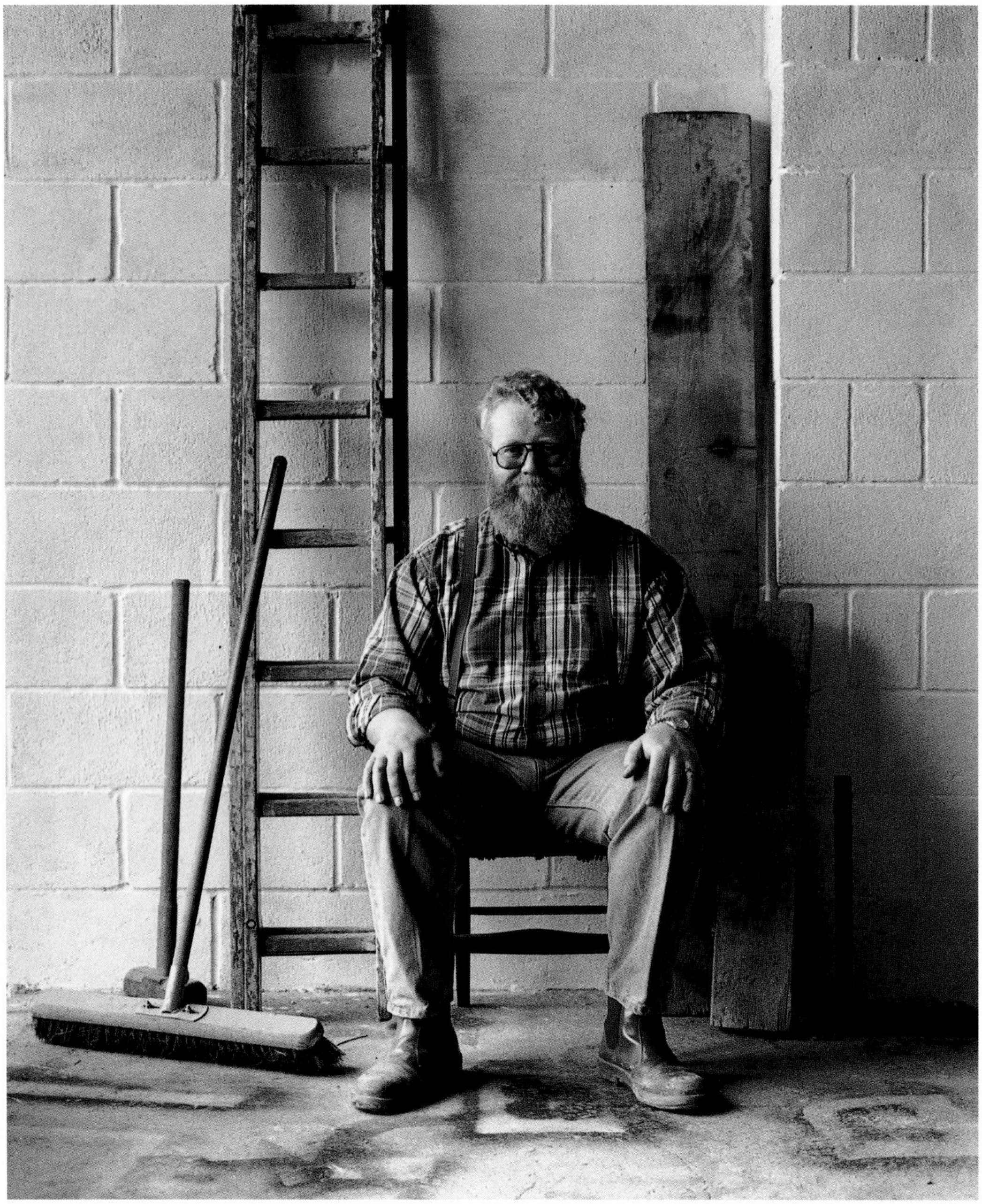

Peter Penfold is an engineer who had just built this brick wall as part of a conversion of a barn into a workshop and gallery for his artist wife. Ronnie Bennett included some props in the composition which give some clues about the subject and his work and also help the formal structure of the picture. She used available window light with a reflector on the right, and placed the camera on a tripod for a long exposure.

Composition

Taken for Dennis Cox's book of photographs of Michigan, USA, this is both a character portrait of the sales assistant in Lexington General Store, and a colourful shot of the unusual and old-fashioned candy-filled environment. Dennis has kept the composition tight to fill the frame with the sweets, including the jar of red candy and the lollipops on the counter to pick up the red colour of the apron. The woman's pose gives her something natural to do with her hands, and also places her clearly in the context of her job.

Technique

Some people will react more kindly than others to being photographed in their workplace and it helps if you can show them previous examples of your work by way of introducing yourself and explaining what you have in mind. Remember that they may be very busy, so you should have a clear idea of the picture you are after to minimise the time you take setting it up and posing the subject.

Lighting

Dennis wanted to bring out the maximum colour saturation here and so he used two 400 W Lumedyne flash units. One was placed on the right in a small light box and the other on the left was bounced from a silver umbrella. Both light box and umbrella had the effect of diffusing and softening the flash for more natural results. Because of all the glass surfaces, the lights were angled to keep reflections to a minimum.

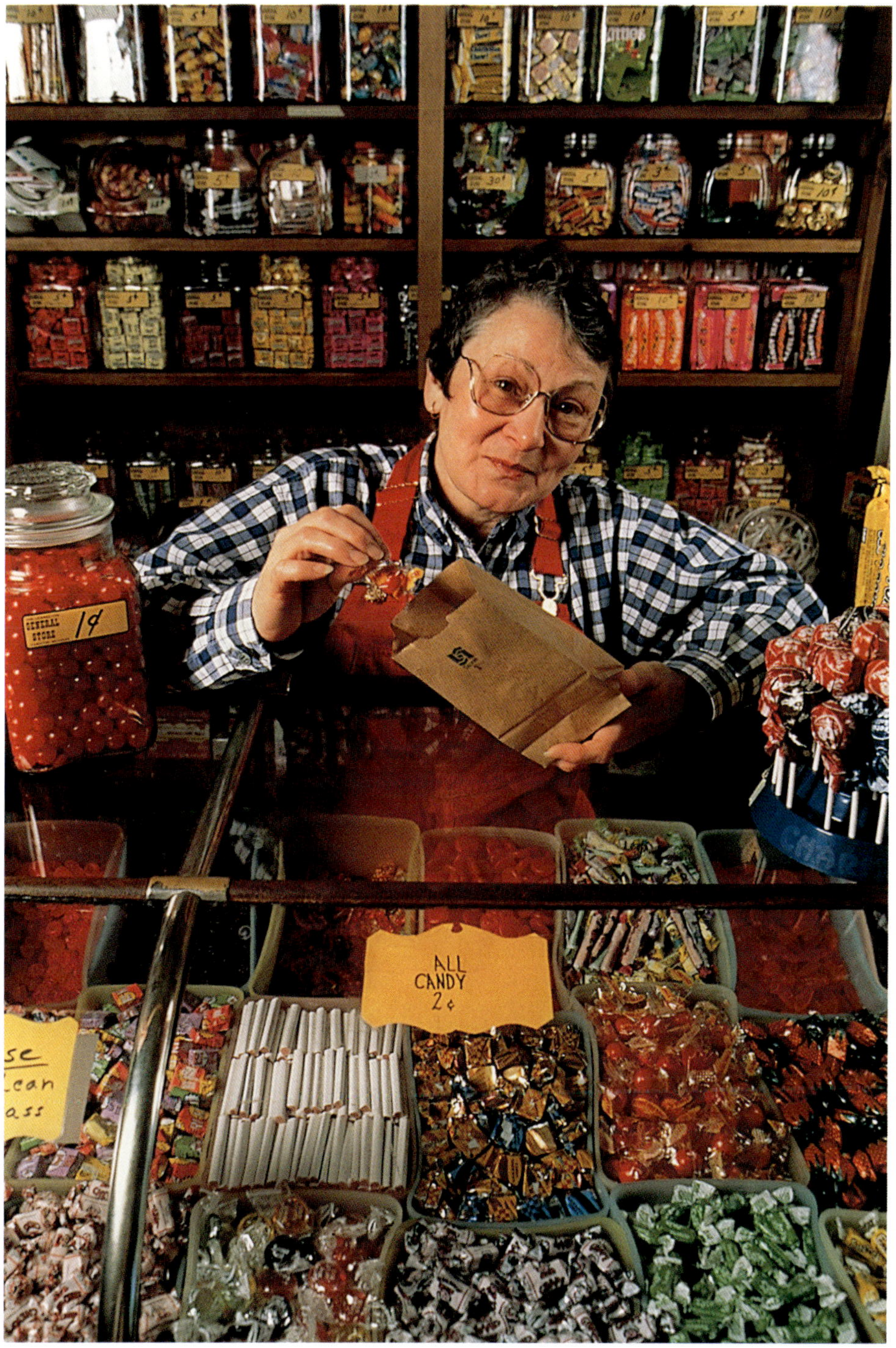

Technical details

Minolta X-700 with 24–35mm lens. Film was Kodachrome 64 and exposures were bracketed.

'For business magazines, the photo editor will usually describe the type of shot or theme they're looking for. The best situation is when they leave it to me to come up with something visually exciting.'

Dennis Cox

For this shot for the Unisys Corporation's magazine, Dennis Cox placed the etch-a-sketches – both traditional and electronic types – in rows on a table in the boardroom. The subject was seated on a stepladder so he could lean over the table. The main light for him was a 400 W Lumedyne in a halo umbrella diffuser to the right. Another Lumedyne flash head with a snoot attached was filtered through a gold gel and placed just in front of the subject to light the circuit panel. The red and blue accent lights were two Vivitar 283 slaved flash units with gels, placed to skim the subject's back.

Technical details

Minolta X-700 camera with 24–35mm lens. Film was Kodachrome 64 with bracketed exposures.

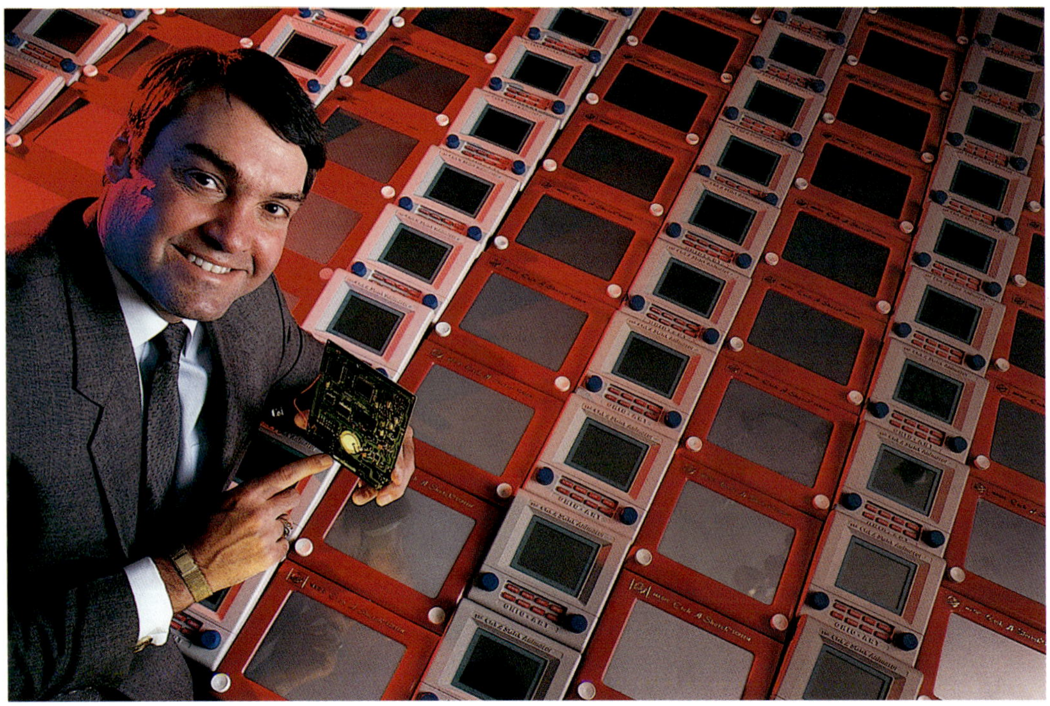

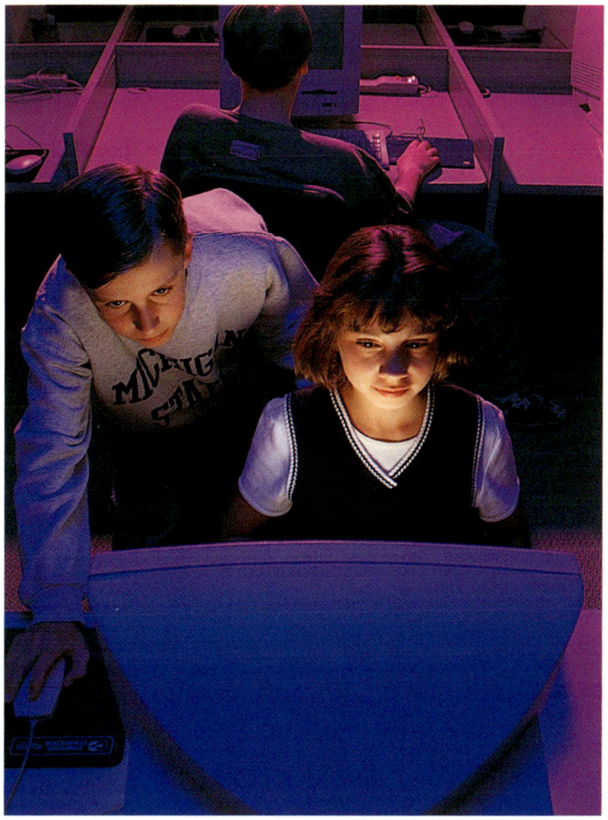

Composition

Taken for a computer magazine, this shows students in the school computer lab. Dennis wanted to show the look of concentration on the young people's faces and so chose a higher viewpoint from behind the monitor. The pose of the boy, leaning down to control the mouse, prevents the shot looking too static and is more interesting than if he had been seated next to the girl. The boy in the background, seen from the back, doesn't detract from the main subject and gives the impression that this is a real computer room and not simply a stage set.

Mood

The lighting provides a dramatic sense of atmosphere here, transforming the mundane atmosphere of a computer room. The light on the children's faces contrasts with the subdued blue and magenta tones and gives the viewer the feeling that they are entering a new and exciting world of technology.

Technique

An 800 W Balcar P4 flash head with a blue gel was placed directly above the camera in a small Chimera lightbox. Another 800 W Balcar head, this time with a magenta gel, was bounced from a silver umbrella directly behind the computer in the background (the light stand is hidden by the computer). The light on the young subjects' faces is from a slaved Vivitar 283 flash with a dome diffuser placed at the base of the computer screen. The shot was metered using a Minolta Flash Meter 111.

Technical details

Minolta X-700 camera with 24–35mm lens. Film was Kodak Ektachrome 100S with bracketed exposure.

Composition
'The first shots I took of Jerome York for Business Week magazine were all full length. Then I moved closer, or used the zoom lens, to take three-quarter length and head shots,' says Dennis Cox. 'I like the symmetry of the painting in the background and the symmetry of the subject's braces, so I set up the lighting symmetrically as well. Often corporate offices are short on visually appealing backgrounds, so I look for any creative technique I can to make an interesting portrait.'

Technique
When a portrait sitting is arranged with a top level businessman, the photographer's time is often limited. Dennis is accustomed to this and has developed a technique for working quickly. 'I can usually work out what will make the best possible shot and make sure I get it nailed down straight away,' he says. 'If I have more time, I can try out different variations or set-ups to give the editor more choices.'

Lighting
The picture was lit with two 400 W Lumedyne flash units, equidistant on each side, through Halo light diffusing umbrellas. These are two umbrellas (one black and one of opaque diffusion material) facing each other on one stem and sealed together. The light (Lumedyne head which is one of the few heads small enough to fit inside the contraption) is bounced off the inside of the black umbrella's reflective silver surface and then through the diffusion side. It gives the best qualities of both types of umbrellas and is great for spreading light about 180 degrees inside a room.

Technical details
Minolta X-700 camera with 50–135mm lens. Film was Kodak Ektachrome Pro Plus ISO 100.

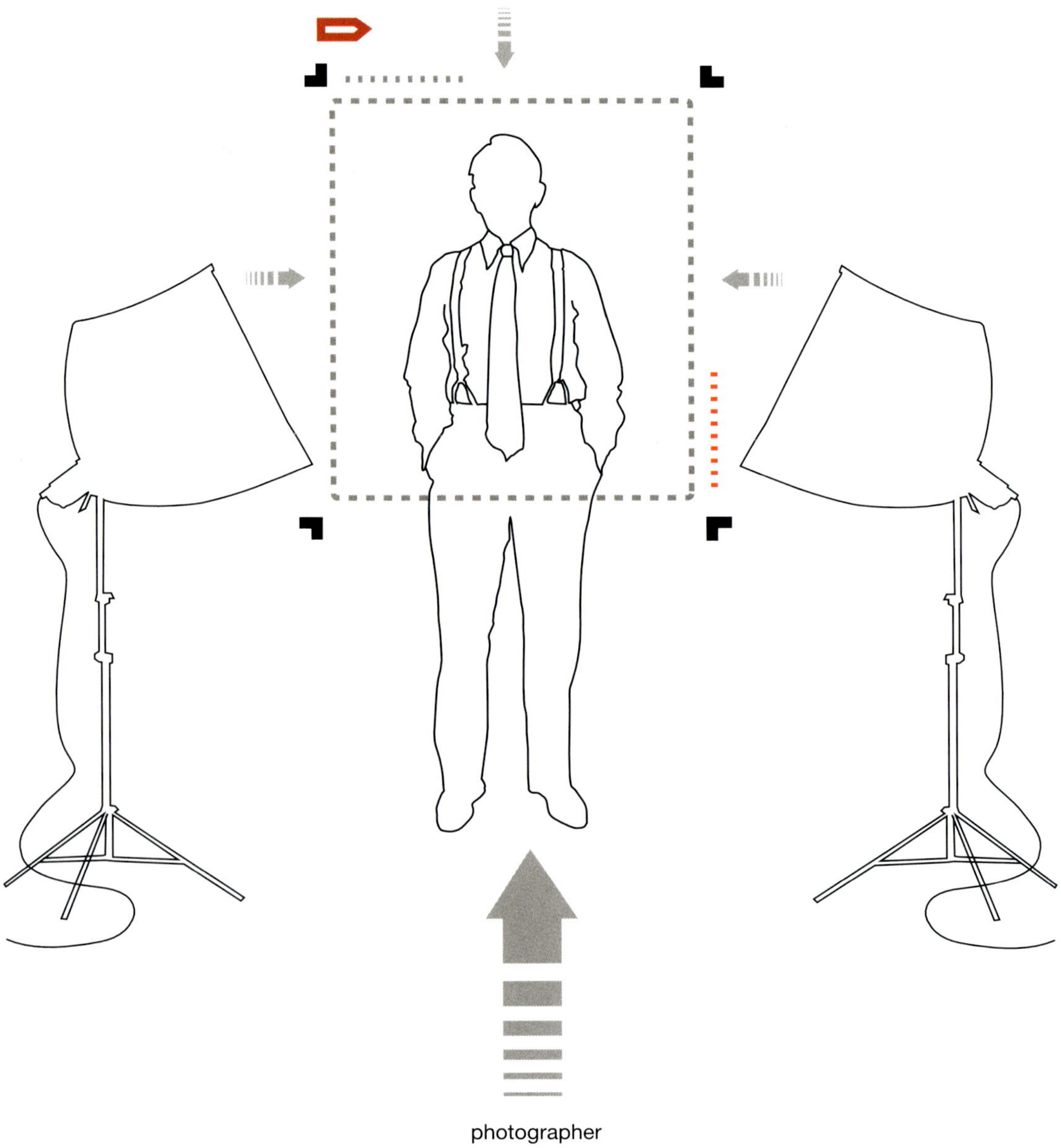

'When I call to schedule the shoot, I try to get an idea of what backgrounds and props may be available. If it's the usual boring office setting, I know I'll have to improvise when I get there.'

Dennis Cox

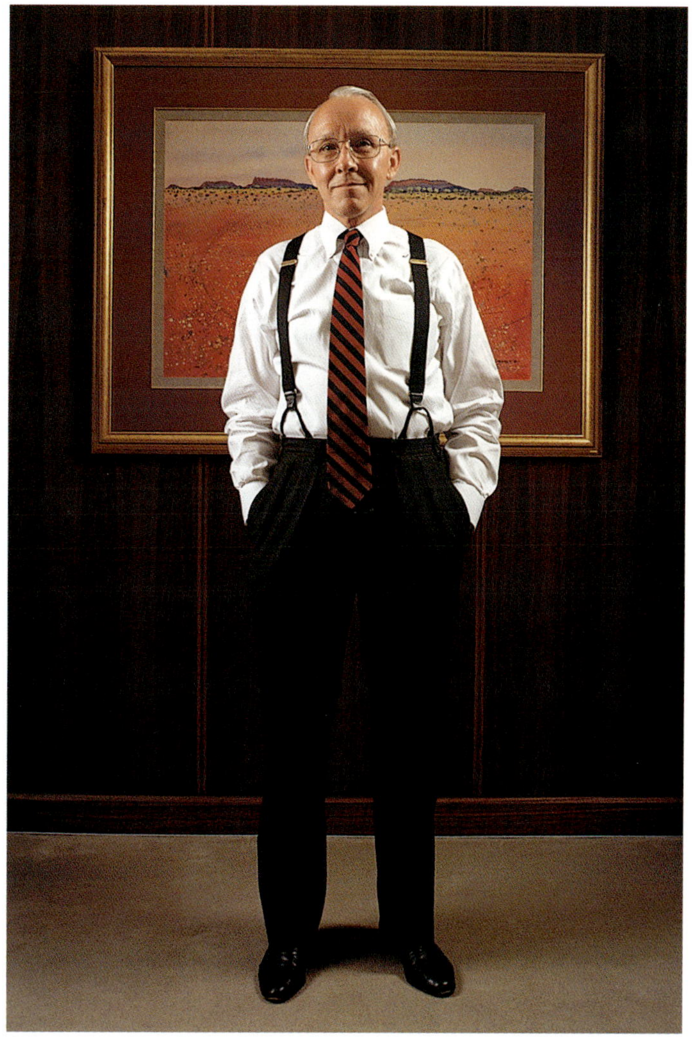

'Carlo is one of my favourite portrait subjects. He's as close as I will come to meeting Rembrandt – he's even Italian.'

Gary Auerbach

Composition

Gary Auerbach was commissioned by a magazine to take this portrait of Carlo Giantomassi, head conservationist at the Vatican. At the time he was leading a restoration project in Tucson, Arizona, at the 18th-century church, Mission san Xavier del Bac. Gary has shown his subject in the context of his work, holding a paintbrush and palette, and with the wall fresco he is restoring clearly visible on the left side of the picture. The use of a large format view camera brings a formal discipline to Gary's work which is suited to the pose here. The direct eye-contact with the subject leaves a strong impression on the viewer.

Technique

Taken from 30 feet high in the scaffolding at the top of one of the church domes, Gary had to haul his equipment up by rope. He had only 30 minutes to work with Carlo and in this time used just two sheets of film with the 8x10 view camera. The print is a platinotype using hand-coated platinum palladium metals.

Lighting

Gary made use of the various lights that the conservationists were using for their work. These were special tungsten lights with no hot spots, which proved ideal for photography. He first lit the wall to the right of the subject and then Carlo himself.

Technical details

Wisner 8x10in camera with 250mm wide field lens. Film was Kodak Tri-X with an exposure of 1/10sec at f/9.

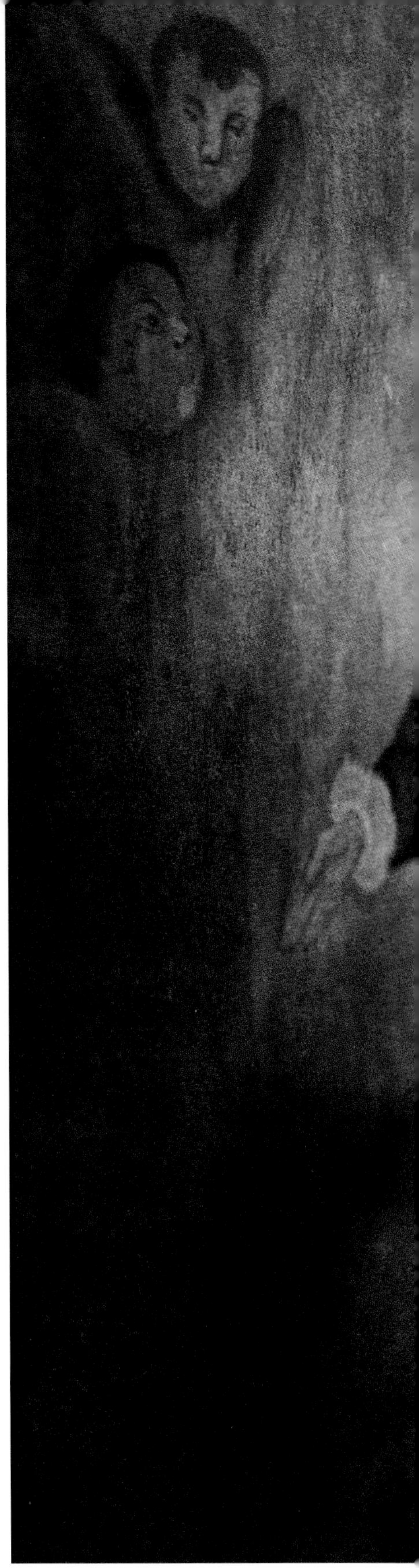

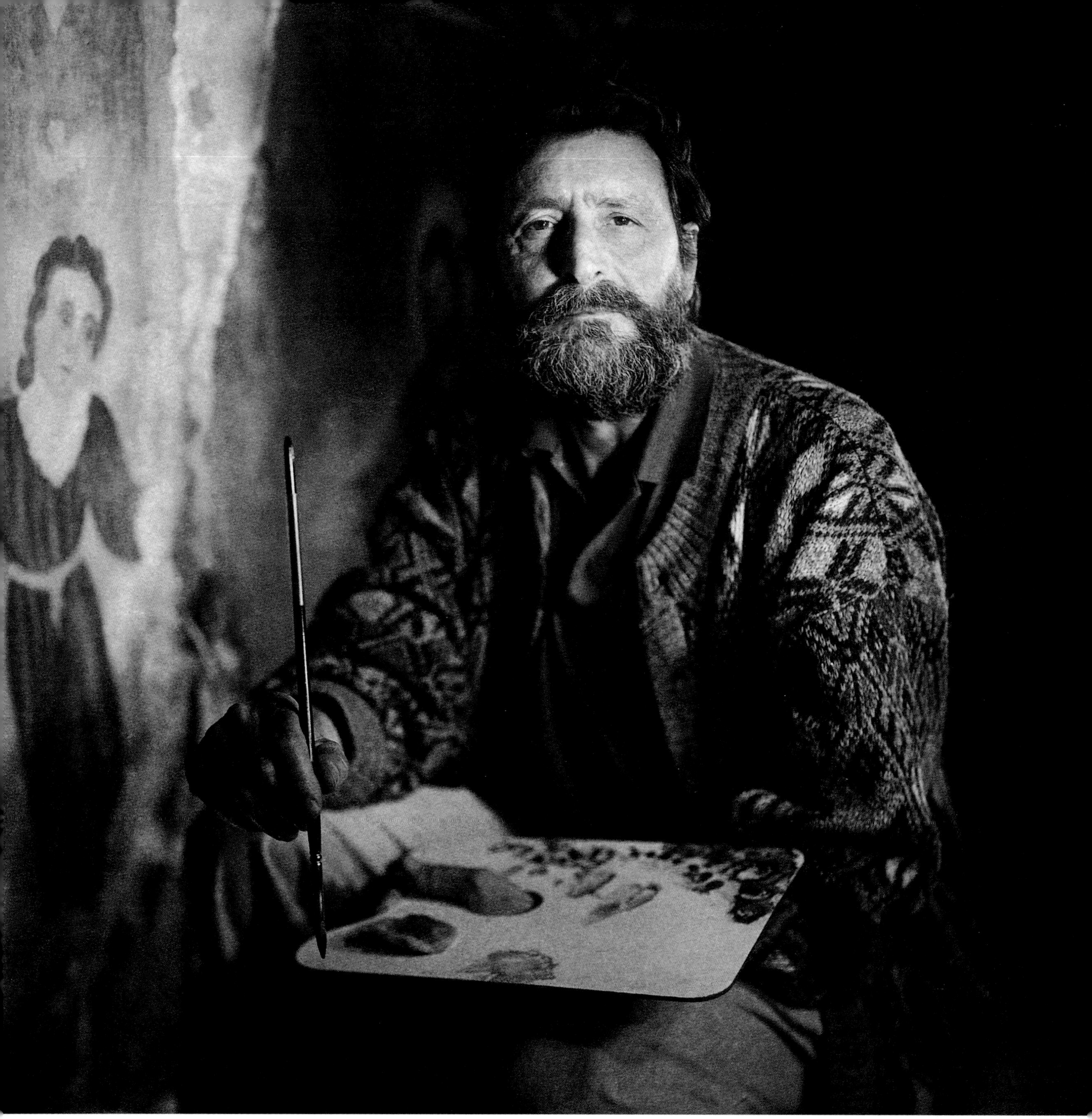

Composition

Photographed in his home, this is 90-year-old Terrence Shaw holding the ukulele he made himself in 1926. The pose is simple and totally natural but very powerful, with the subject forming a triangular shape, cut across by the diagonal of the ukulele. The prominence of the hands is appropriate because these are what made and played the instrument. The low camera angle and direct eye contact have the effect of making the subject appear dominant.

Technique

Sandy Huffaker wanted a gritty, textured quality to the image to suit the age and character of the subject. Flash would have destroyed this effect so he used the existing light in the room. A high speed film of ISO 3200 provided him with sufficient exposure and also resulted in a slight graininess to the print.

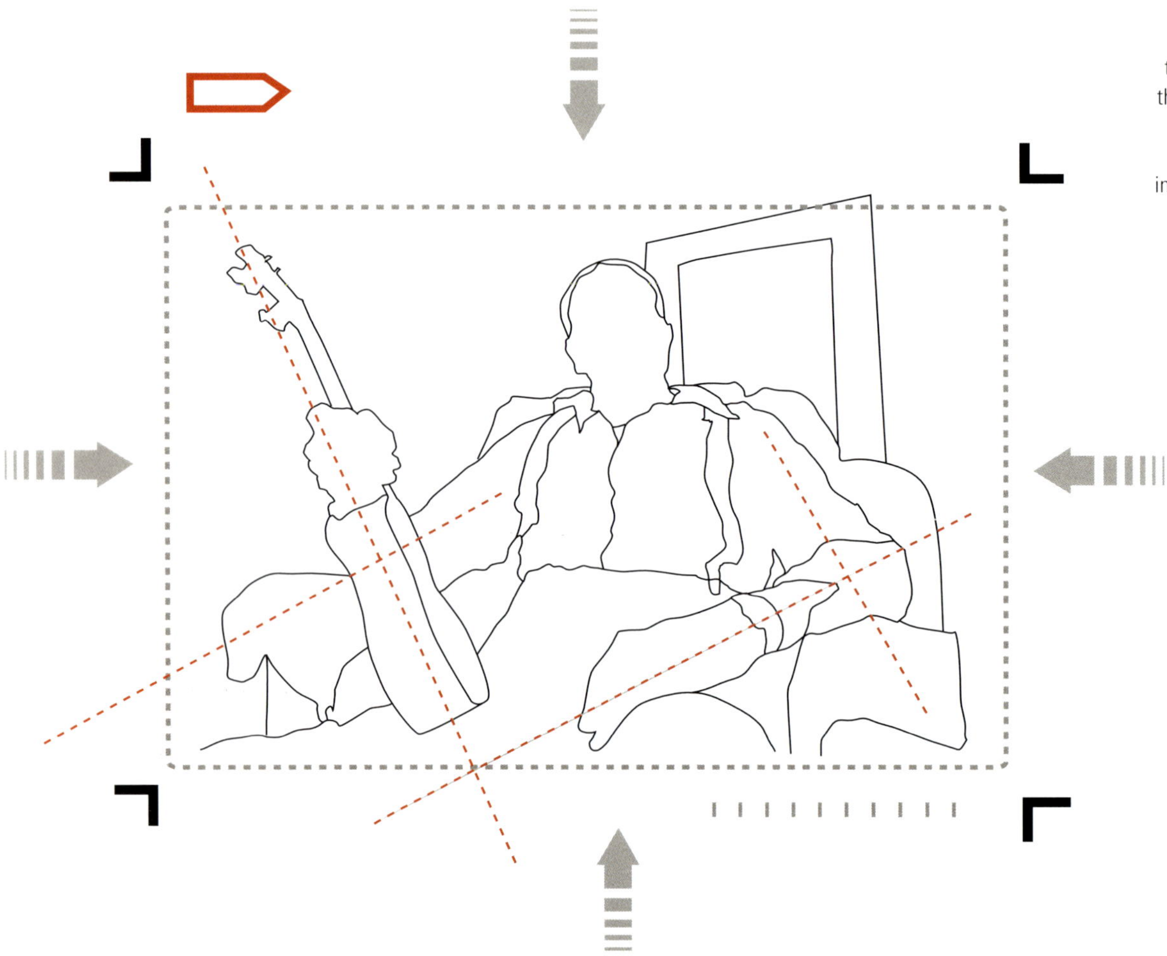

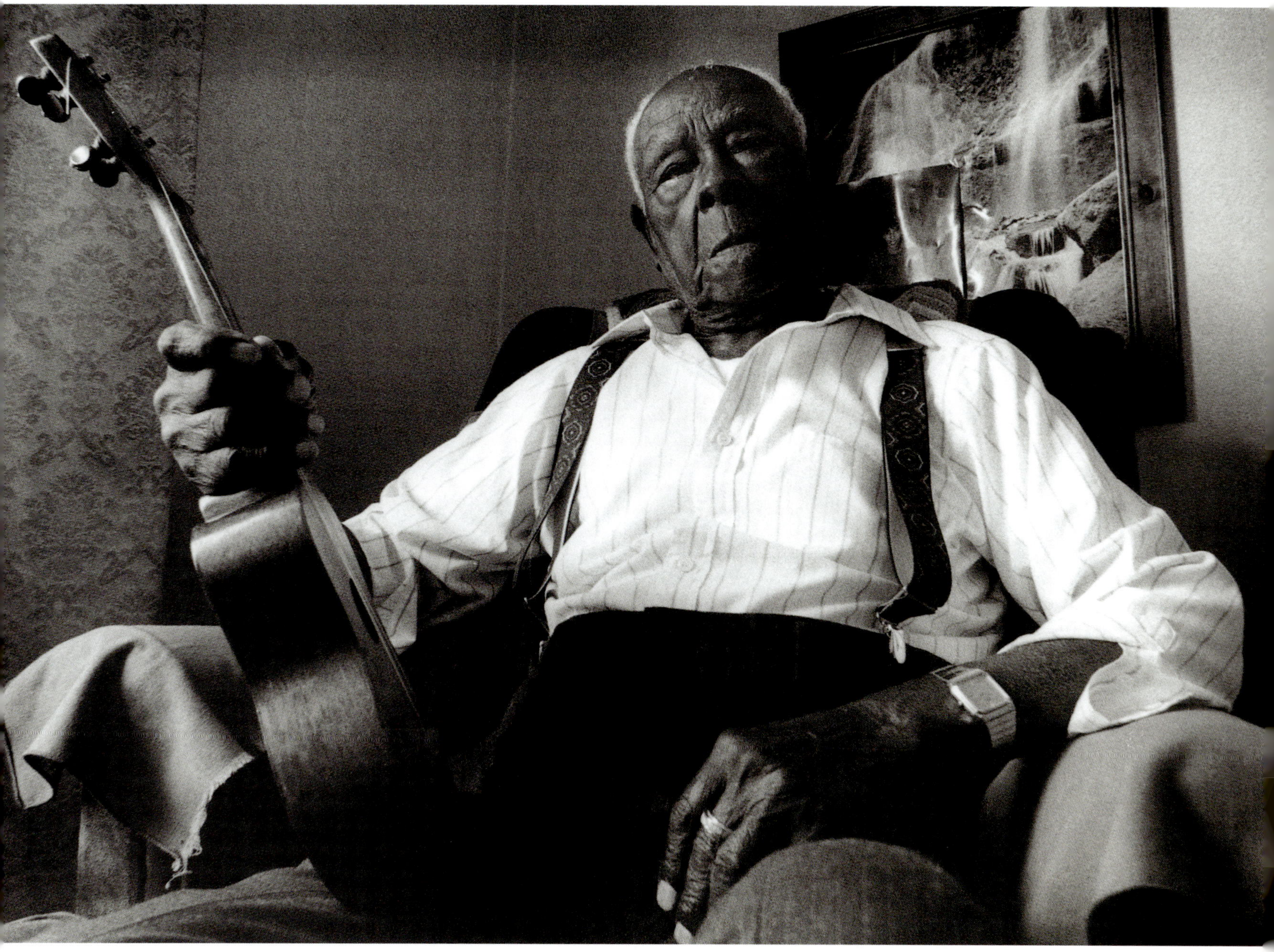

Technical details

Nikon F4 camera with 24mm lens. Film was Kodak T-Max 3200 with an exposure of 1/60sec at f/8.

3

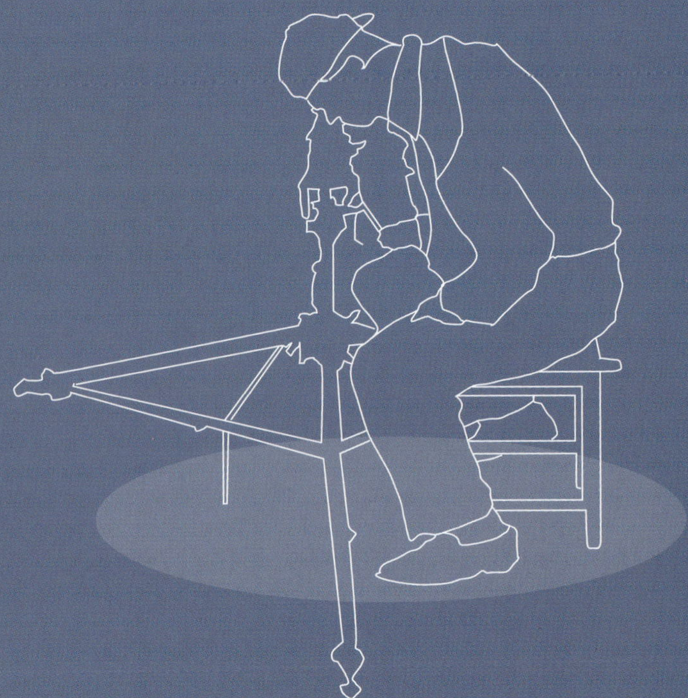

leisure

People relaxing and at ease during their leisure time offer great scope for the photographer and there are many different markets for these kind of pictures, from magazines to picture libraries. Public parks, festivals and sporting events offer opportunities for candid shots, although you may need to obtain permission in advance to take pictures at the latter.

Composition
This was from Sandy Huffaker's personal project on the Knights of Southeast San Diego – a baseball team formed by a group of kids from an impoverished area. The picture shows a spontaneous moment as team member Robert Shannon plays around with his mother, while Grandma sits in the background. 'It's indicative of family life for many of these teenagers in that their mother and extended family are the ones raising the kids without the presence of the father.'

Technique
It isn't easy to capture natural emotions from such a close distance as this, and a certain amount of trust and familiarity between the photographer and the subject is essential. Sandy built this relationship up by spending a whole season following the baseball team, going to their practice sessions, games and homes.

Lighting
You have to take whatever light nature gives you with unposed outdoor shots like this. Fortunately for Sandy the overcast sun provided adequate light here. He selected a fast shutter speed of 1/250sec to capture the movement and, although there is still some blur in the mother's arm, this adds to the lively mood of the picture.

Technical details
Nikon F4 with 24mm lens. Film was Kodak Tri-X with an exposure of 1/250sec at f/8.

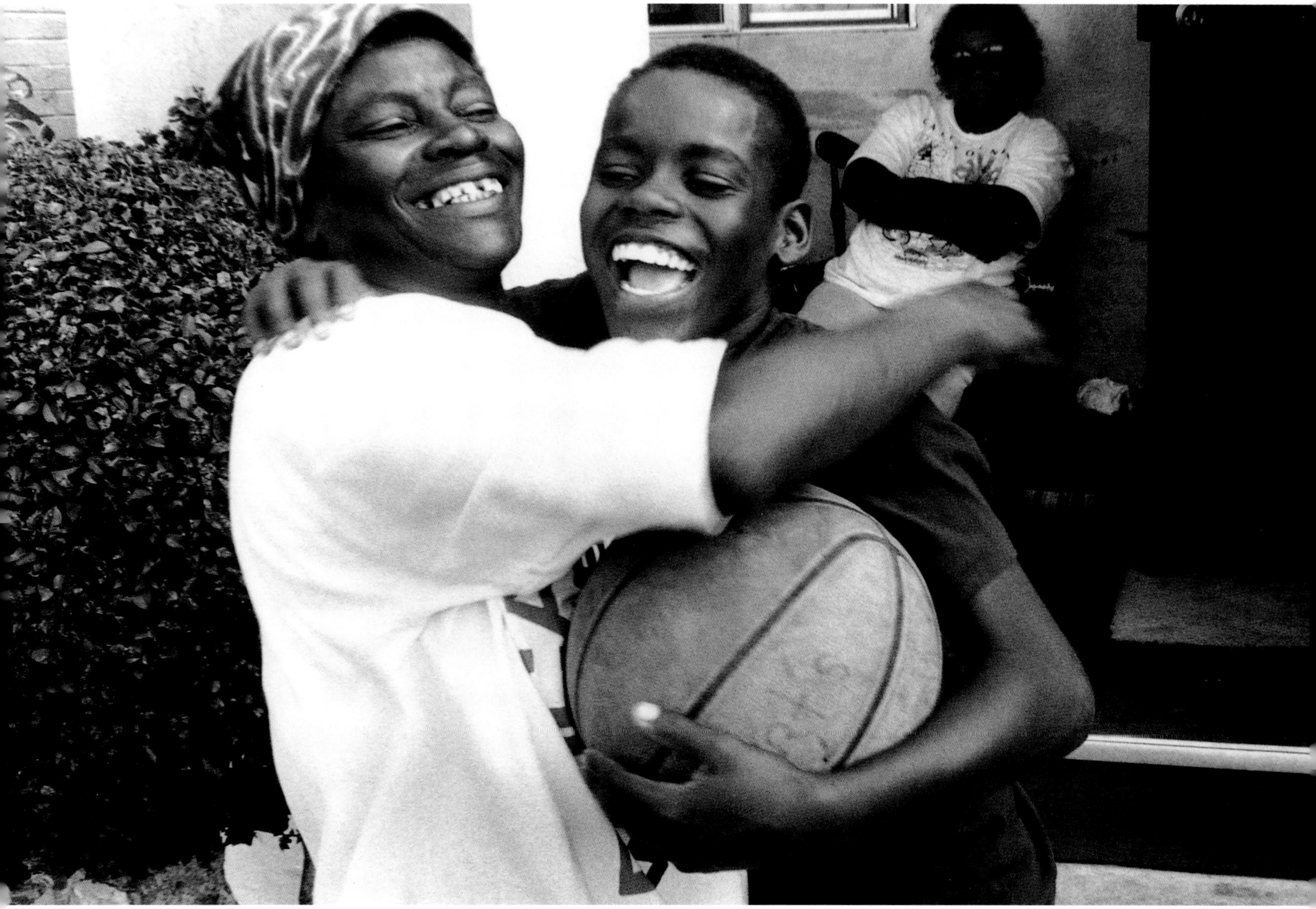

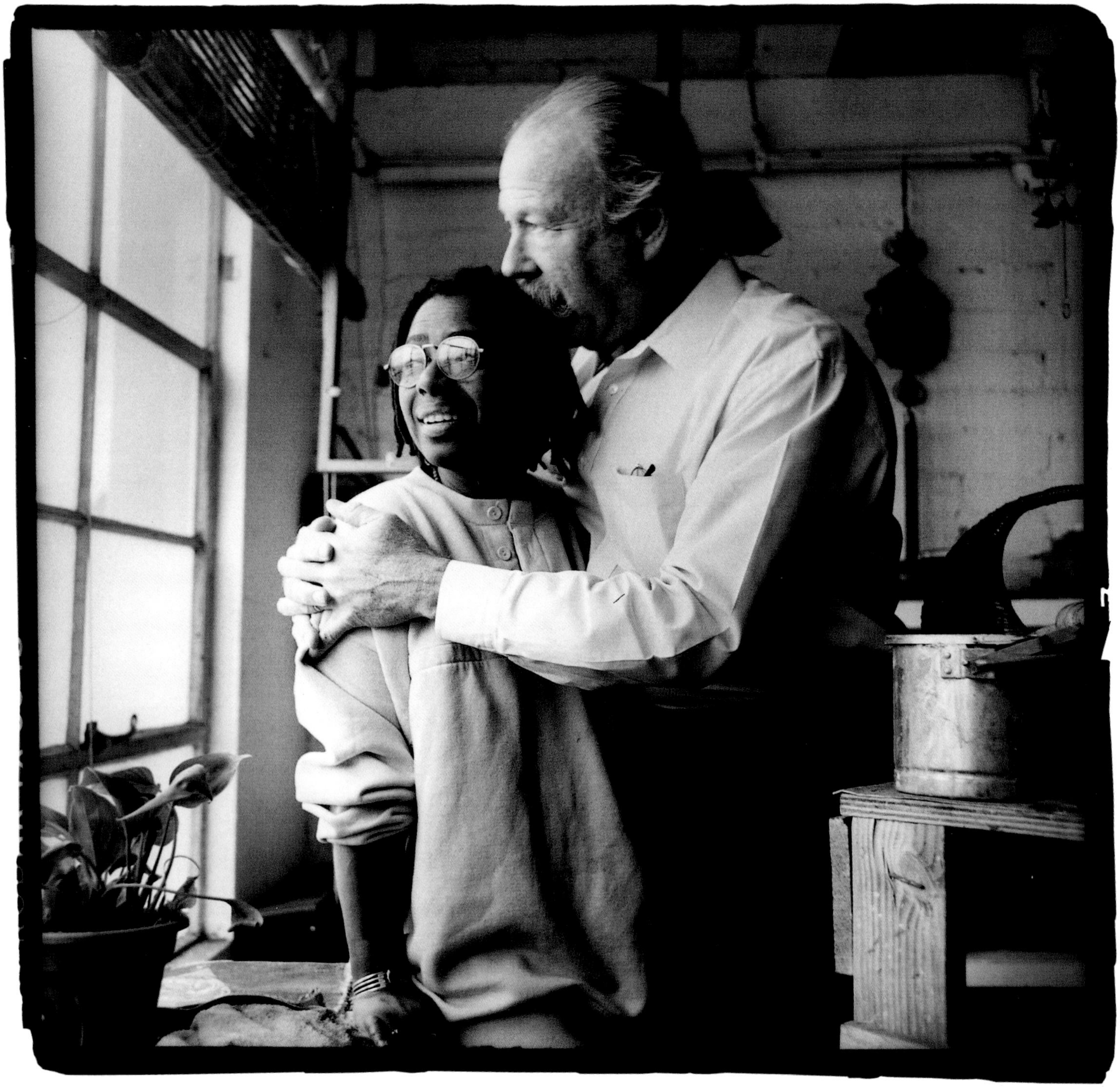

The way the couple are looking outside gives a pensive, reflective quality to this intimate portrait, which is enhanced by the light coming in from the window.

Technical details
Mamiya C330 camera with 65mm lens. Film was Tri-X Pan 400, pushed to ISO 800 with an exposure of 1/125sec at f/4.

Sandy Huffaker used a Powerlight strobe flash light to provide additional light in the bedroom. The boy was very keen on using his computer so Sandy included it in the frame, along with the posters in the background which give clues about his interests. The off-centre angle of the camera and the foreground clutter give the impression that this was a grab shot of the boy rather than a formal, posed portrait.

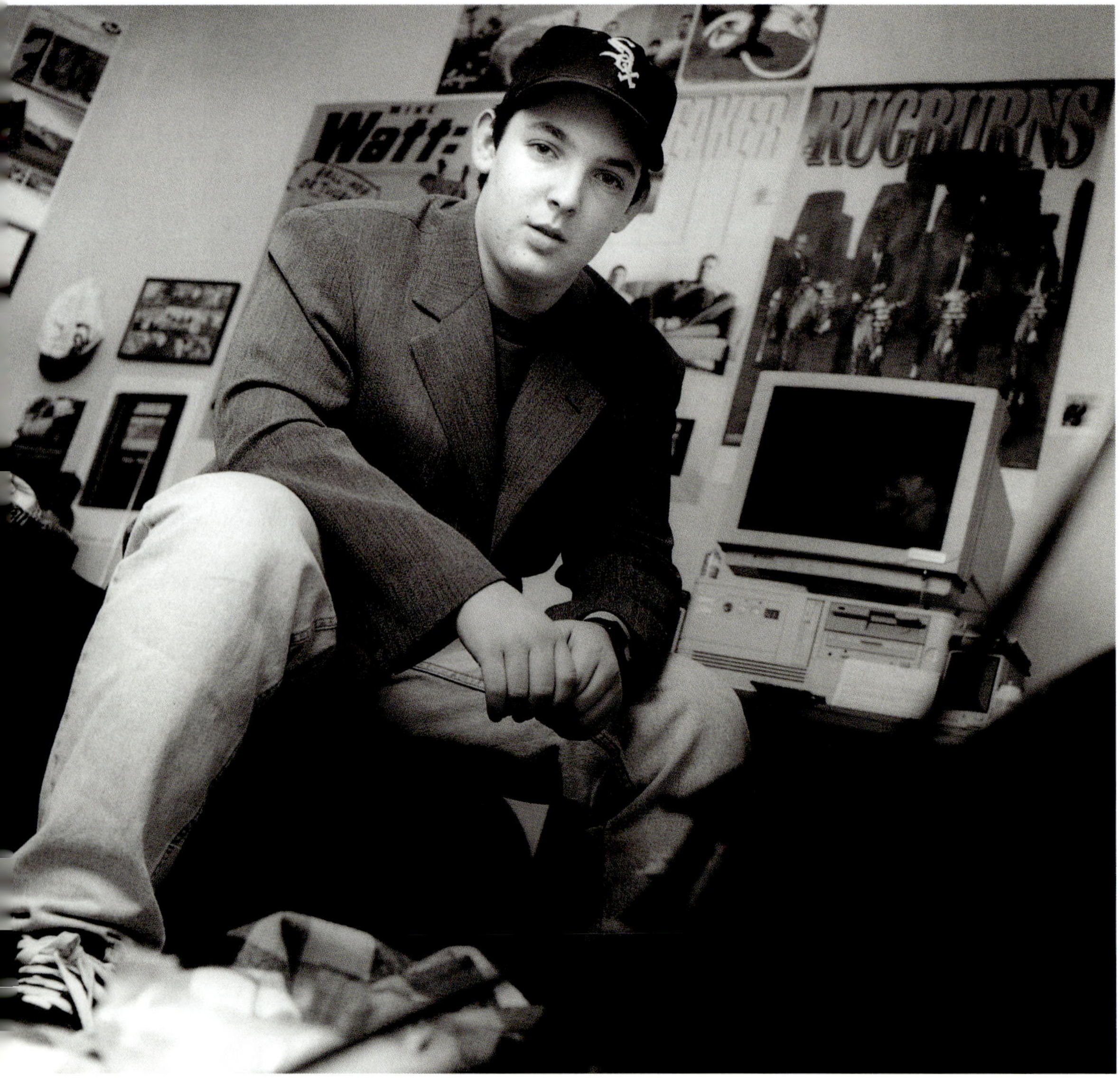

Technical details

Mamiya C330 camera with 65mm lens. Film was Kodak Tri-X Pan 400 with an exposure of 1/60sec at f/11.

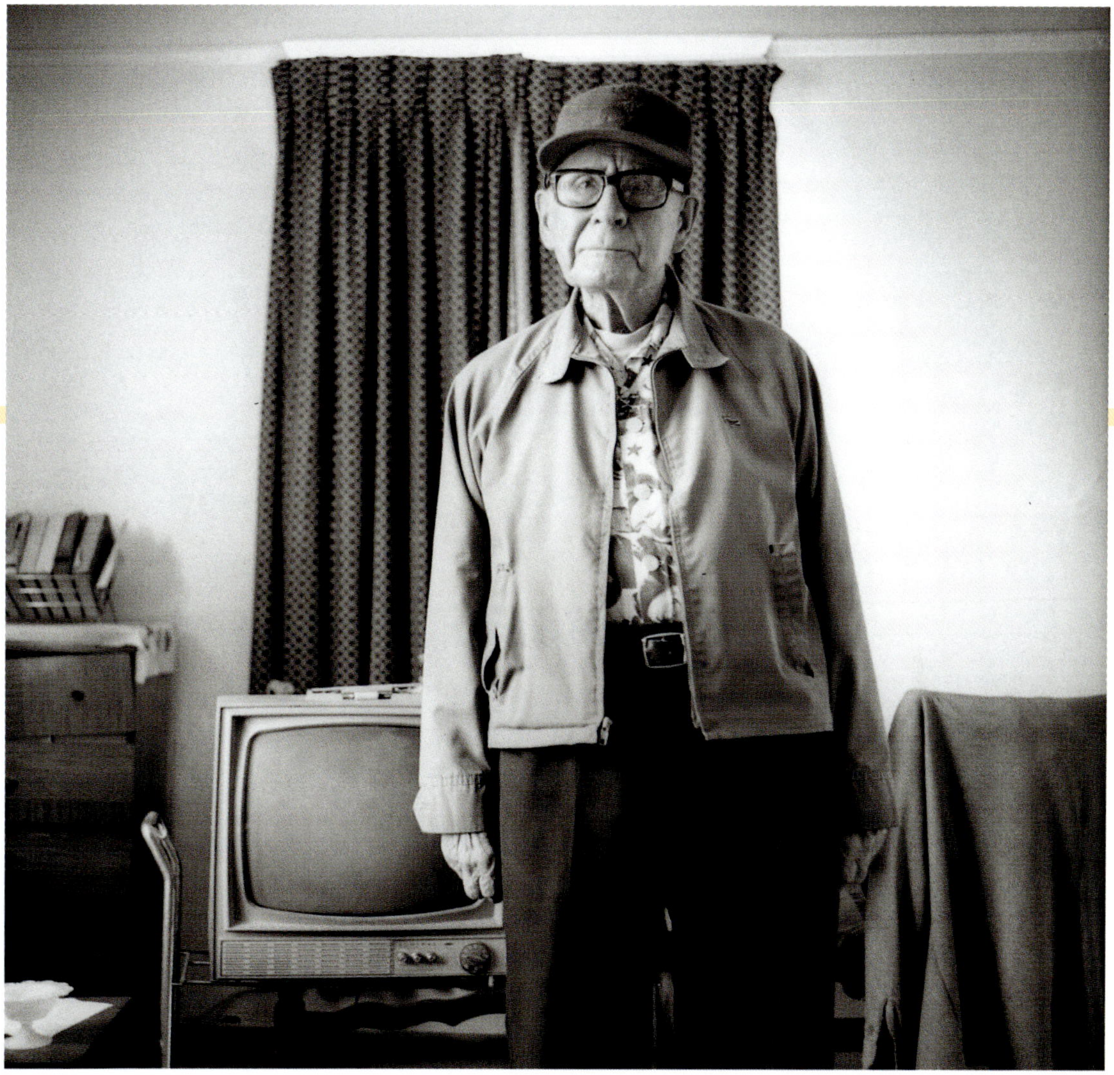

Composition

'I liked the askew posture of this old man as well as some of the outdated items like the TV in his apartment,' says Sandy. This picture is about showing the real life of the subject and so Sandy photographed the room as he found it, simply asking the subject to stand in position. The background details are important, but it is the man himself, and the expression on his face, that is the real focus of interest in the picture. It's an intimate portrait, revealing much about the old man's character and lifestyle.

Technique

In low available light, Sandy pushed the ISO 400 film by one stop to ISO 800 to give him a useable shutter speed of 1/60sec. The lens was wide open at f/2.8 but the use of a wide-angle lens has kept the background details in focus.

Technical details

Mamiya C330 camera with 65mm lens. Film was Kodak Tri-X Pan 400 with an exposure of 1/60sec at f/2.8.

'It's good to include details in a room because it tells you something about the subject's life.'

Sandy Huffaker

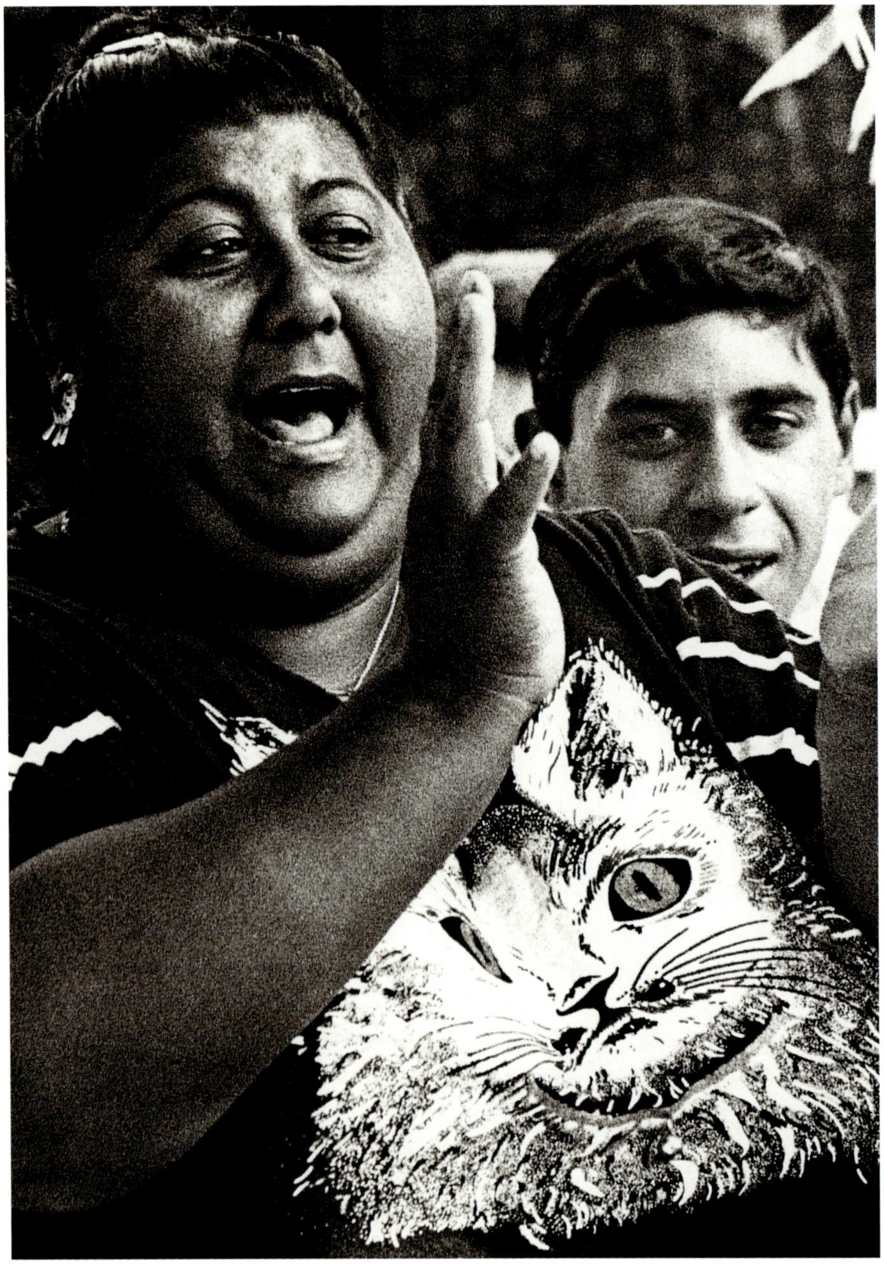

Composition

This was taken at an annual gypsy pilgrimage to a mountain-top sanctuary in southern Spain. Singing and flamenco dancing play a large part and there were many people enjoying the festivities. Carlo Chinca spotted this mother of a large family and saw her potential as a subject. He took several frames, but this was the most successful. Her expression and movements are animated and the way the boy behind her is, in contrast, looking at the camera, works well within the composition. The original negative included another woman to one side, but Carlo cropped in during printing to fill the image with the main subject.

Technique

Carlo was one of only three non-gypsies at the festival and was fairly conspicuous with his camera. Initially he was regarded with some suspicion but was able to explain, in Spanish, what he was doing. 'They posed a bit for the camera to begin with, but soon became used to me being there and ignored me taking pictures. I find it best to be open in these situations, rather than try to sneak pictures when the subject is unaware.'

Lighting

Taken in natural light, Carlo used ISO 400 film, pushed to ISO 800. The grain is very obvious because the image was enlarged from a section of the negative and printed on hard grade paper. In this case it helps add some atmosphere to the image.

Technical details

Nikon F3 camera with 135mm lens. Film was Kodak Tri-X 400 with an exposure of 1/125sec at f/5.6.

These children were watching the dancing at the same gypsy festival. Carlo cropped the negative in the darkroom to focus attention on the line of children, and burned-in the right side of the image to highlight their faces.

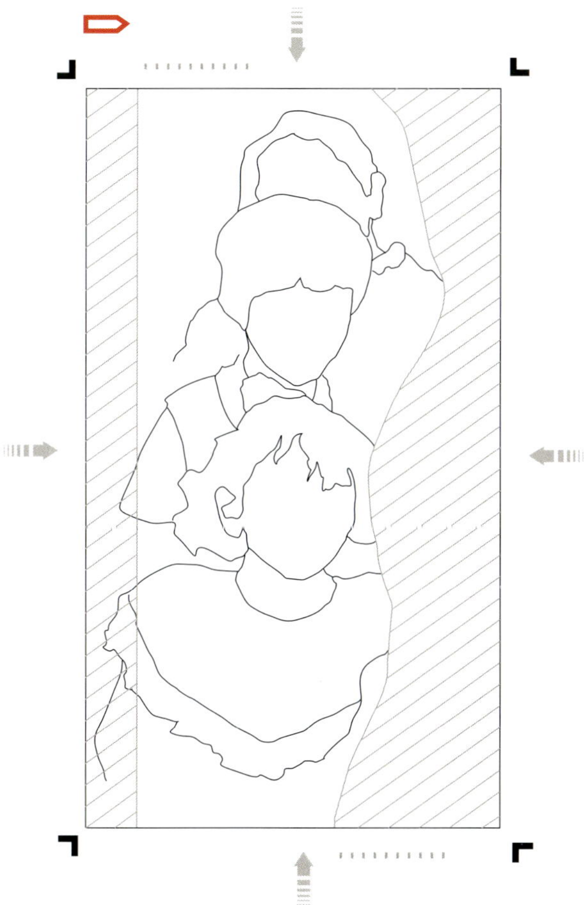

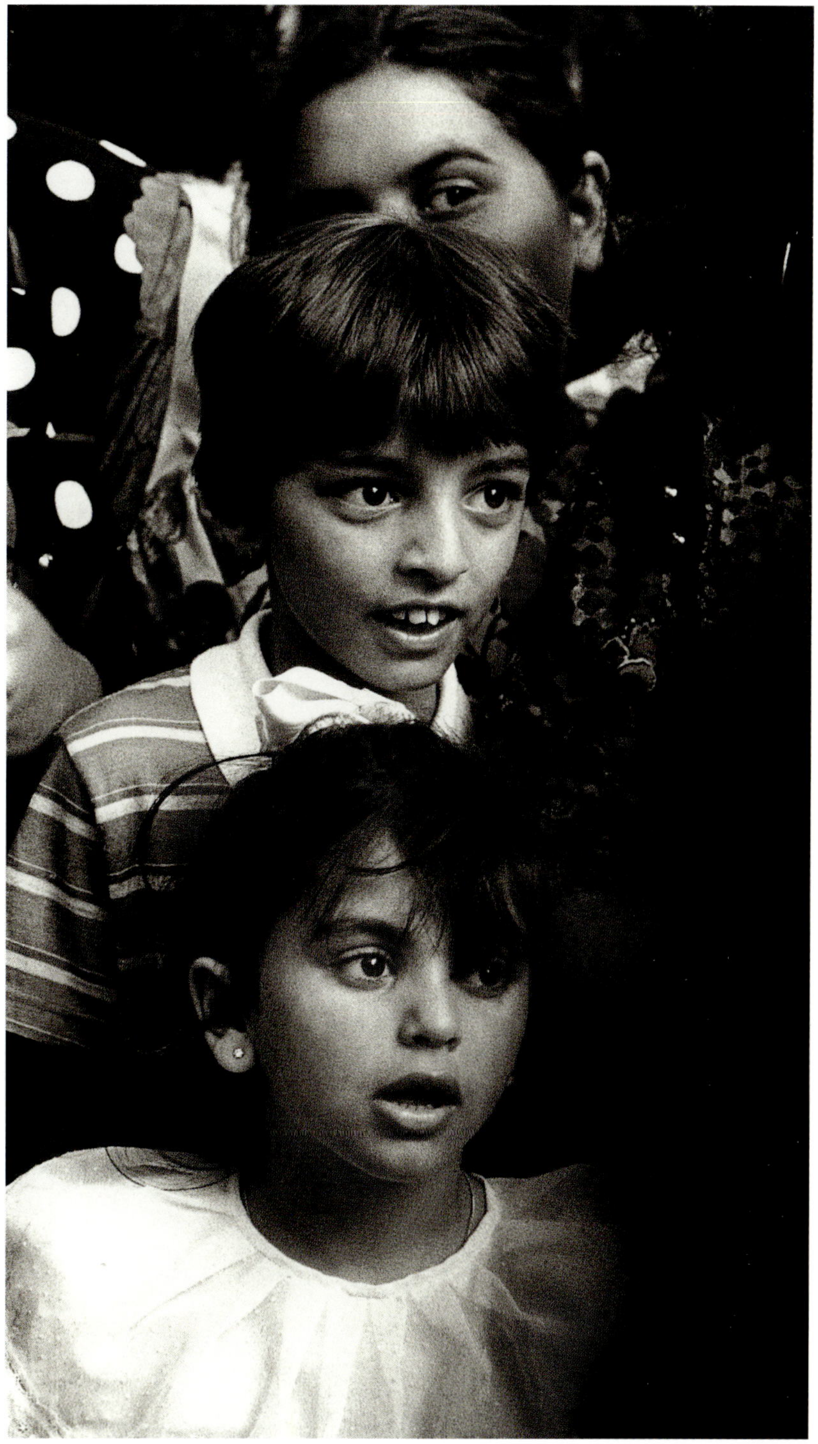

Technical details

Nikon F3 with 135mm lens. Film was Tri-X 400 with an exposure of 1/60sec at f/3.5.

Technical details
Nikon F4 camera with 24mm lens. Film was Kodak T-Max 3200 with an exposure of 1/60sec at f/2.8.

Composition
A San Diego newspaper commissioned Sandy Huffaker to do a photo story on a small wrestling gym in Tijuana, Mexico. 'I found the gym while wandering around one day and was immediately attracted by its unpolished, neighbourhood feel,' he says. For this shot, Sandy wanted to capture a split frame image, with the boys wrestling at the bottom and the arena at the top. 'I like the way your eye goes immediately to the boy looking at the camera, and then wanders around to other elements in the frame. My thoughts were that maybe someday those boys would be in the ring.'

Lighting
The light was extremely low here, with just one overhead source. Sandy used high speed ISO 3200 film and shot with his wide-angle lens wide open at f/2.8. The speed of the film has resulted in noticeable grain in the print, but Sandy likes the way that gives the image a gritty, textured quality. 'I think that using flash would have sterilised the image and not given a true feeling of the situation,' he says.

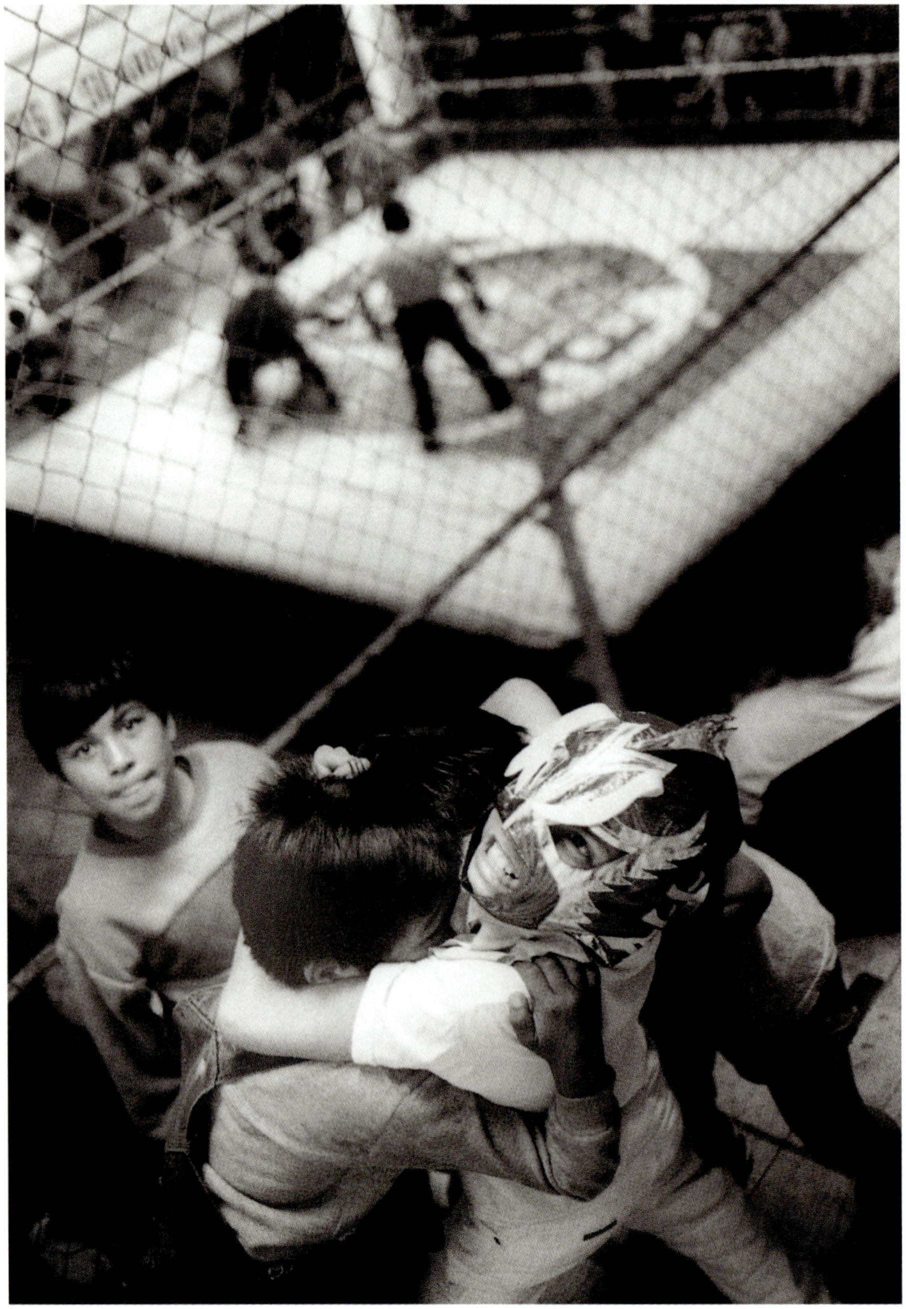

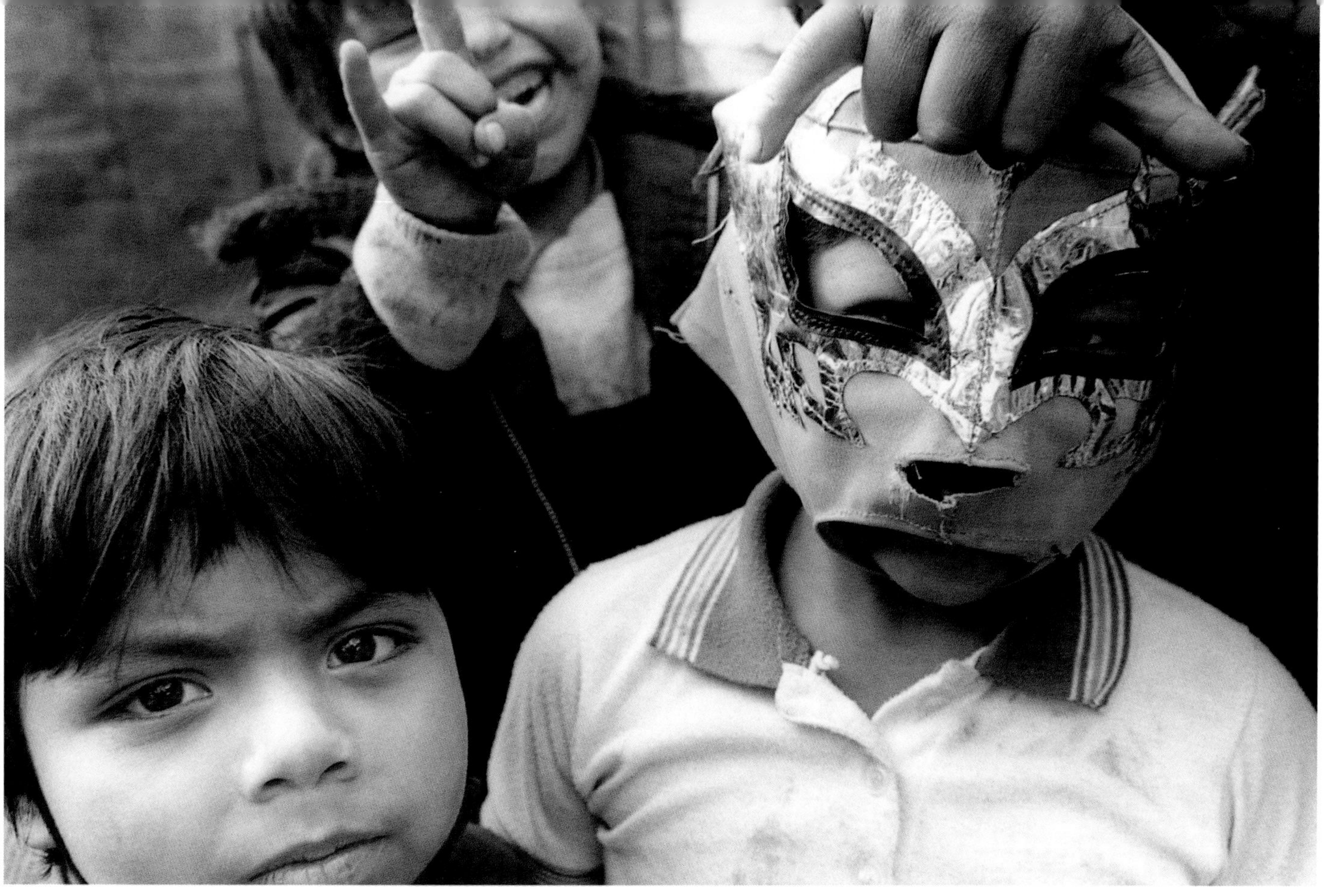

This was part of the same story on the wrestling gym. 'I wanted to see the impact of the gym on the community so I hit the streets and found these kids staging a battle in an alleyway a few blocks away. After I shot a few frames they noticed I was there and started interacting with the camera.'

Technical details
Nikon F4 camera with 24mm lens. Film was Kodak Tri-X Pan 400 with an exposure of 1/125sec at f/8.

'I shot about 10 frames of this scene and liked this one because of the spontaneity and the different expressions of each kid.'
Sandy Huffaker

4

with the family

A few years ago families wanting a professional portrait of the children, or a record of a special occasion, had little choice but to pose in the confines of a studio. Today there is a demand for a more natural and lively style that can best be achieved in a real-life setting.

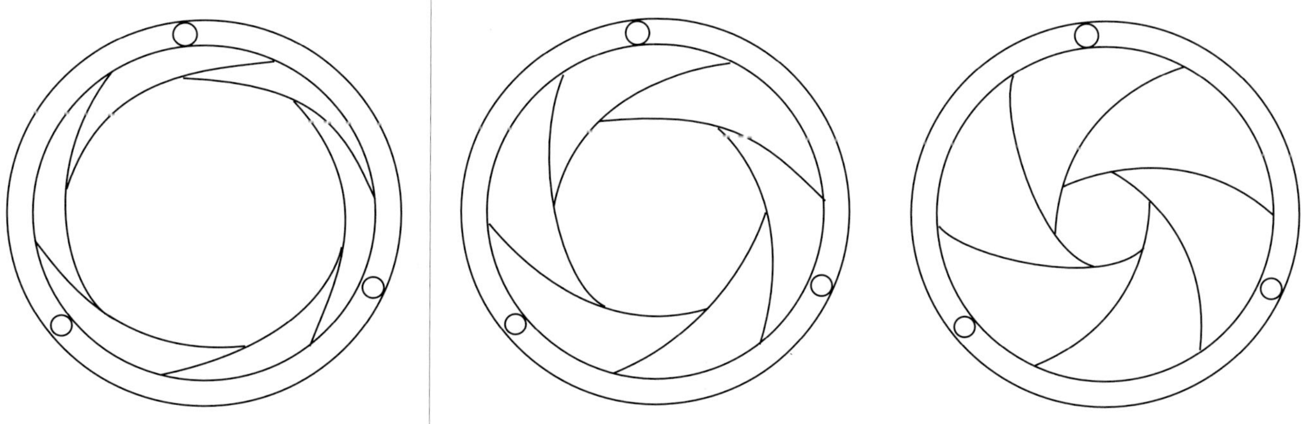

Tip
On a dull day, or even a bright day in open shade, there is usually an excess of blue and a deficiency of red in the light. An 81B warm-up filter redresses the balance, adding more warmth to the colours which is more pleasing to the eye.

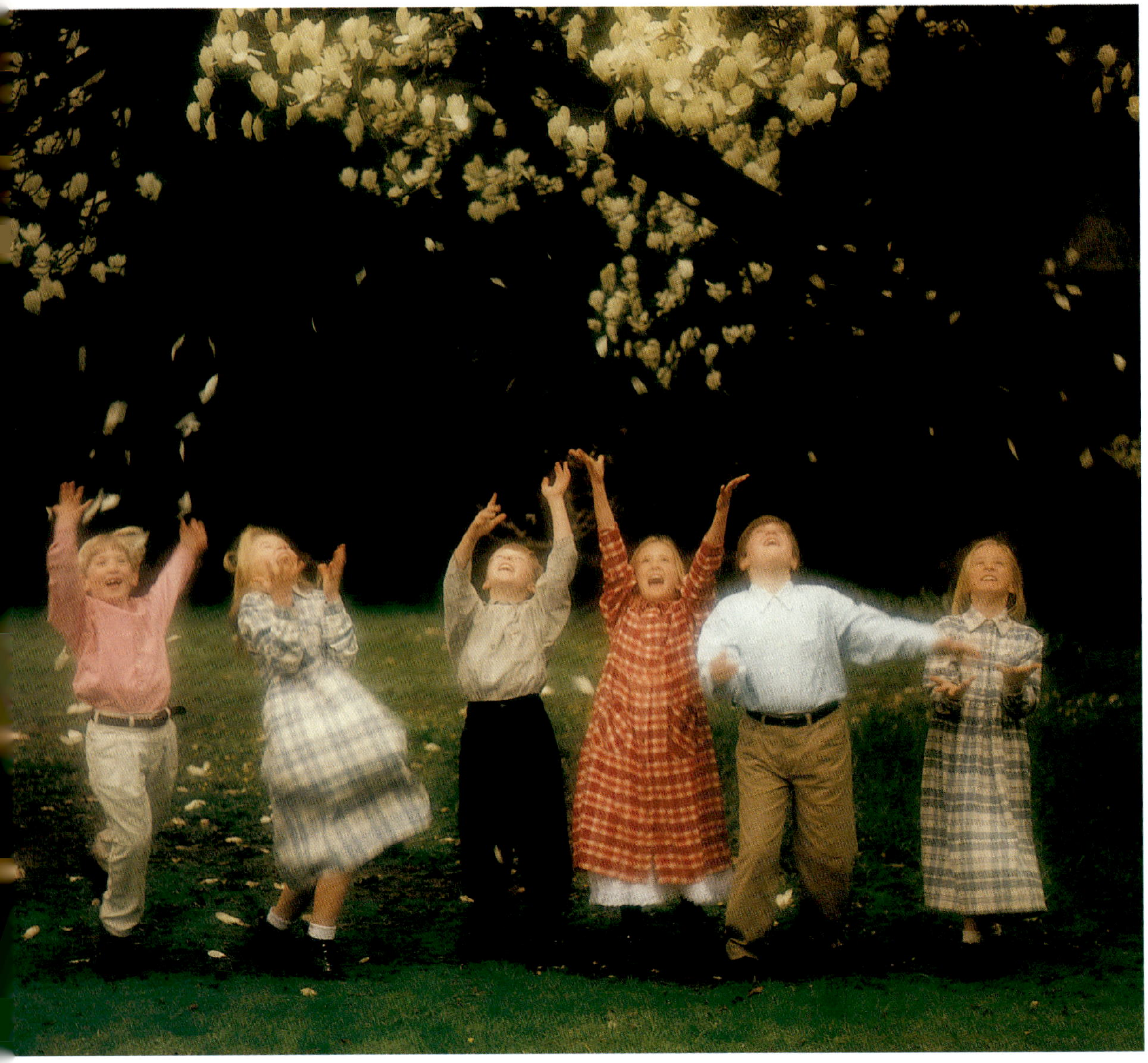

Ronald Turner had just one exposure left on the film and wanted a fun shot to complete a commission to photograph a group of young cousins. His daughter Tracy collected some leaves and asked them to throw the leaves into the air at the word 'go' to give a lively action picture. 'We asked them to stay in the same spot and make sure they didn't cover their faces with their arms,' he says. 'We had one practice go first and then took just the one shot. The expressions were probably so exuberant due to the fact we told them: "This is the last shot". It was a very dull day and I used the lens at its widest aperture of f/4 to give me the highest shutter speed the light would allow.'

Technical details
Hasselblad 205 TCC camera with 120mm Makro-Planar lens. Film was Kodak GPX Gold 160 with soft focus and 81B warming filters.

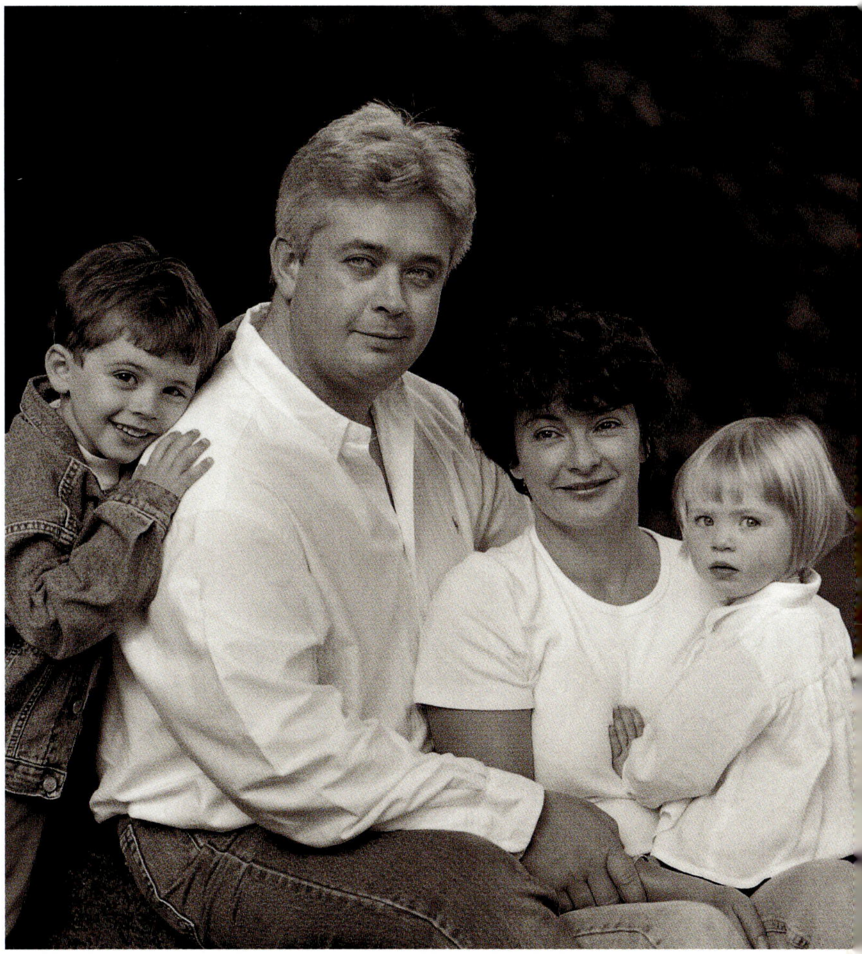

Composition
This was taken in a woodland park near to Ronald's studio, which he often uses for portraits. He looks for backgrounds that don't overpower the subject, particularly for tight family groups such as this where the background needs to be relatively neutral. The body language between the group is important and all the figures are leaning slightly into the centre with a pleasing arrangement of the heads. It's also vital that they all look at the camera at the same time, with relaxed and happy expressions on their faces.

Lighting
In the middle of woodland the light tends to have a muddy quality so Ronald picked a location on the edge of a glade where there was an opening in the trees. This gave him soft directional light on the faces of his subjects, which he enhanced by bouncing light from an area of open sky with a reflector.

Technique
Ronald used a subtle soft focus filter which is barely noticeable in the final print but has a flattering effect on adult skin, spreading the highlights into the shadows and softening facial lines. Black and white is increasingly popular with his clients and he presents them with prints on fibre-based paper, sepia toned in thiocarbamide for both appearance and the enhanced archival properties of this process.

Technical details
Hasselblad 205 TCC camera with a 120mm Makro-Planar lens. Film was Kodak T-Max 400 CN.

Composition

This was taken at the beach where the subtle variation in tones between the sky, sea and dune grass provide an attractive but unobtrusive background, contrasting with the brightness of the girl's face and dress. The portrait has a slightly nostalgic mood to it, partly due to the soft focus, her long dress and also the way she is looking away from the camera which is much more effective here than direct eye contact would have been. The straw hat is a nice touch and a useful compositional device because it gives her something to do with her hands.

Technique

Ronald Turner took a stepladder to the location with the intention of gaining a higher viewpoint for some of the poses. For this shot it became a useful posing aid as the girl used it as a seat. The camera was set up on a tripod directly in front of the girl and Ronald used a long cord with a bulb air release to fire the shutter. This enabled him to stand four or five feet to the right of the camera and ask the girl to look at him, thus holding her attention and directing her gaze precisely.

Lighting

The so-called golden hour – half an hour before and after sunset – is Ronald's favourite time for beach portraits. 'The surrounding sky becomes almost as bright as the sun, which accentuates textures and gives that porcelain look to the skin,' he says. 'It's a light we treasure because on location you have to take what you are given and work around it. If it had been a dull day, I would have taken different pictures – you have to work with whatever Mother Nature dishes out'.

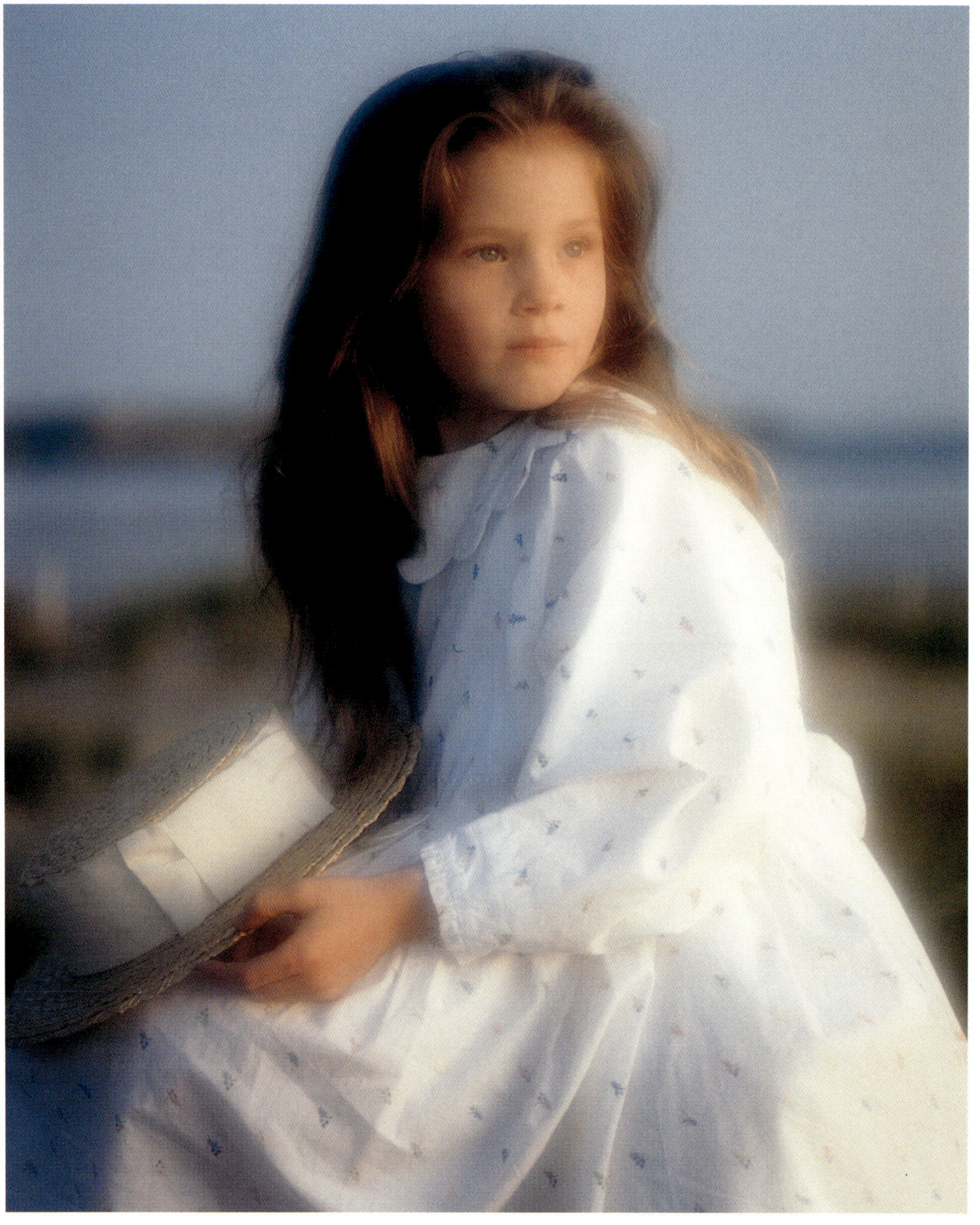

Technical details

Hasselblad 205 TCC camera with 180mm Sonnar lens. Film was Kodak T-Max 400 CN with an aperture of f/4.

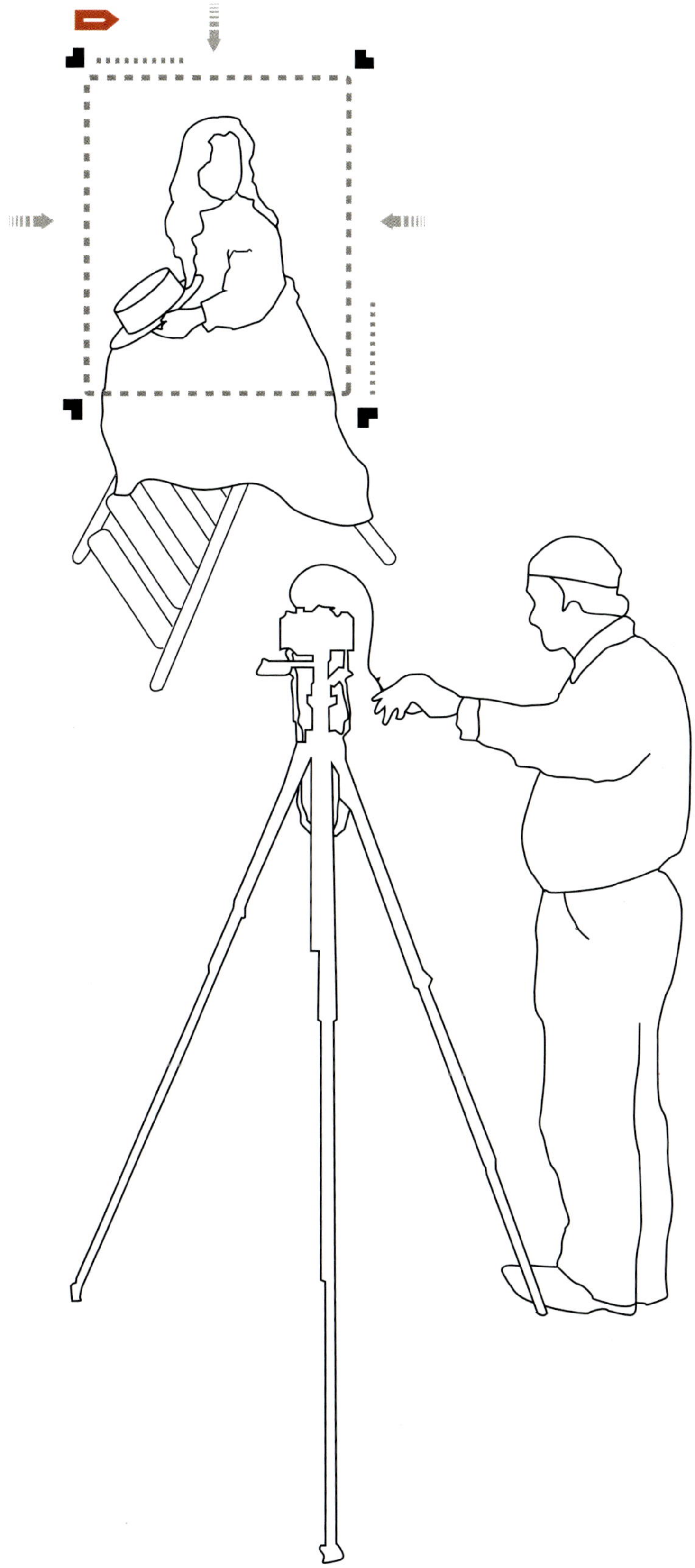

'Just before sunset the surrounding sky becomes almost as bright as the sun, which accentuates textures and gives that porcelain look to the skin.'

Ronald Turner

Composition
The landscape here is almost as important in the picture as the people and the technique of combining the two elements is becoming increasingly popular. On a clear day, when the horizon is clearly defined it's important to ensure the horizon line does not cut through the heads. At normal eye level this can be hard to avoid so look for a raised viewpoint such as a rock to take the picture from, or consider taking a stepladder to the location.

Technique
Having decided on the composition of the image, Ronald Turner asked the mother to crouch down and call her child towards her for a spontaneous and natural-looking shot. When a picture involves movement and an interaction between the subjects, rather than with the photographer, Ronald prefers to use a 35mm camera which is faster to use and can be hand held more easily than his medium format camera.

'During autumn we collect bags of leaves and keep them in our garage. We take them along to our location shoots and make autumn colour extend until March.'
Ronald Turner

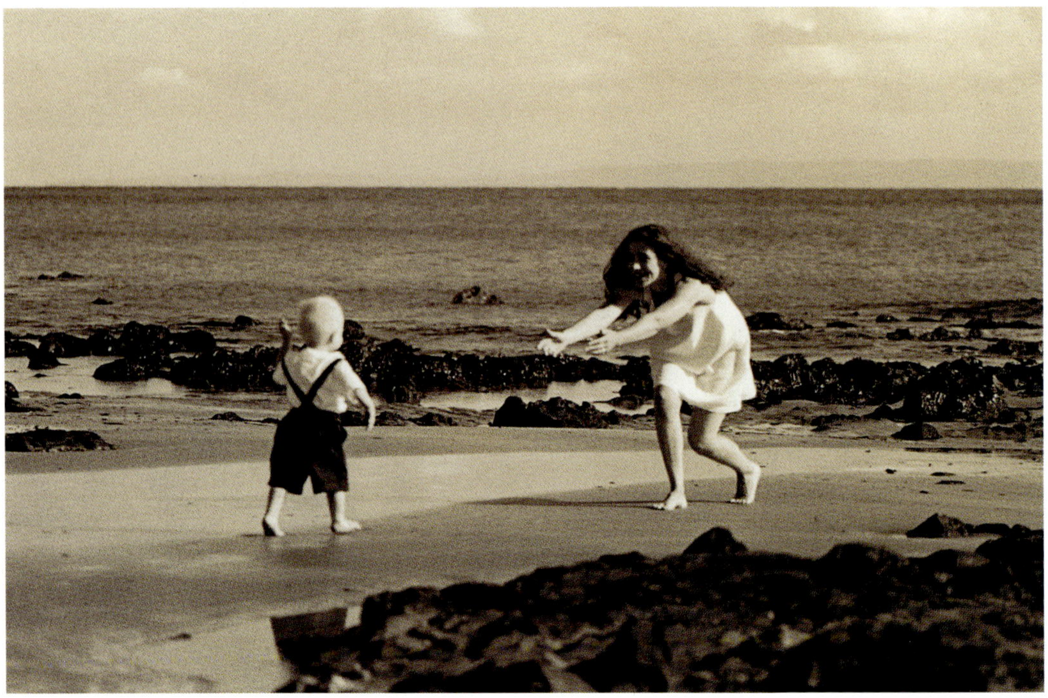

Technical details
Contax RTS 111 with 100mm Macro Planar lens. Film was Kodak Tri-X rated at ISO 200.

This pose is a simple but effective way to keep a small child 'contained' for a photograph. Ronald and his daughter Tracy, kept his attention and enjoyment of the session by talking to him constantly and playing little games to make him smile. The 'huggy' pose of the father, apart from being great body language, helps prevent his young son from running off.

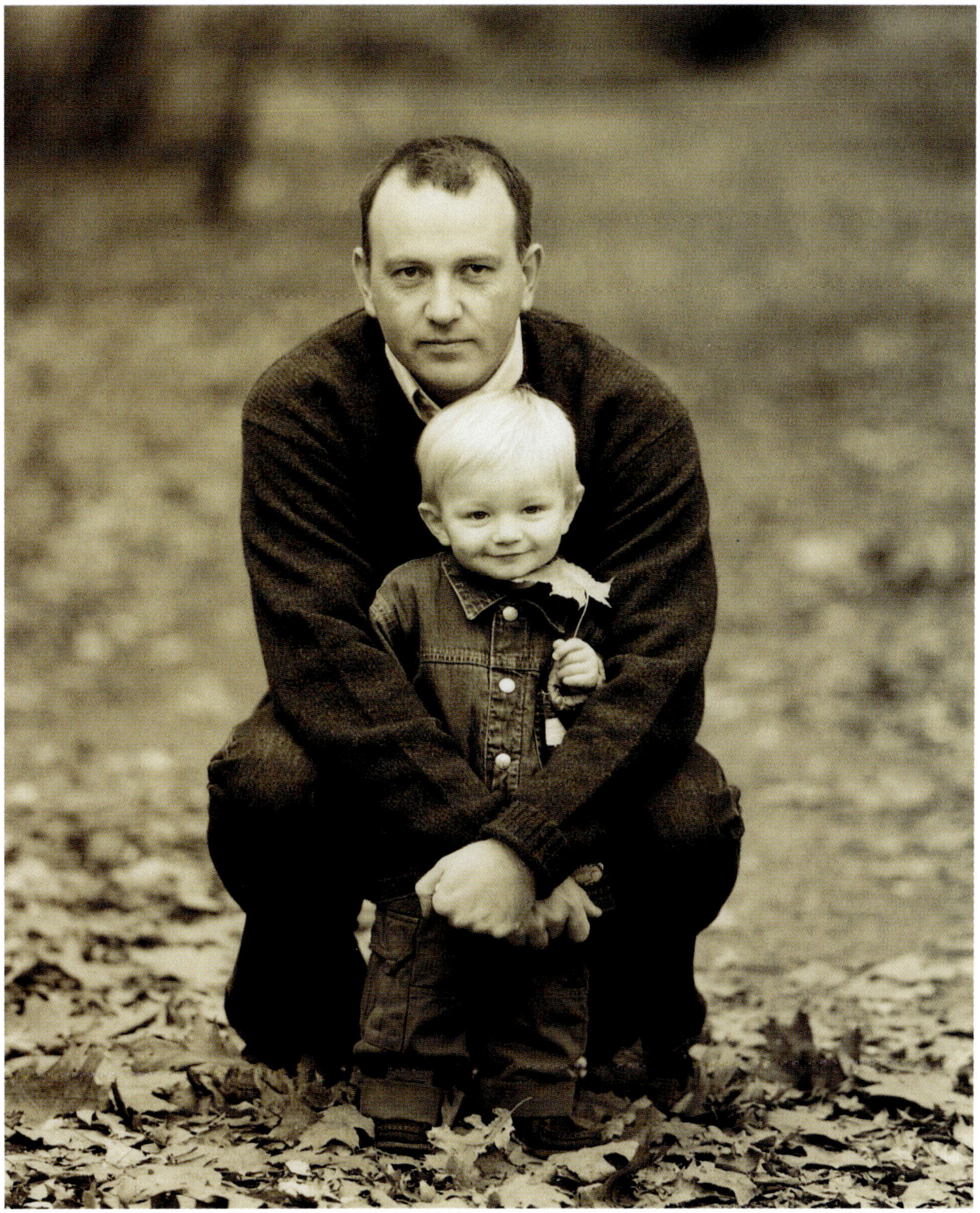

Technical details
Hasselblad 205 TCC camera with 180mm Sonnar lens. Film was Kodak T-Max 400 CN.

Composition

Ronald Turner frequently uses beach locations because they can make for such a variety of backgrounds at all times of the year and you can choose how much detail you want to include or omit. The effect of this winter shot is very minimalist, with the pale sand and sea in black and white providing a neutral but authentic setting for mother and daughter. The inclusion of so much empty space around them emphasises the contrast in their size while the eye contact and movement towards each other tells of the closeness of their relationship.

Technique

Ronald wanted to make this shot look as natural and believable as possible but paradoxically that requires a little planning. Mother and daughter had several practice goes at running together before getting it just right. Ronald used his 35mm camera here. The lightness, ease of use and speed of this format make it ideal for action shots. He used a hand-held meter to take an incident light reading from the subject.

Mood

The starkness and simplicity of the composition is perfectly suited to black and white film, which pares an image down to its basic elements. The picture has something of the feel of a fashion magazine shot and is as far removed from the traditional, formal studio portrait as you can imagine.

'I try to make every location session really enjoyable. Then the client will see the pictures in a far better light than if they've had an excruciating experience comparable to a visit to the dentist.'

Ronald Turner

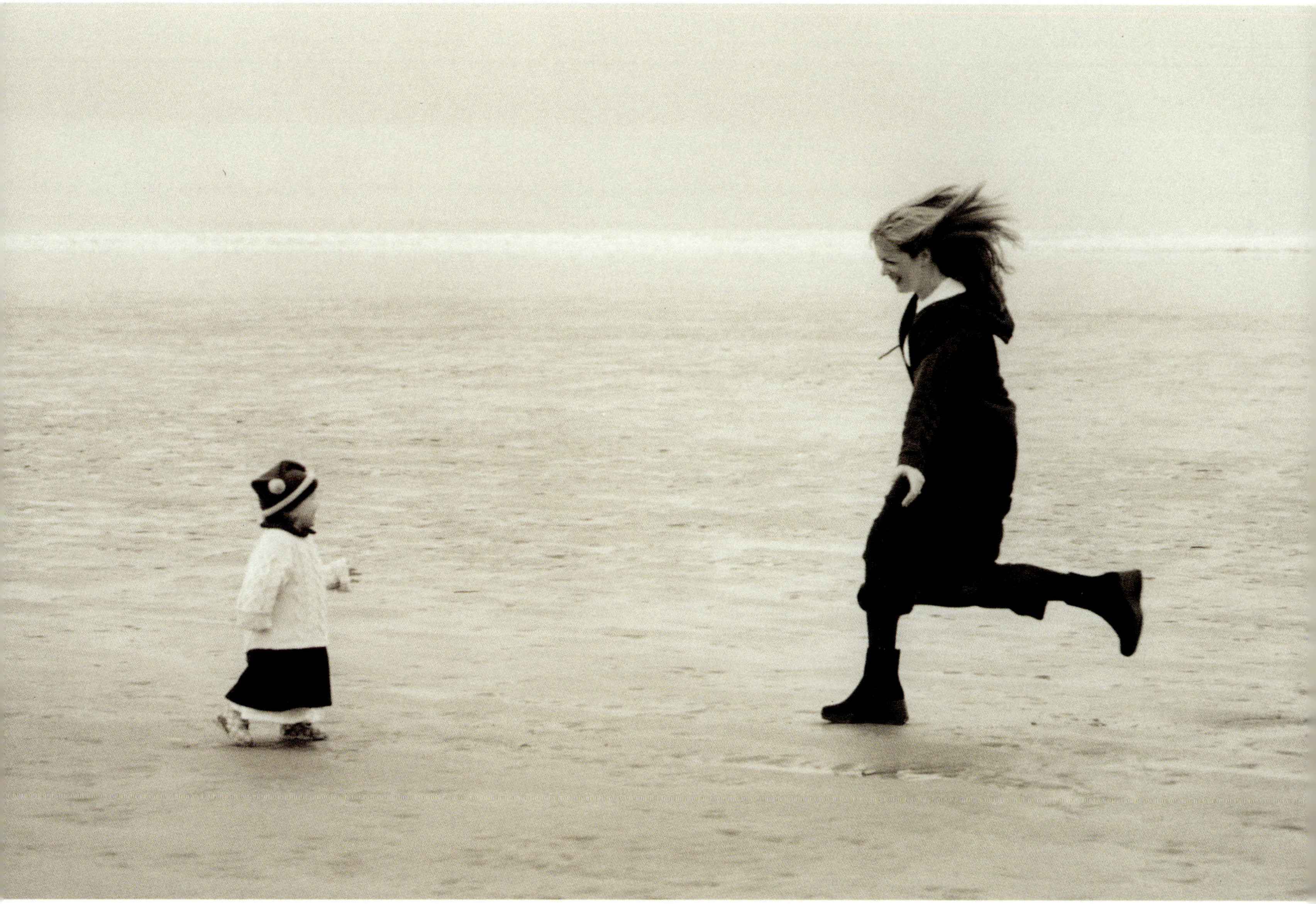

Technical details
Contax RTS 111 camera with 100mm Macro Planer lens. Film was Kodak Tri-X rated at ISO 200.

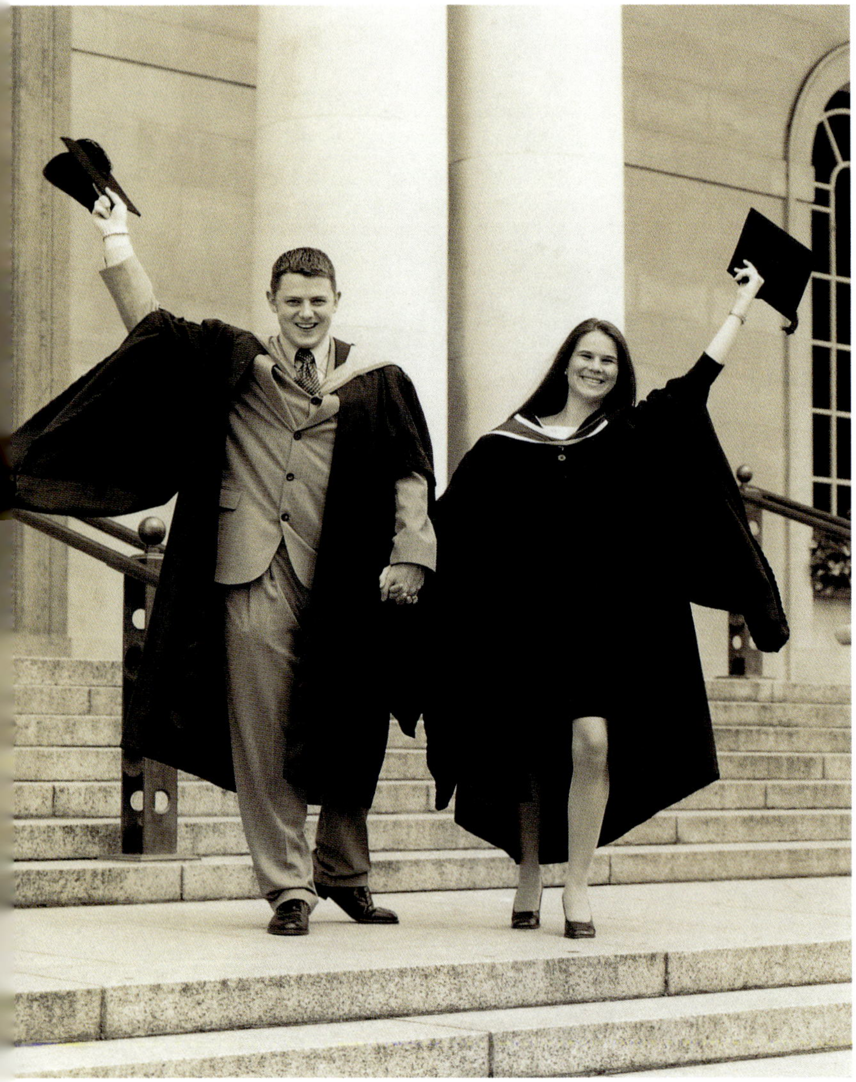

Graduation portraits can look stiff and artificial in the studio. Ronald Turner found a public building that looked suitably academic and, with the couple in a lively pose, has captured a fitting air of celebration.

Technical details
Hasselblad 205 TCC camera with 120mm Makro-Planar lens. Film was Kodak T-Max 400 CN.

Composition

For all their wedding commissions, Ronald and Tracy Turner offer a free location portrait after the wedding. This was planned as an autumnal shot in November but, on the day, there was thick snow on the ground at the Brecon Beacons. Tracy and the bride trekked for 15 minutes up a mountain to arrive at this location and turned the snow to their advantage by including a large area of the wintry landscape in the shot. The result is far from a conventional bridal portrait but one which will certainly stand out in the album. Since the bride was wearing a white dress, it was important to place her against the dark background of foliage to make her stand out from the snow.

Lighting

This was taken in weak directional light and the bride was asked to pose with her face looking up to catch as much of the light as possible. When taking pictures in situations such as this the camera's meter can be fooled by the reflectivity of the snow into giving the wrong exposure. In such conditions an incident light reading will usually give a more accurate reading.

Colour

This picture is virtually monochromatic, consisting largely of the white and grey tones of snow and foliage in the late afternoon of a heavily overcast day. Colour film was important to the success of the shot, however, because the bride's skin tones stand out from the background and so naturally attracts our eye.

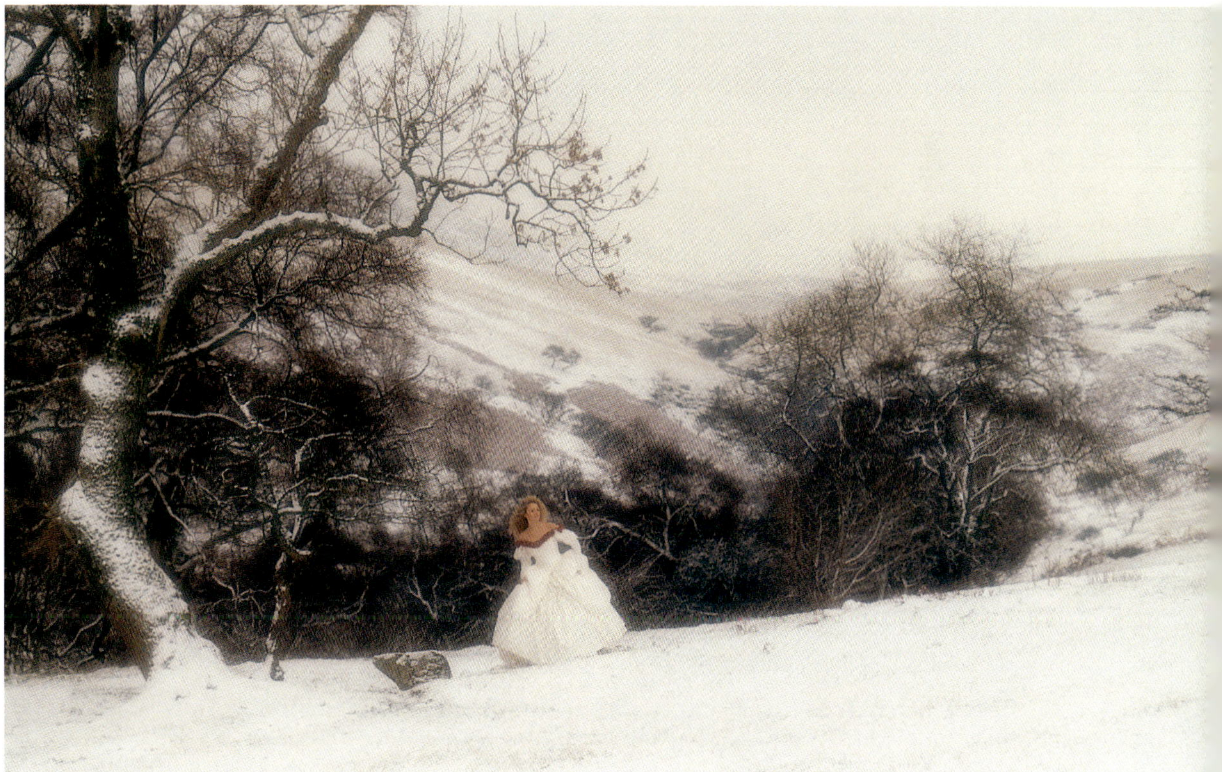

Technical details

Hasselblad 205 TCC with 120mm lens. Film was Kodak GPX Gold 160.

photo-journalism

Reportage photography is essentially about capturing real life as it happens, although the term can also describe a story told through pictures. Both rely heavily on location portraiture to show the subject in the context of their everyday life.

Black and white is the traditional, although by no means exclusive, medium for reportage. By using fast emulsions or up-rating the film speed, you have greater flexibility to work in low or artificial light. Black and white has a starkness and simplicity perfect for portraying people and events in everyday situations without the added gloss and distraction of colour.

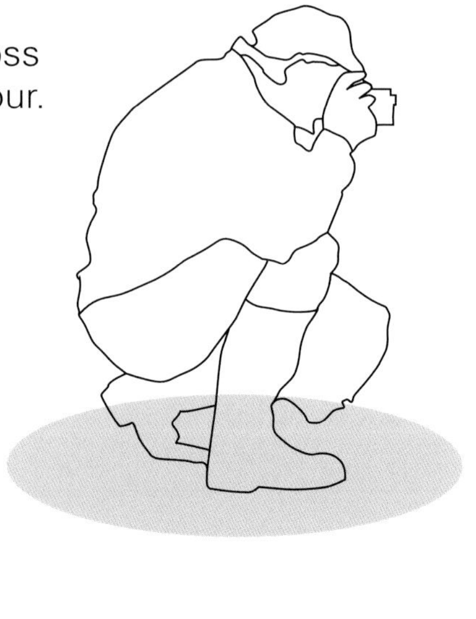

5

Background
The British athlete Chris Hallam MBE has won numerous medals in the wheelchair track event at Seol, Barcelona and Atlanta Paralympic games. He is one of the subjects of an award-winning book called The Road to Glory: Portraits of Britain's Paralympians by Richard and Fiona Bailey. The idea for the book began when the couple, commissioned by a magazine, visited a training session for disabled athletes. They decided there was potential for a large scale project, aiming to emphasise their subjects athleticism before their disability.

Composition
Richard wanted to capture the spirit, drive and commitment of his subjects and frequently chose an unusual camera angle to achieve a dynamic effect. Here, he lay on the ground and used a wide-angle lens to emphasise the wheelchair. The low angle and tilted camera give the impression of the athlete powering forward out of the picture.

Technique
Richard and Fiona took all the pictures for the book on location at training centres for the various sports they covered. The images were printed through a soft focus filter which gives a halo effect with the blacks bleeding into the white background. They were then sepia toned. By employing the same distinctive technique for all the pictures, they work together as a set, which is particularly important for a book which tells a story.

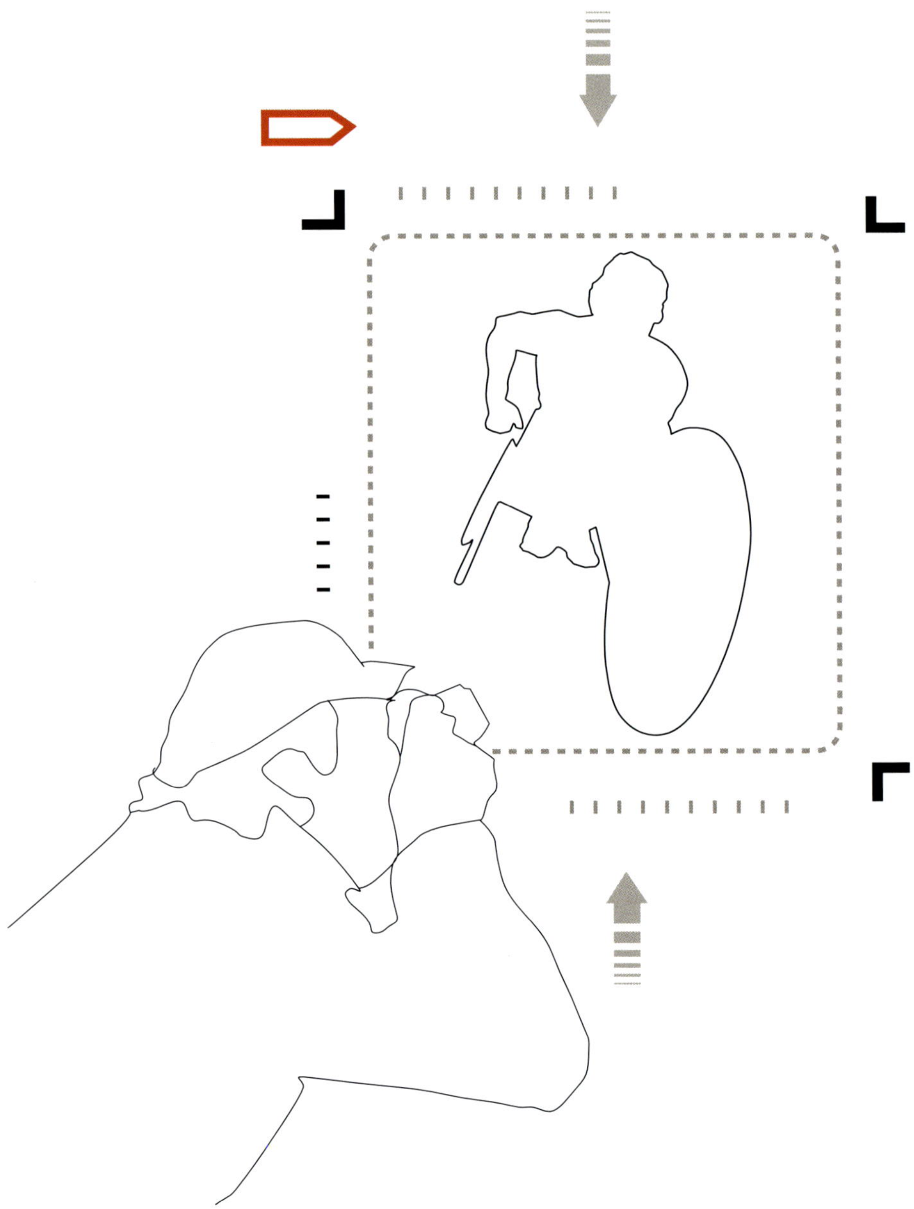

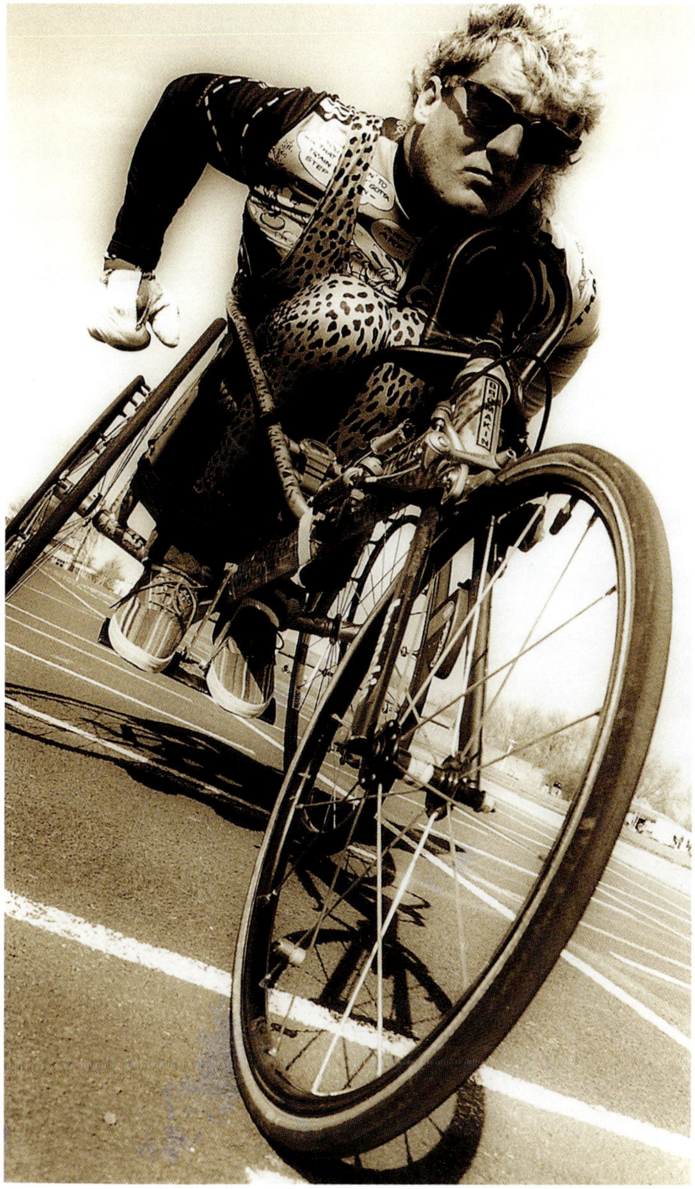

Technical details
Nikon FE camera with 24mm lens. Film was Ilford FP4 with an exposure of 1/125sec at f/8.

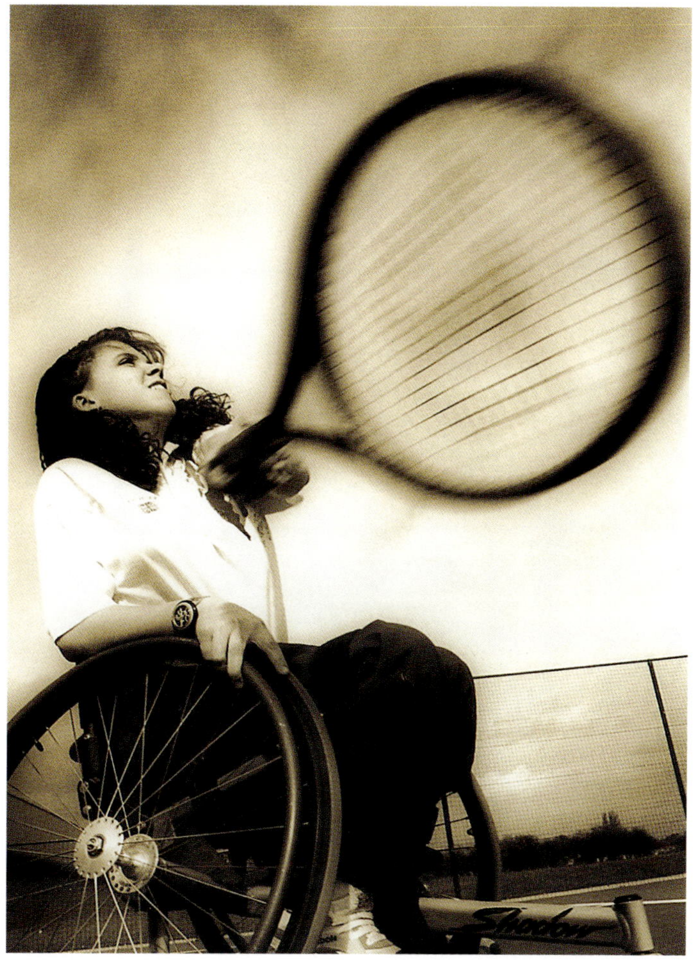

Again, Richard chose a very low, tilted camera angle to show the movement and power of Kimberley Dell swinging the racket. He set the camera on shutter priority at 1/15sec to allow for some blur around the racket.

Technical details
Nikon FE camera with 24mm lens. Film was Ilford FP4 with an exposure of 1/15sec.

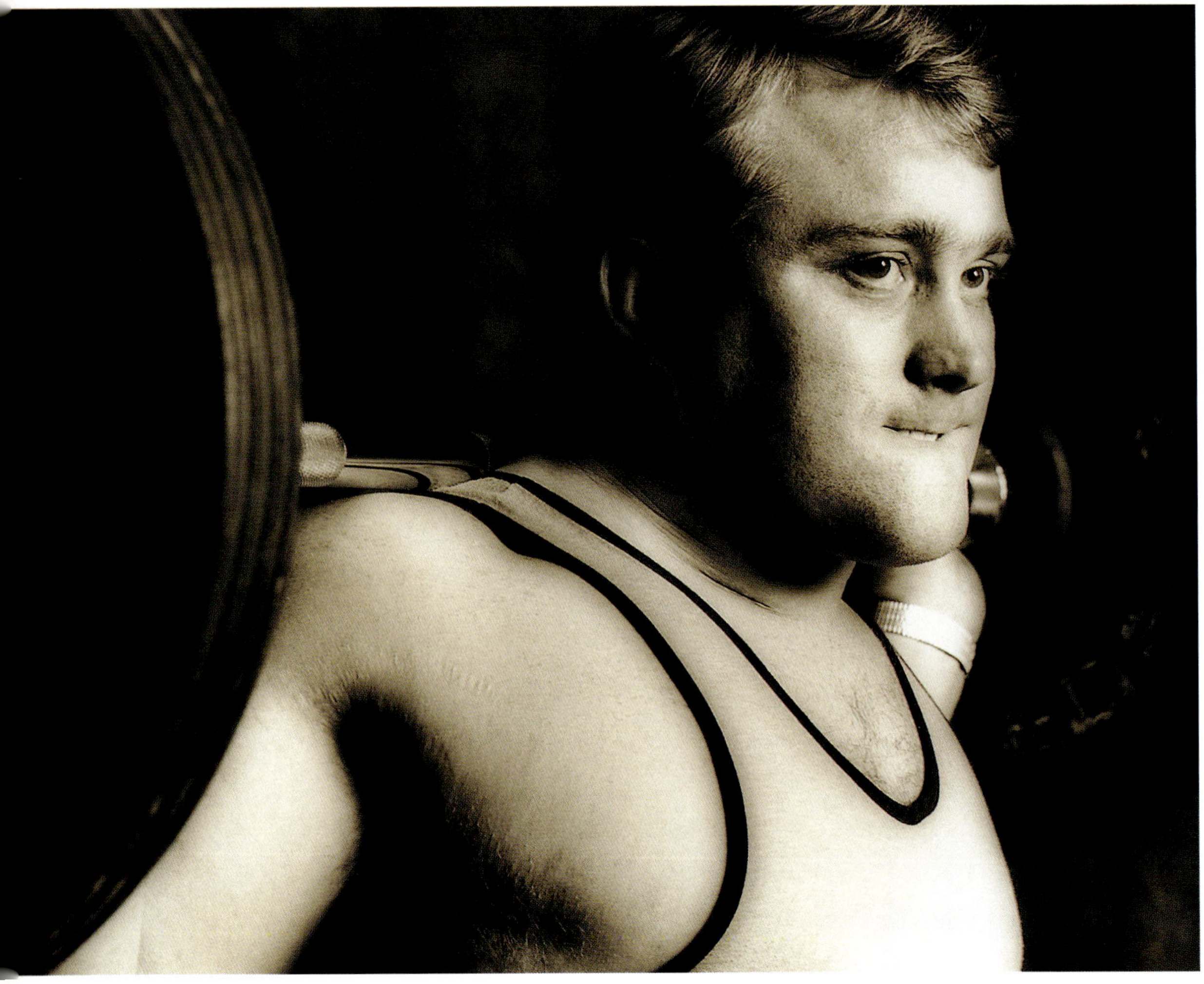

Composition

Richard Bailey set up a backdrop in the gym where the power-lifter Nicholas Slater was training, turning the location into a make-shift studio and eliminating the distracting background. He set the medium format camera on a tripod close to the subject for a tight portrait, showing the gritted teeth and look of determination on the face of the athlete.

Lighting

Because he was interrupting training sessions, Richard needed to work quickly. He kept the lighting simple, using just one Bowens flash unit with a softbox, positioned slightly to the side of the subject. The shadow areas were printed even darker to make a dramatic contrast with the face and body.

Technical details

Mamiya RB67 camera with 90mm lens. Film was Ilford FP4 with an exposure of 1/125sec at f/8.

'We used two different styles in the book. The slightly more formal close-up portraits which barely show the disability, contrast with the immediacy and realism of the action pictures.'

Richard Bailey

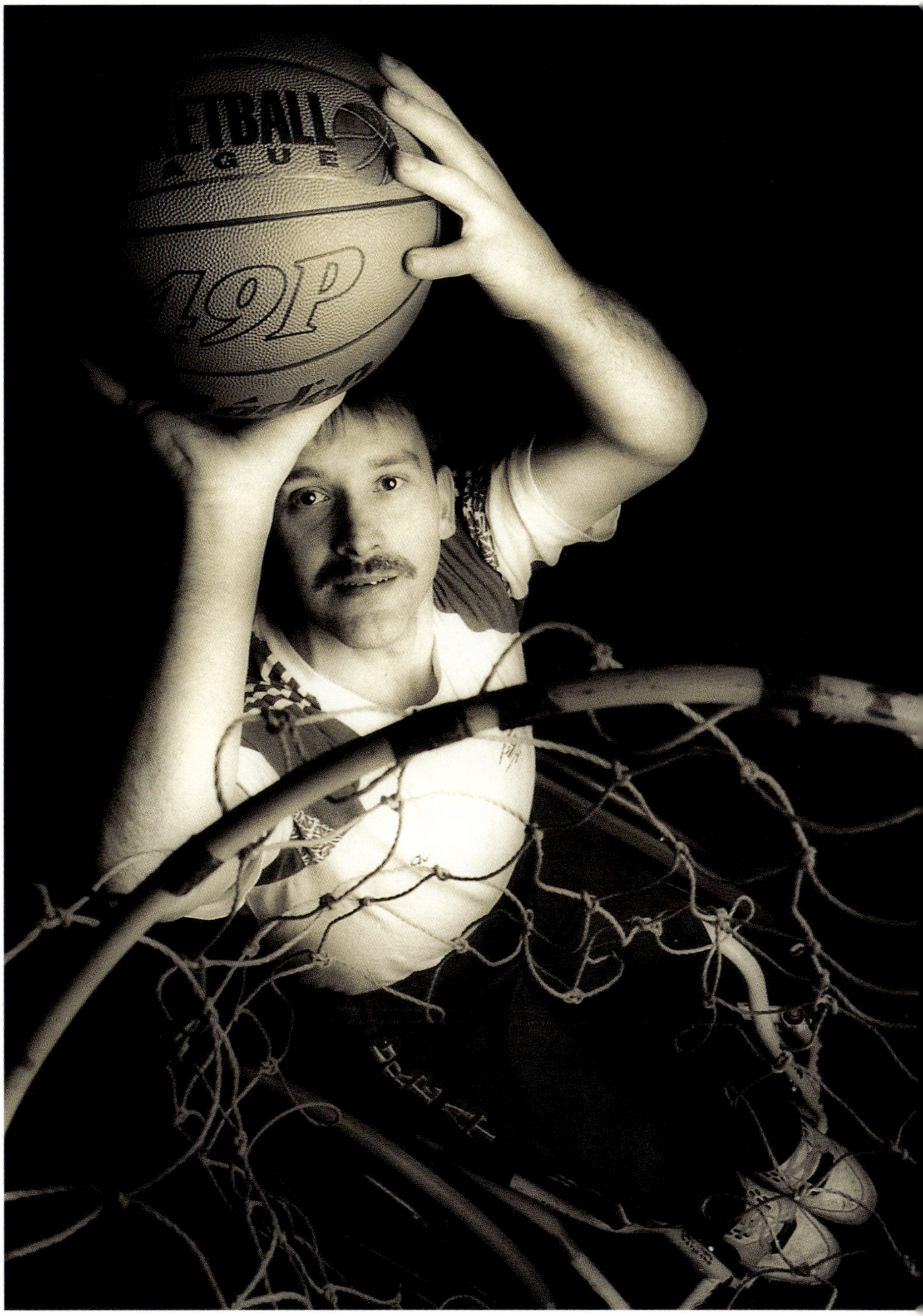

The wheelchair is barely noticeable in this portrait of basketball player, Gary Peel. Richard brought the loop of the net down lower and stood on a ladder to include all the elements of the player and his sport in a tight composition. The lighting came from a Bowens flash unit with softbox, placed to the right of the subject as you look at the picture.

Technical details
Mamiya RB67 camera with 65mm lens. Film was Ilford FP4 with an exposure of 1/125sec at f/8.

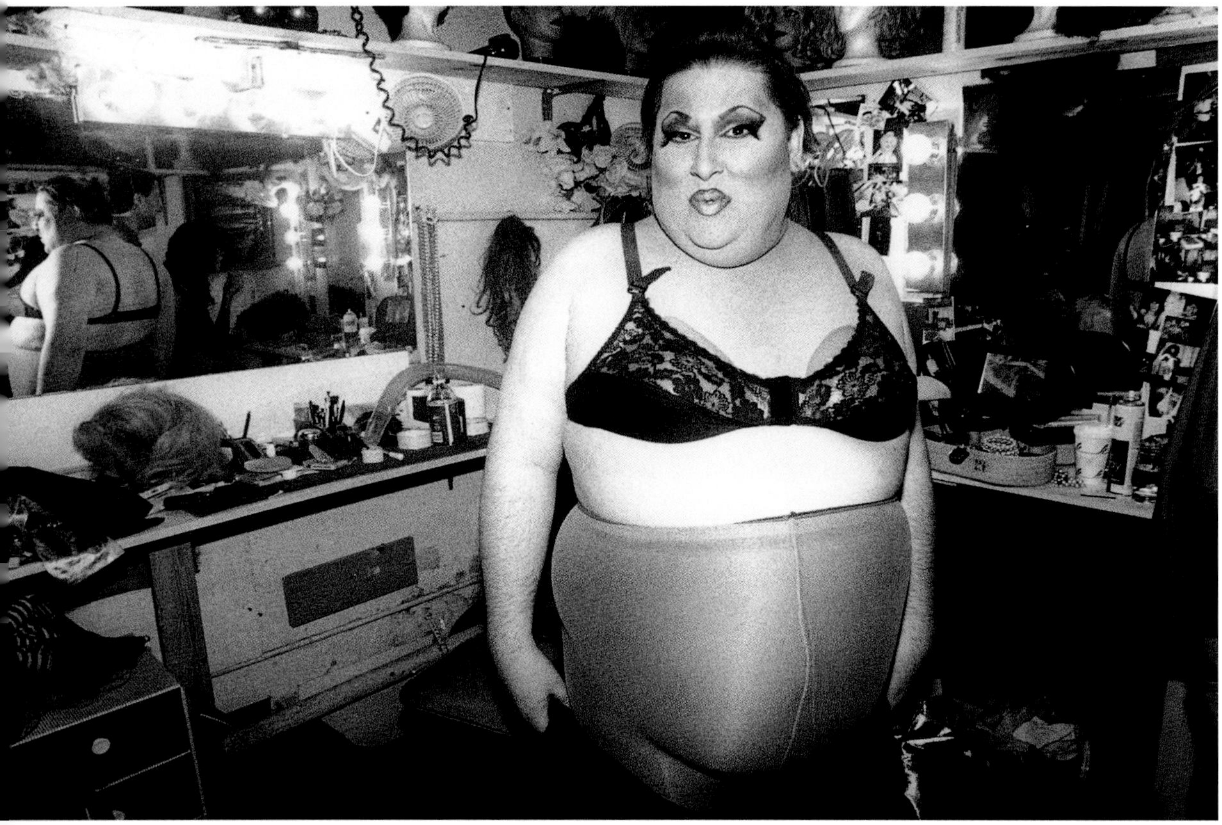

Composition
Both these pictures were part of a project on drag queens, commissioned from Sandy Huffaker by a newspaper in San Diego. 'This picture was very straightforward,' says Sandy. 'I walked into the dressing room of "De la Licious" and he struck a pose for the camera straight away. I usually like to put the subject off to the left or the right of the frame, but I liked the directness of him in the centre, looking straight at the camera. The stuffed bra and the wigs lining the wall provide humorous elements and the whole image feels very candid.'

Technique
Sandy used a wide-angle lens to include as much as possible of the cramped dressing room. He usually prefers to avoid flash where possible but it is effective here, providing strong light on the drag queen and giving the impression that he has been caught in the spotlight.

Mood
Although hardly a flattering portrait, this picture tells a story about life behind-the-scenes for a drag queen, in contrast to his glamorous image on stage. It's this candid, real-life element that forms the essence of a reportage portrait.

Technical details
Nikon F5 camera with Nikkor 20mm lens. Film was Tri-X Pan 400 rated at ISO 800 with flash.

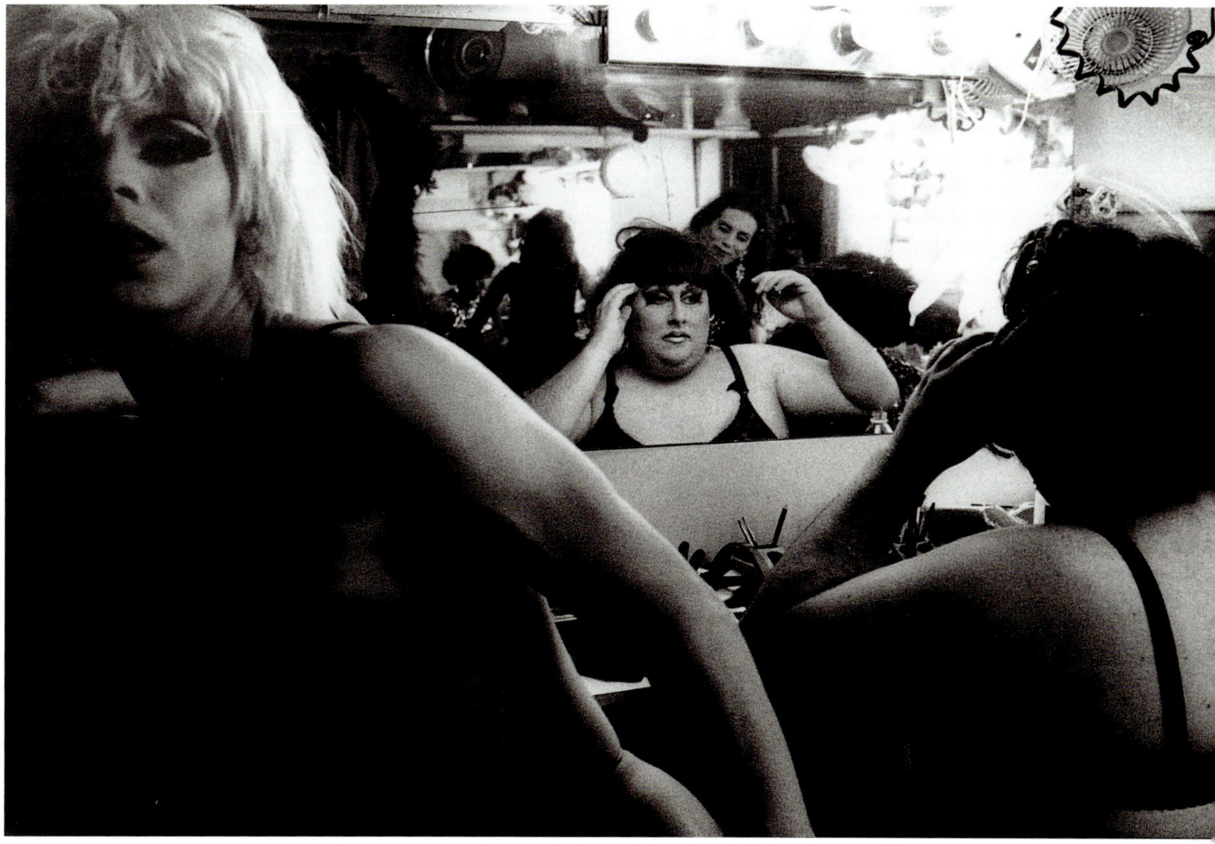

Technical details
Nikon F5 camera with 20mm lens. Film was Kodak Tri-X Pan 400 rated at ISO 800 with an exposure of 1/15sec at f/2.8.

Sandy used available light here rather than flash in order to capture the mood of the dressing room. The necessary slow shutter speed has blurred the figure on the right, adding to the candid feel of the image.

Composition
This was part of Sandy Huffaker's personal project on his travels through Haiti. 'I wanted to show a more human side to Haitians because they have often been misrepresented through the media. They are not just poor, needy people, but have strong family units and a certain spirituality that is beautiful. I like the way this family looks so proud.' The tight framing and the triangle formed by the three heads make this a very strong composition. The eye contact between the subjects and the camera is also very powerful.

Lighting
The daylight here was perfect for portraiture because the overhead clouds diffused the sunlight, giving a glow to the skin tones. If there is no cloud cover, it's best to find an area of open shade to avoid the harsh, contrasty light of direct sun.

Technique
Sandy switches from a 35mm camera to a 6x6cm Mamiya medium format camera for portraits which have a slightly more formal feel. The quality is slightly higher from the larger negative and the square format is suited to a structured composition.

Technical details
Mamiya C330 with 80mm lens. Film was Kodak Tri-X Pan with an exposure of 1/125sec at f/8.

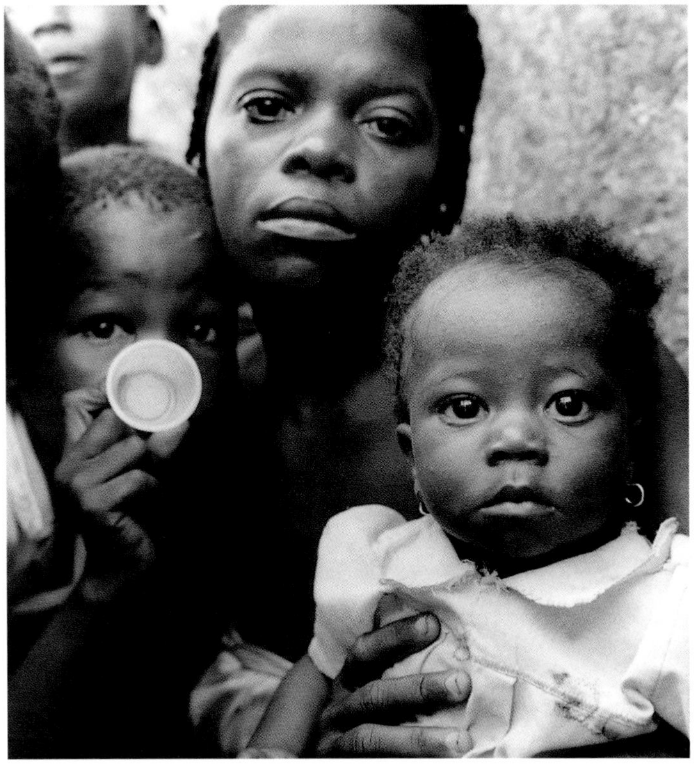

'This was a personal photo I shot while wandering round Tijuana, Mexico,' says Sandy. 'I peeked my head into this family's ceramics studio and they invited me in to shoot pictures. The child was acting up for the camera for the first dozen or so frames, but he finally lost interest and I was able to get a more honest shot.'

Technical details
Nikon F4 with 24mm lens. Film was Kodak Tri-X Pan with an exposure of 1/30sec at f/5.6.

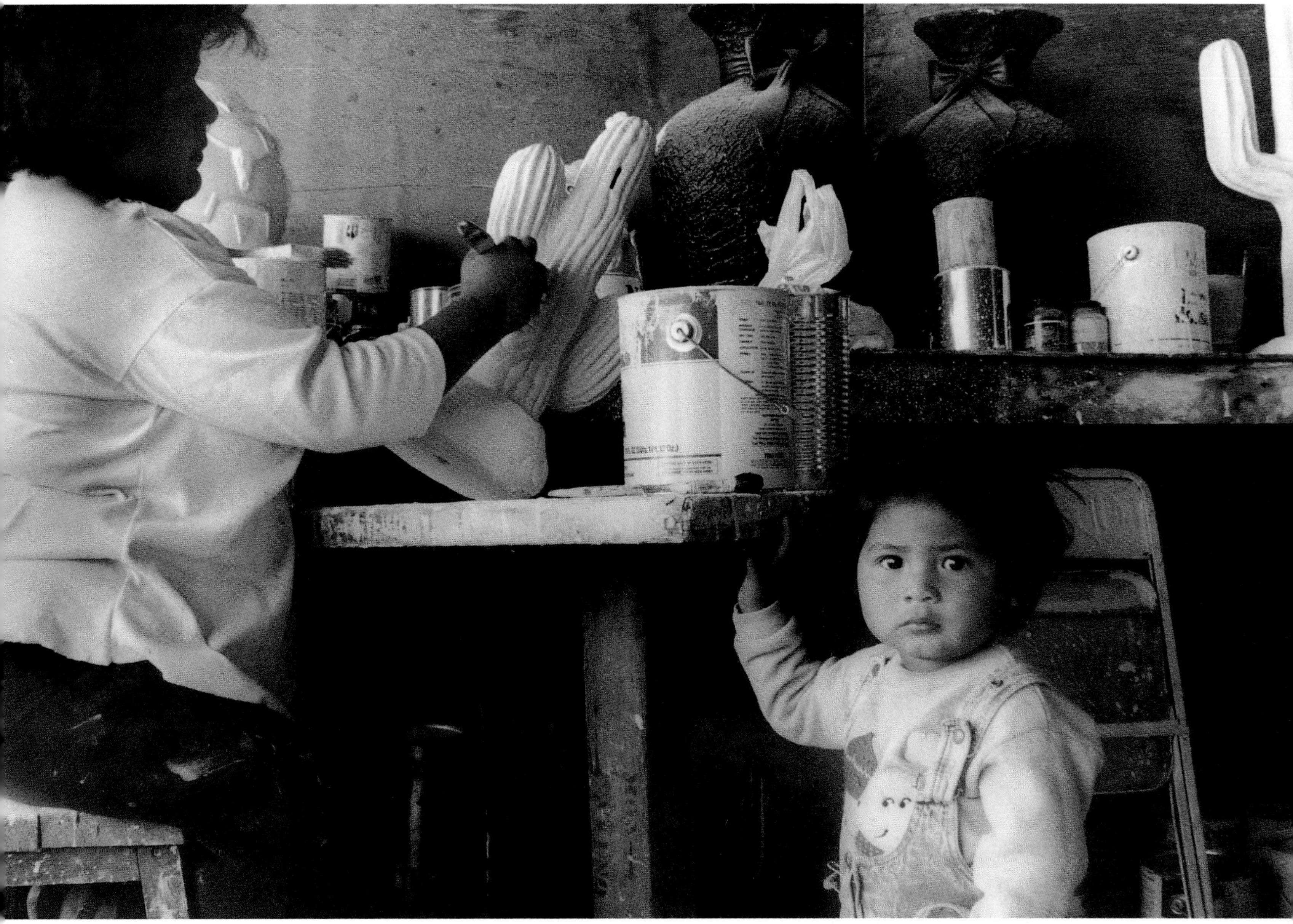

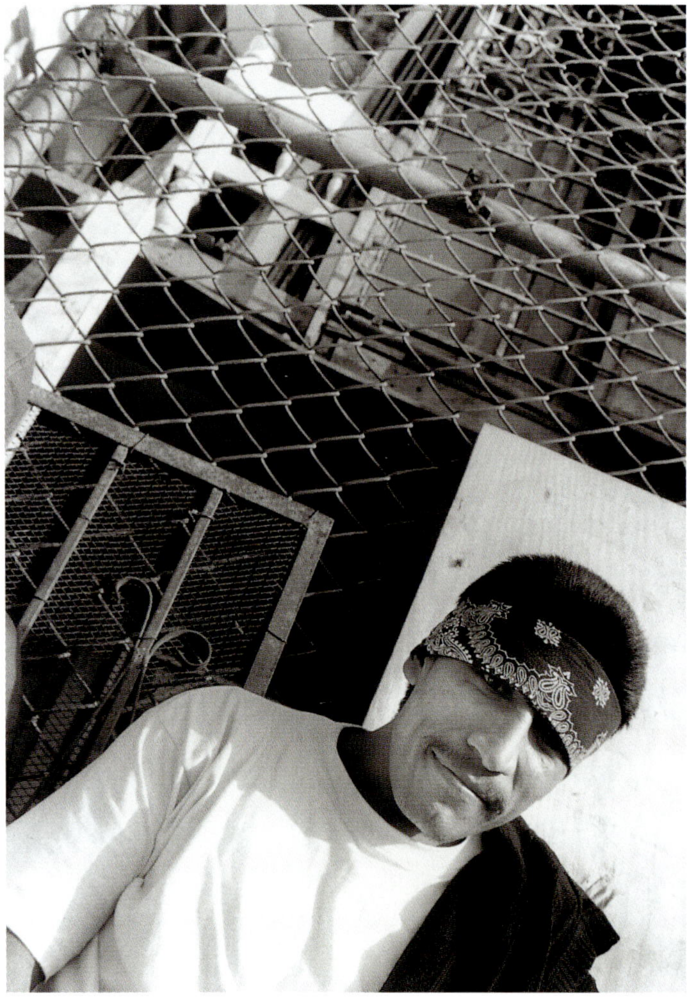

Composition
Sandy Huffaker was commissioned by the San Diego Reader newspaper to do a four-part picture story on La Mesa penitentiary in Tijuana, Mexico. As he approached this prisoner, he liked the way the wooden board framed his head. 'I also felt that the vertical length of the fence gives the viewer a sense of being caged in,' he says. 'By tilting the camera slightly, you see more of the fence height. The subject conveys a kind of sullen but tough look which is indicative of the attitude many of the prisoners projected.'

Technique
This picture demonstrates how it's worthwhile experimenting with camera angles and your own viewpoint as the photographer. A straightforward eye-level portrait may not always lead to the most dynamic composition. Sandy uses a 35mm camera with a 24mm lens for most of his location work. The wide-angle lens allows him to place the subject in the context of his environment and this simple, one camera, one lens set-up allows him to shoot quickly, when the opportunity arises.

Lighting
The hazy sunshine provided excellent natural lighting conditions without unwanted harsh shadows from direct sun, or the need for fill-in flash to brighten the subject's face. Sandy uses ISO 400 film on assignments like this because it has the latitude to capture good images in both light and dark situations.

Technical details
Nikon F4 camera with 24mm lens. Film was Tri-X Pan 400 with an exposure of 1/250sec at f/11.

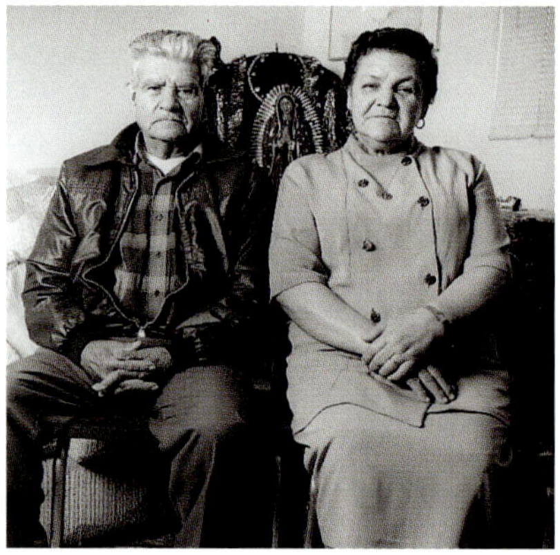

'I wanted to shoot an honest, straightforward portrait of this couple, which was commissioned by a newspaper, to show how two people can almost look alike after 50 years of marriage,' says Sandy. 'The religious icons also tell a lot about their strong faith.'

Technical details
Mamiya C330 camera with 80mm lens. Film was Kodak Tri-X Pan with Powerlight strobehead and an exposure of 1/125sec at f/16.

Commissioned by a newspaper for a story on Okies living in San Diego, this was the only unposed shot on a roll of film. Sandy liked the way the wife looks a little uneasy about her husband's prized ram skull. The lighting came from a large window and Sandy pushed the ISO 400 film by one stop to ISO 800 to give him better depth of field.

Technical details
Mamiya C330 camera with 65mm lens. Film was Tri-X Pan with an exposure of 1/60sec at f/4.

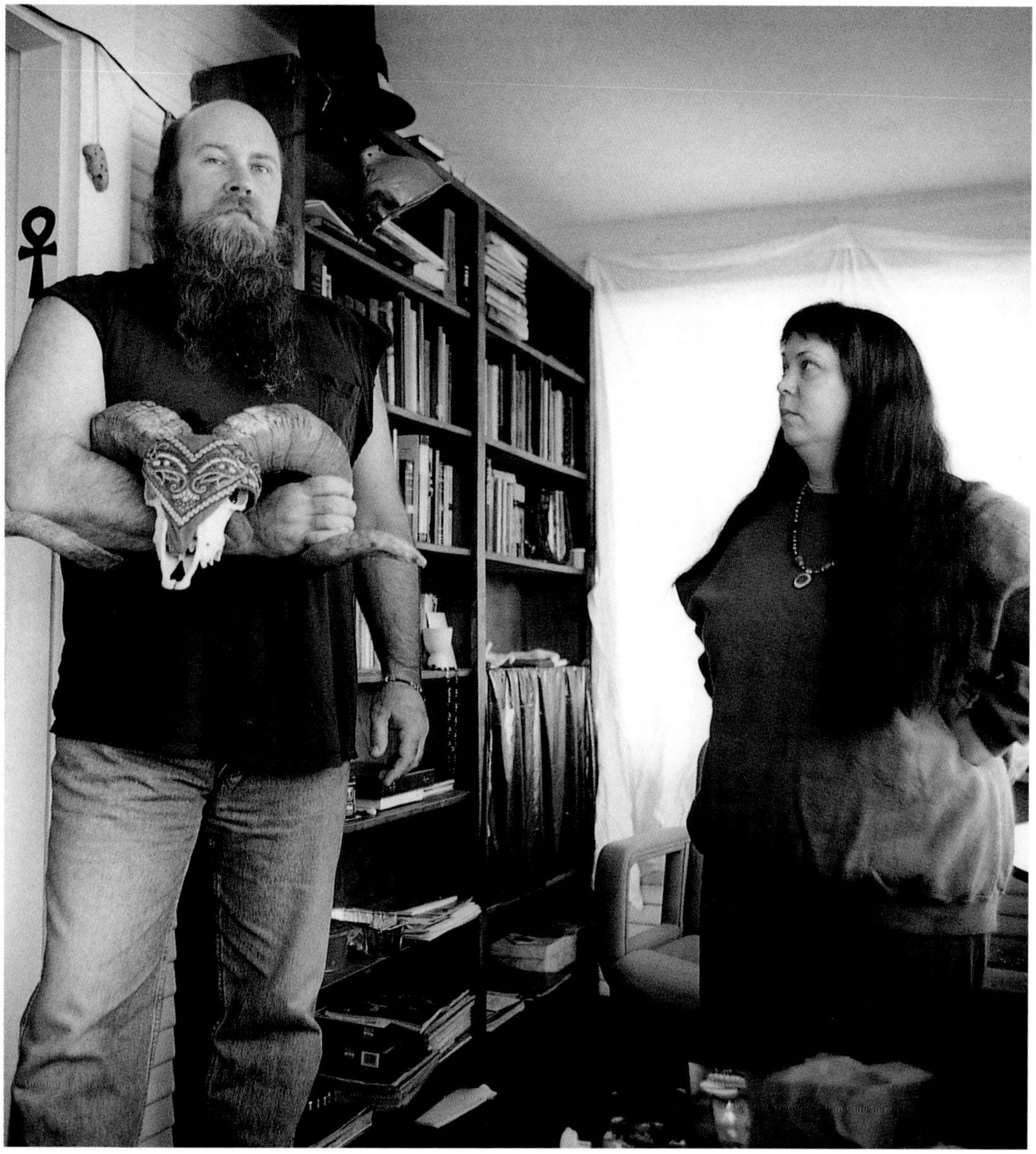

'I think this shot leaves the viewer with questions about the couple's relationship. I like it when a portrait makes me feel uneasy.'
Sandy Huffaker

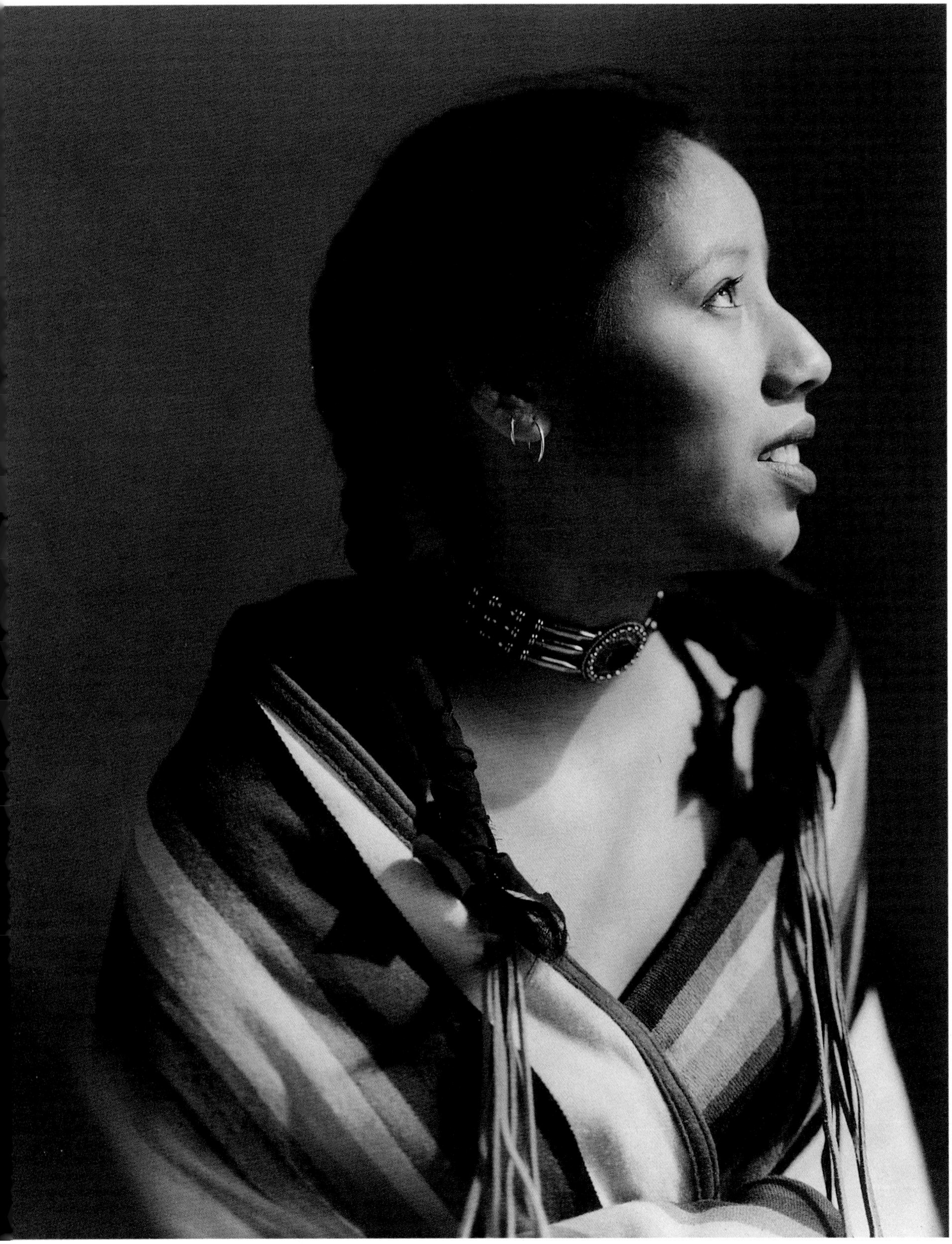

Rebekah, an Apache girl, photographed in her home on San Carlos Indian Reservation with a large format camera and lit with two kerosene lamps. The print was made using the platinum process.

Technical details

Wisner 8x10in camera with 450mm Nikkor lens. Film was Kodak Tri-X with an exposure of 1/10sec at f/9.

Composition
This portrait of Tiffany, an Apraho Indian, is from Gary Auerbach's series on Native Americans. These pictures have a formal and timeless style which is partly due to his use of large format 8x10in or 11x14in cameras. 'You go under a black hood and it's a very precise and formal process,' he says. 'I'm not looking for smiles from my subjects, unless that is a normal element in the image. Connecting with the eyes is a way to see into my subject.' This picture has been acquired by the US Library of Congress.

Technique
'Having seen Tiffany at a Native American banquet, I asked her to return the next day to be photographed,' says Gary. 'High winds prevented me shooting outside so I asked the hotel manager for a room on the sunny side of the building. I used a blanket from the bed as a backdrop with a reflector to fill in the light on the other side to the window.'

Printing
The 8x10in negative was contact printed on to Cranes' watermarked paper. This has a felt nap which gives an etched charcoal look when coated with platinum palladium metals.

Technical details
Rajah 8x10in camera with 450mm Nikkor lens. Film was Kodak Tri-X with an exposure of 1/10sec at f/9.

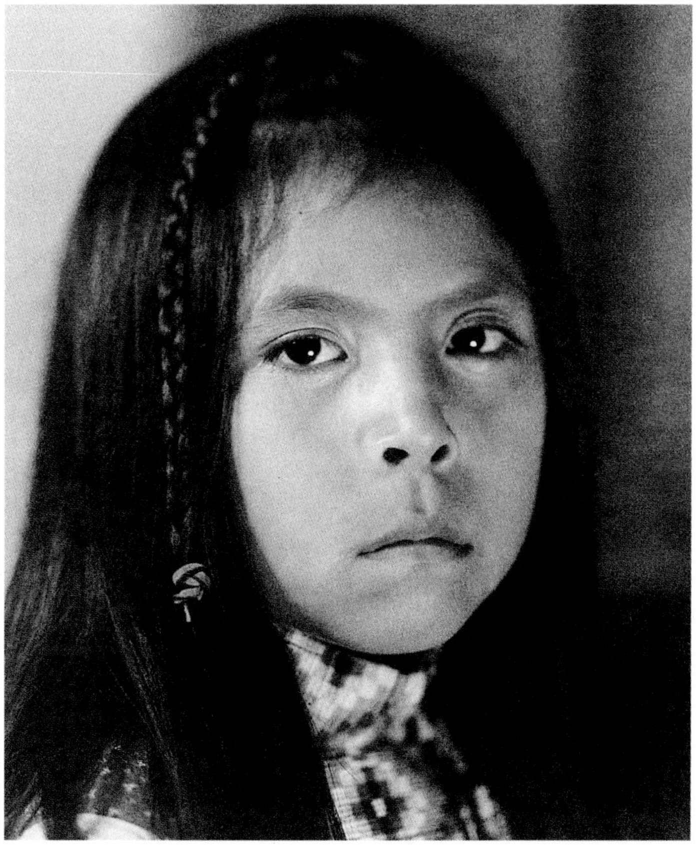

'Being a native New Yorker, I've always been fascinated by our Native American peoples. Now I have the opportunity to meet and photograph them, it's an honour.'
Gary Auerbach

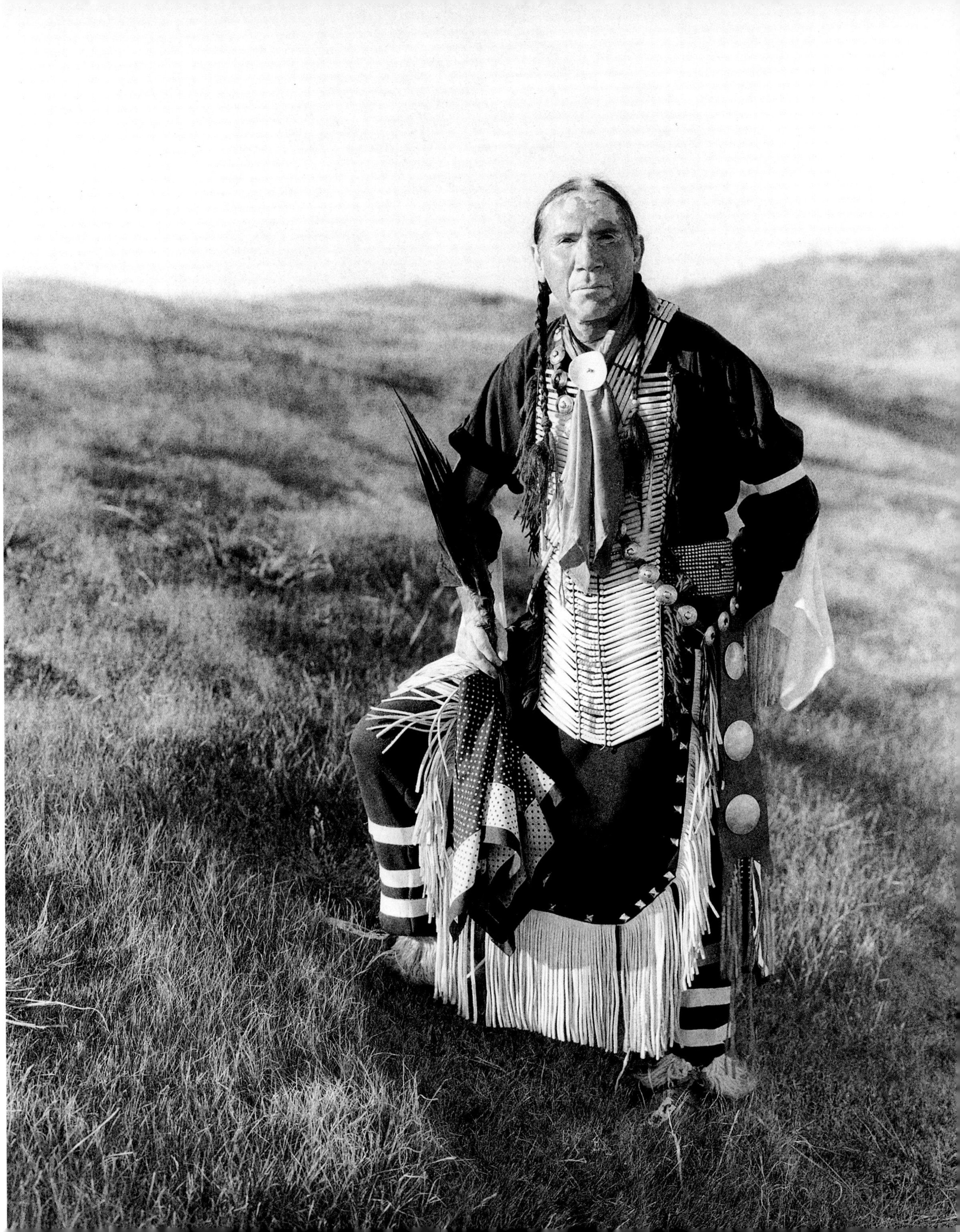

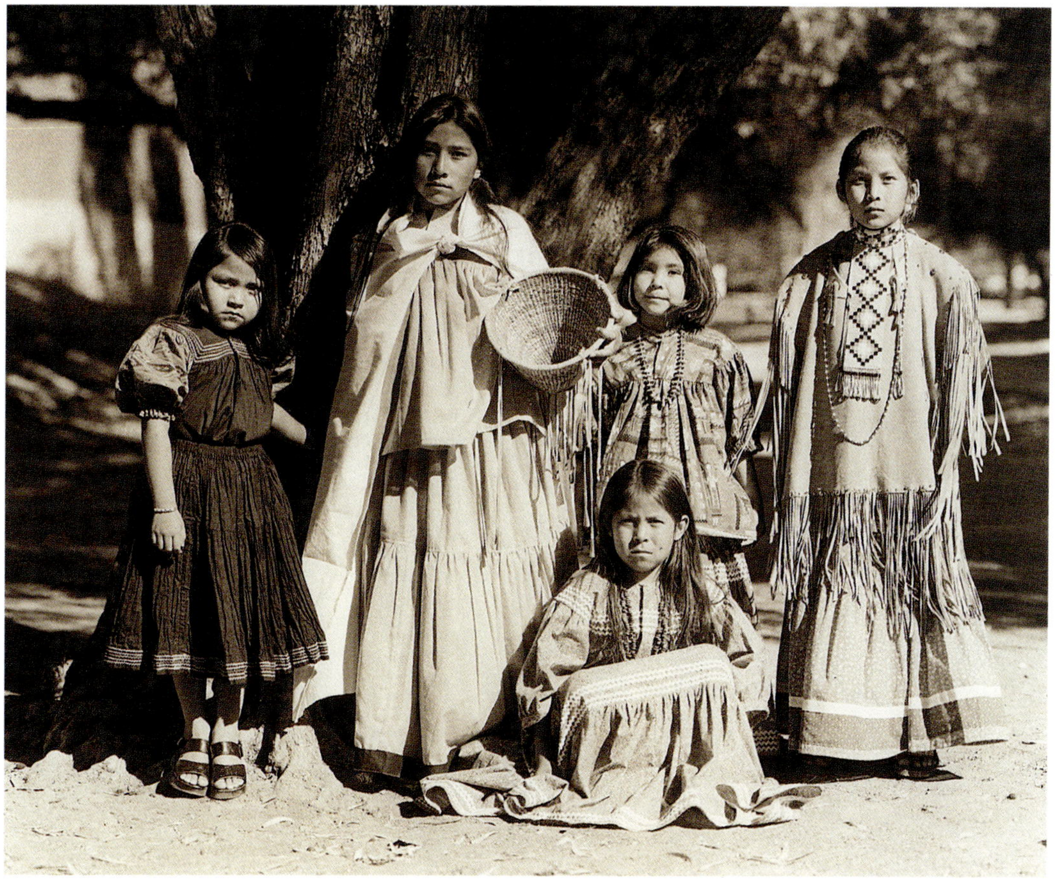

Composition
At an Indian arts fair in the San Carlos Reservation, Arizona, these children were doing an Apache fashion show and were happy to pose for Gary Auerbach. The clothing and setting look so authentic, it's hard to believe this photograph was taken in 1999. Even the way the girls are posed is reminiscent of much earlier portrait styles and it is easy to see that Gary is influenced by some portrait artists from the past. Since taking this picture, Gary has returned to the reservation five times to photograph these children.

Technique
Taken in directional sunlight, Gary used a reflector to fill in the shadows on the dark side of the subjects. He used a small aperture for good depth of field, but a slow shutter speed, which meant that the children had to practice standing very still.

Printing
Gary specialises in the platinum process, which involves working on the print with metallic emulsions. 'I was searching for a style of print making that would be relatively permanent because silver-based photographs have an image permanence problem,' he says. 'Platinum photographs will last as long as the paper lasts – 500 years or more.'

Technical details
Wisner 8x10in camera with 450mm Nikkor lens. Film was Kodak Tri-X with an exposure of 1/10sec at f/11.

Having gone to an Indian pow-wow, Gary chose to photograph Bob Red Elk out of 300 Native Americans. 'I knew his black and white outfit would translate well into the platinum print,' he says. It was taken in direct sunlight, with a reflector placed to the right of the camera to fill in shadows.

Technical details
Wisner 11x14in camera with 450mm Nikkor lens. Film was Ilford FP4 with an exposure of 1/10sec at f/11.

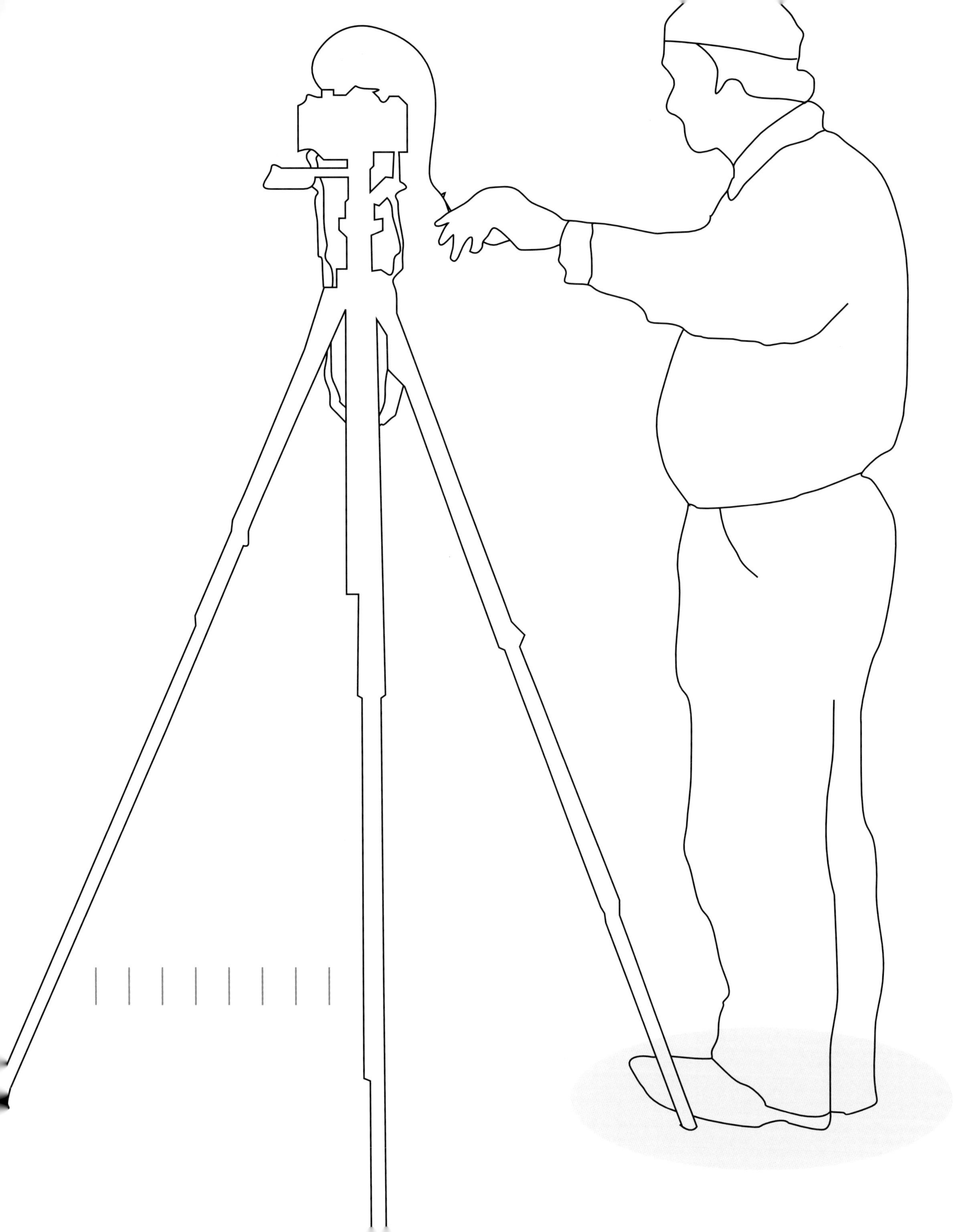

editorial assignments

6

If travel broadens the mind, then it also greatly increases the scope for the portrait photographer. Immersing yourself in a different culture is a sure-fire way of finding new inspiration, with numerous commercial opportunities for good quality results. Always show respect for your subject, and never ignore their wishes if they decline to be photographed.
The promise of prints in return for a picture is good practice, so long as you stick by your word.

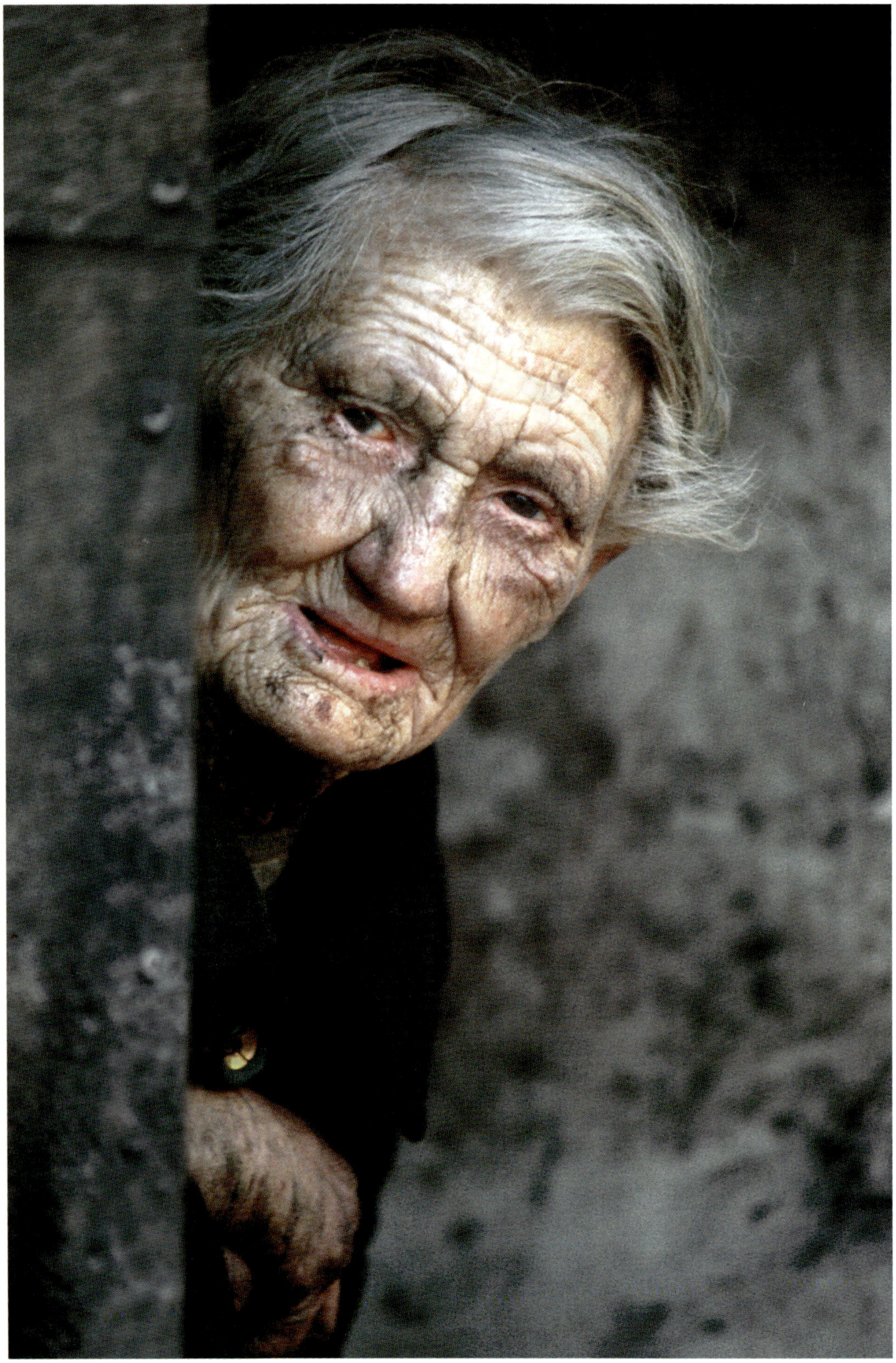

'Bertha lived about eight miles from me and could often be seen in the city centre,' explains Philip. 'I found out she lived in an old caravan and went there to see if I could take some pictures. She was reluctant at first but I took some prints back for her on a second visit, when this was taken, and she was more open then.'

Technical details
Canon T90 camera with 80–200mm lens. Film was Kodachrome 200 with an exposure of f/8.

Composition
This was taken in the town of Bhaktapur, about ten miles from Kathmandu in Nepal. 'I spent the day wandering around and happened across this old lady, sitting in a doorway with a friend,' says Philip. 'She was embarrassed when I asked to take her picture and declined but a small crowd, mainly children, had gathered and were all coaxing her to agree. She did, but stood, staring straight ahead like a soldier. I took a few pictures anyway and an even bigger crowd gathered. After five or ten minutes she started enjoying herself and I caught this lovely cheeky expression.'

Technique
Philip always carries a solid tripod on location, even when he's trekking. 'I don't see the point of spending money on good lenses to have the pictures spoiled by camera shake,' he says. 'You don't always have time to use a tripod for portraits, but in this case I was taking a series of pictures and so I was able to set the camera up on it.'

Lighting
The light here was ideal for a portrait. The sky was bright but overcast which produced a soft light on the subject, accentuating the lines and contours of her interesting face. Philip used a wide aperture to minimise the background.

Technical details
Canon T90 camera with 80–200mm lens. Film was Fujifilm Sensia 100 with an exposure of f/4.

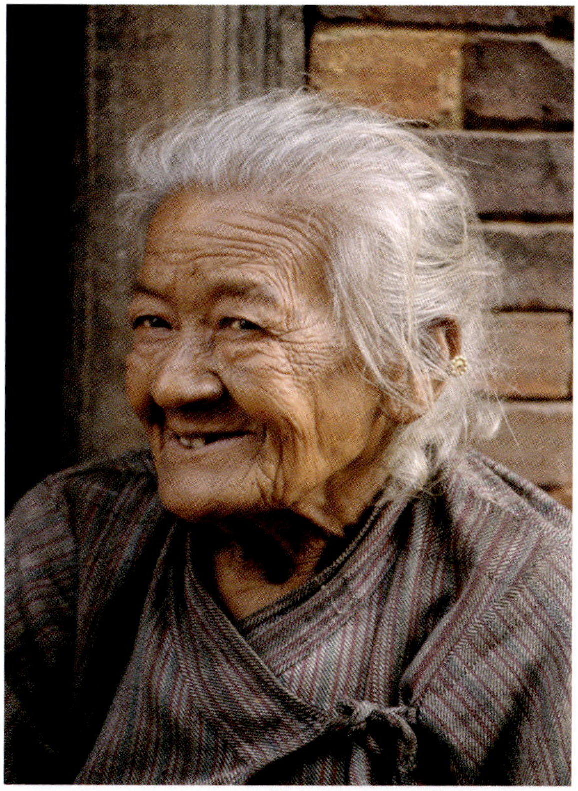

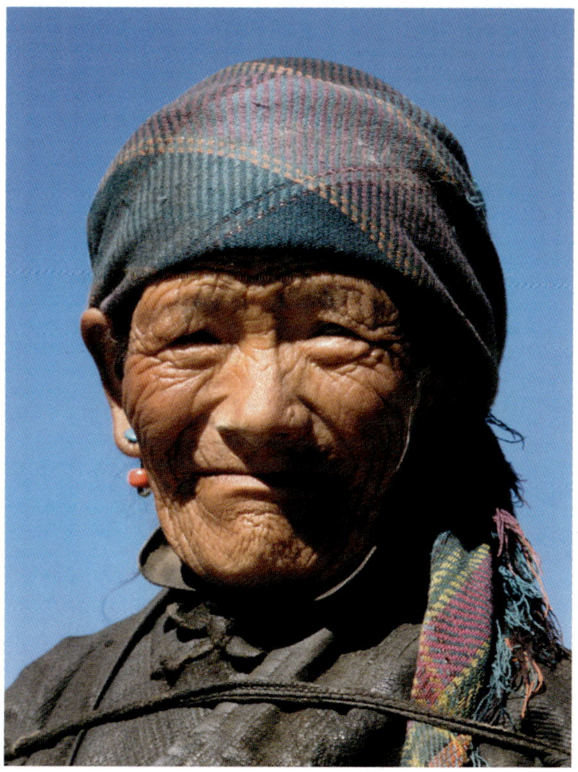

Philip Sprague came across this old lady in a village on the main road between Nepal and Tibet. 'She was standing outside a petrol station which didn't make a good background, so I took a low viewpoint to make the sky the background. I was fascinated by her clothing and the very hard life she must have. It was October then, and already very cold.'

Technical details
Canon T90 with 28–85mm lens. Film was Fujifilm Sensia 100 with an exposure of f/5.6.

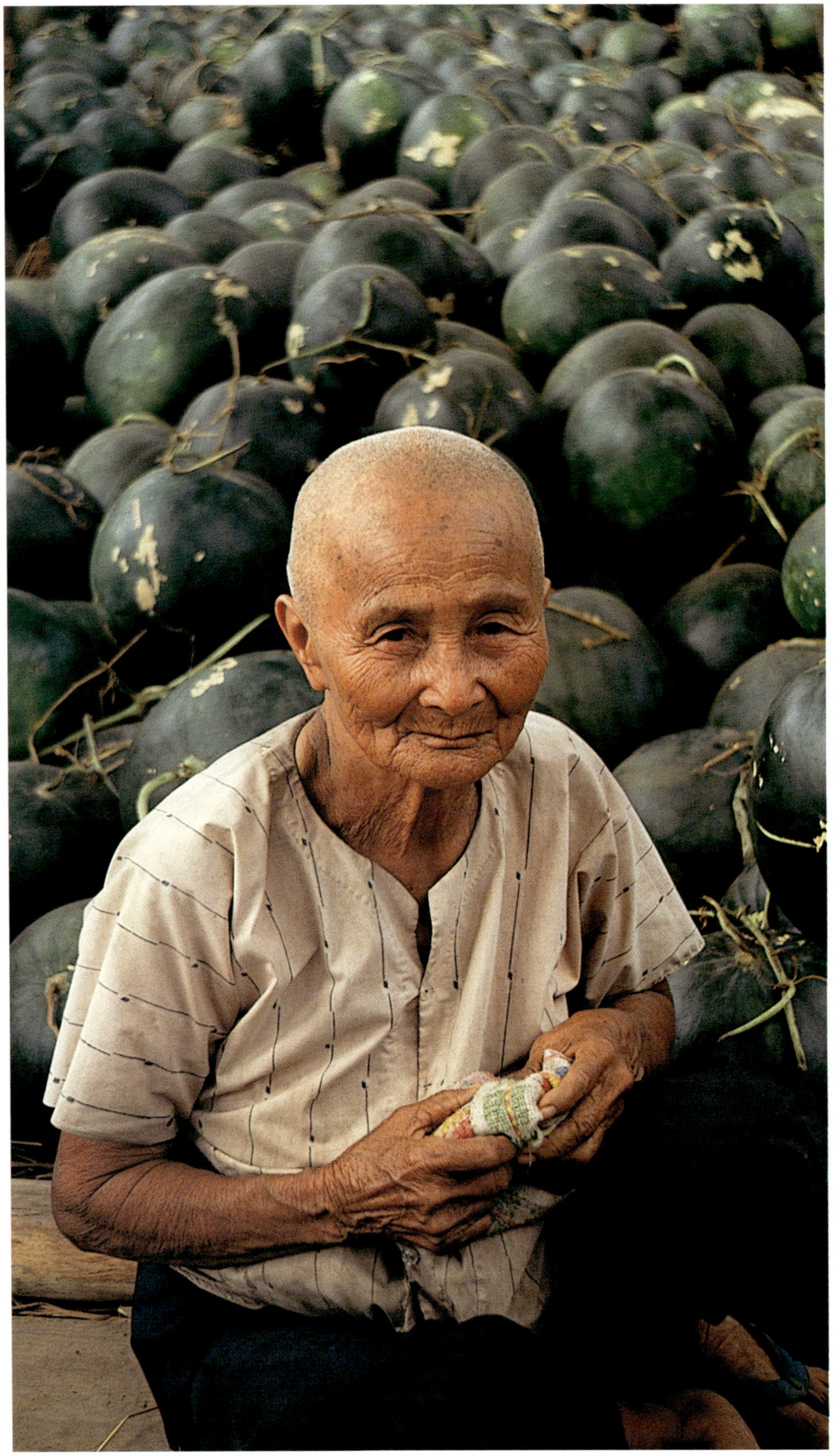

'I was on a tour in Vietnam and spotted this woman selling melons by the side of the road, so I yelled to the driver to stop,' says Joan Wakelin. 'She reminded me of the melons!'

Technical details
Minolta 7Xi camera with 28–105mm lens. Film was Kodak Pro 64 with program exposure.

Composition

This grandmother belongs to the ethnic group Sgaw Karen, and lives in a village in Chiang Mai Province, Northern Thailand. 'I met her while I was visiting the village and, after showing her a snapshot of my wife to break the ice, she consented to have her portrait taken,' explains EJ Haas. 'I indicated that I would like her to sit in the shade of her porch out of the glaring tropical sun. She did so and then took out her pipe and tobacco which many older Karen women like to smoke. As you can see, she enjoyed herself, contentedly smoking away while observing these odd western tourists taking her portrait.'

Technique

EJ Haas used a zoom lens on his 35mm camera for a fairly tight crop on the seated figure. His companion held a white Photoflex reflector to bounce some light on to her face to help make her stand out from the background which was in shadow. 'Later I had prints made of her portrait which I gave to the tour guide to deliver to her next time he went to the village.'

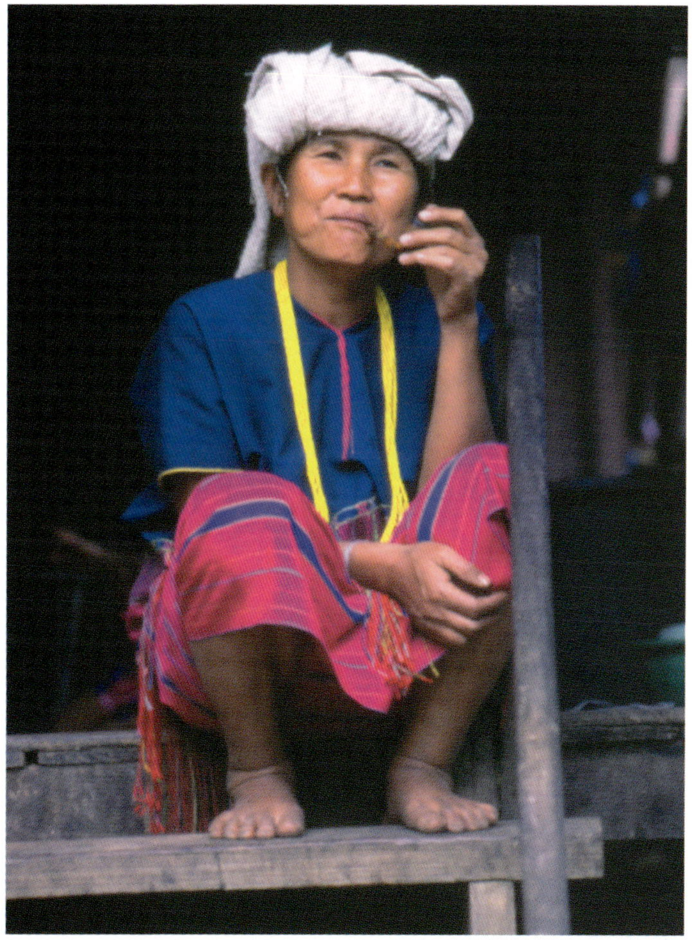

Tip

Haas feels it's degrading to people to offer them money for being photographed. 'I feel that making a small gift, such as pens, or buying something from them is more appropriate – many tribal people have fruit, vegetables or handcrafts for sale.'

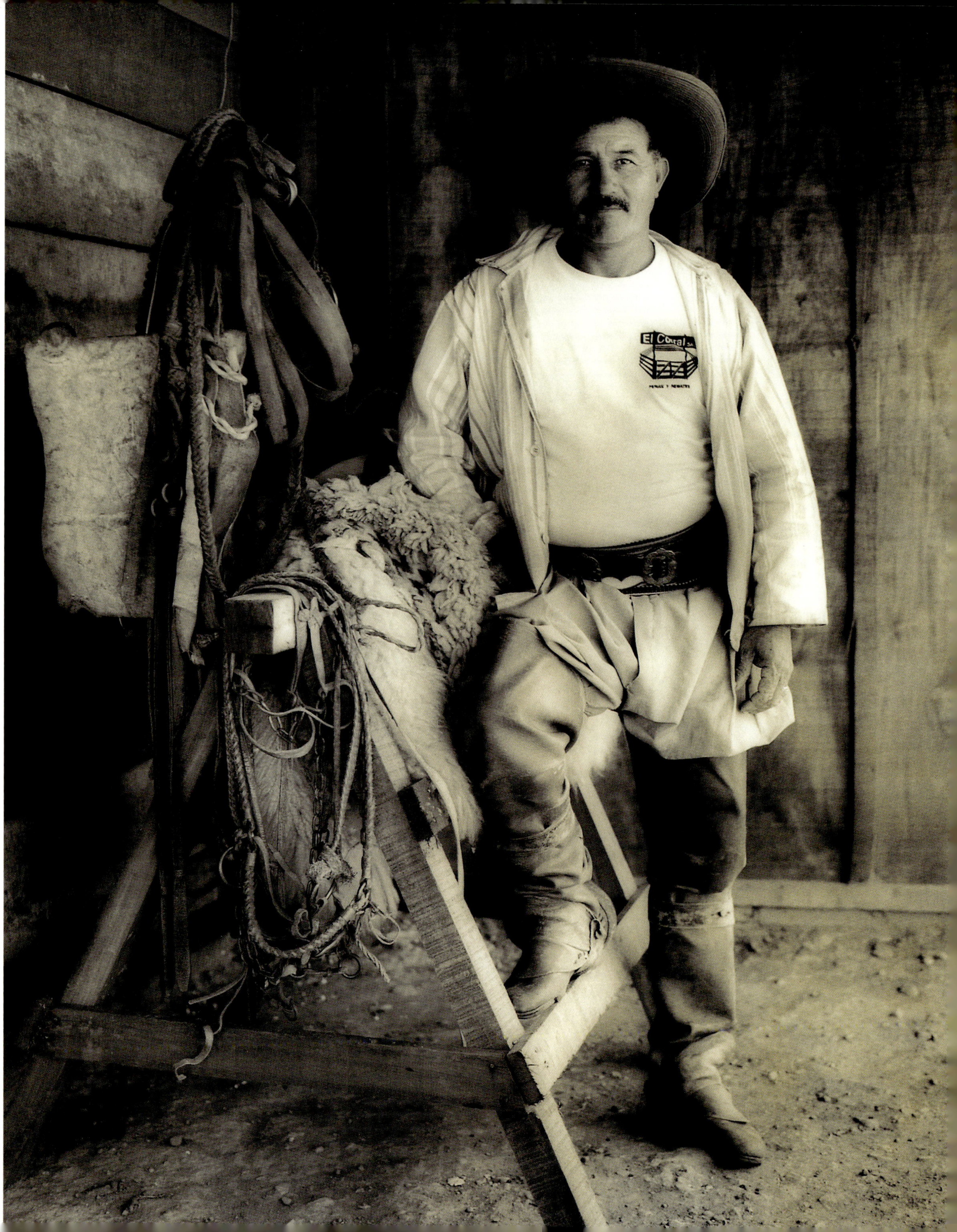
El Corral

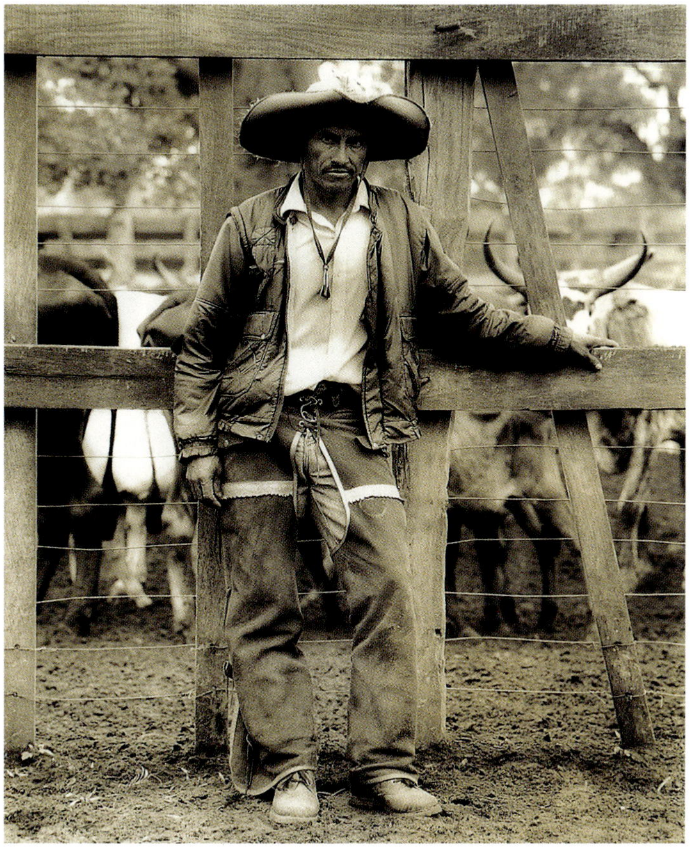

Composition

Richard spent three months travelling in Paraguay, photographing the many different types of people who live there. He wanted to give an idea of what their everyday lives are like and showing them in their environment was the best way of doing this. He found this ranch on the border with Bolivia where the men work in much the same way as they have for decades. For this portrait, he asked the rancher to stand in front of the wooden fence which provides an attractive prop. The inclusion of the cattle in the background help to place the man in the context of his work.

Technique

The picture was taken on a medium format camera on a tripod which gave Richard optimum image quality and allowed him to take his time over the composition. Many photographers choose 35mm SLRs for travel work, chiefly because they are lighter and easier to carry and this format is readily accepted by most picture libraries. Richard was after quality rather than quantity on his trip and had in mind producing exhibition prints on his return. The larger negative has the edge over 35mm when it comes to making enlargements.

Lighting

Taken in daylight on a bright but slightly overcast day, there was no problem here with excessive contrast or unwanted shadows. The negative was printed through a soft focus filter and the print was then sepia toned.

Technical details

Mamiya RB67 camera with 80mm lens. Film was Ilford FP4 with an exposure of 1/125sec at f/8.

Richard Bailey spent a few minutes arranging the items in this stable to make sure they worked well within the composition. He took a Polaroid picture first which enabled him to check the lighting. It also made a welcome gift for his subject who was then only too happy to pose for another few frames on the medium format camera.

Technical details

Mamiya RB67 camera with 80mm lens. Film was Ilford FP4 with an exposure of 1/125sec at f/8.

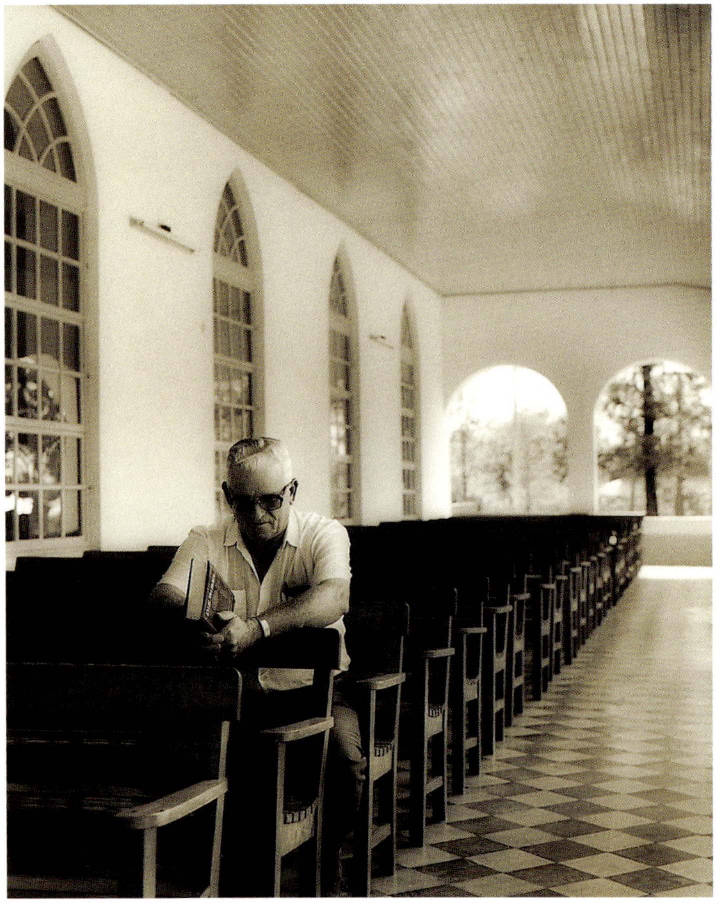

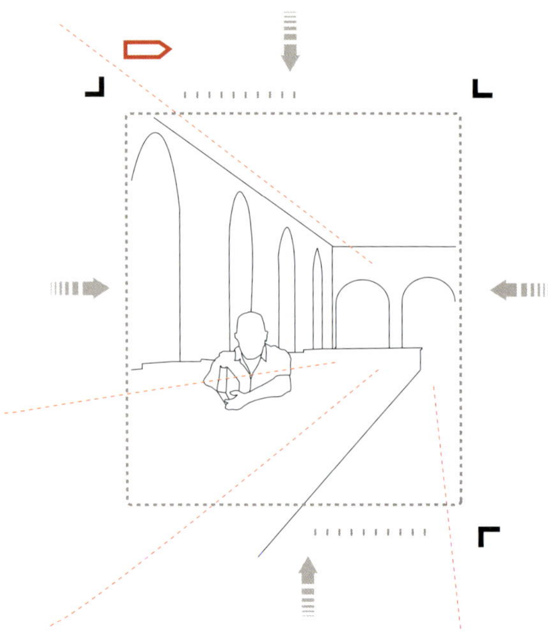

Composition

A Mennonite preacher in the town of Filadelfia in Paraguay. 'I turned up there and explained to the preacher what I was doing and asked if I could take some pictures,' says Richard Bailey. 'The church was quite stark and too dark inside. This is outside, where they have pews to use in hot weather.' The composition of the picture is very graphic, with the line of the pews leading the eye through the window on the end wall, the 180mm lens giving a foreshortening effect.

Technique

By explaining his motives for taking pictures, Richard found all his subjects were happy to oblige and usually proud to show off their environment, whether it was their workplace, home or, in this case, church. It's important to gain this kind of rapport if you want to take your time to seek out the best possible location and encourage the subject into the pose you require.

Lighting

The sunlight entering this outside area through the colonnade was quite adequate for an exposure and Richard didn't need any additional light source. He does all his own printing and was able to darken the far side of the pews slightly to contrast with the lighter tones of the walls and ceiling.

Technical details

Mamiya RB67 camera with 180mm lens. Film was Ilford FP4 with an exposure of 1/125sec at f/5.6.

Another Mennonite preacher, this time in the village of Rio Verde in Paraguay. Richard asked him if he could take a picture but he didn't alter his subject's location or pose in any way. Like the other portraits in this series, it was printed through a soft focus filter and sepia toned.

Technical details
Mamiya RB67 camera with 90mm lens. Film was Ilford FP4 with an exposure of 1/125sec at f/8.

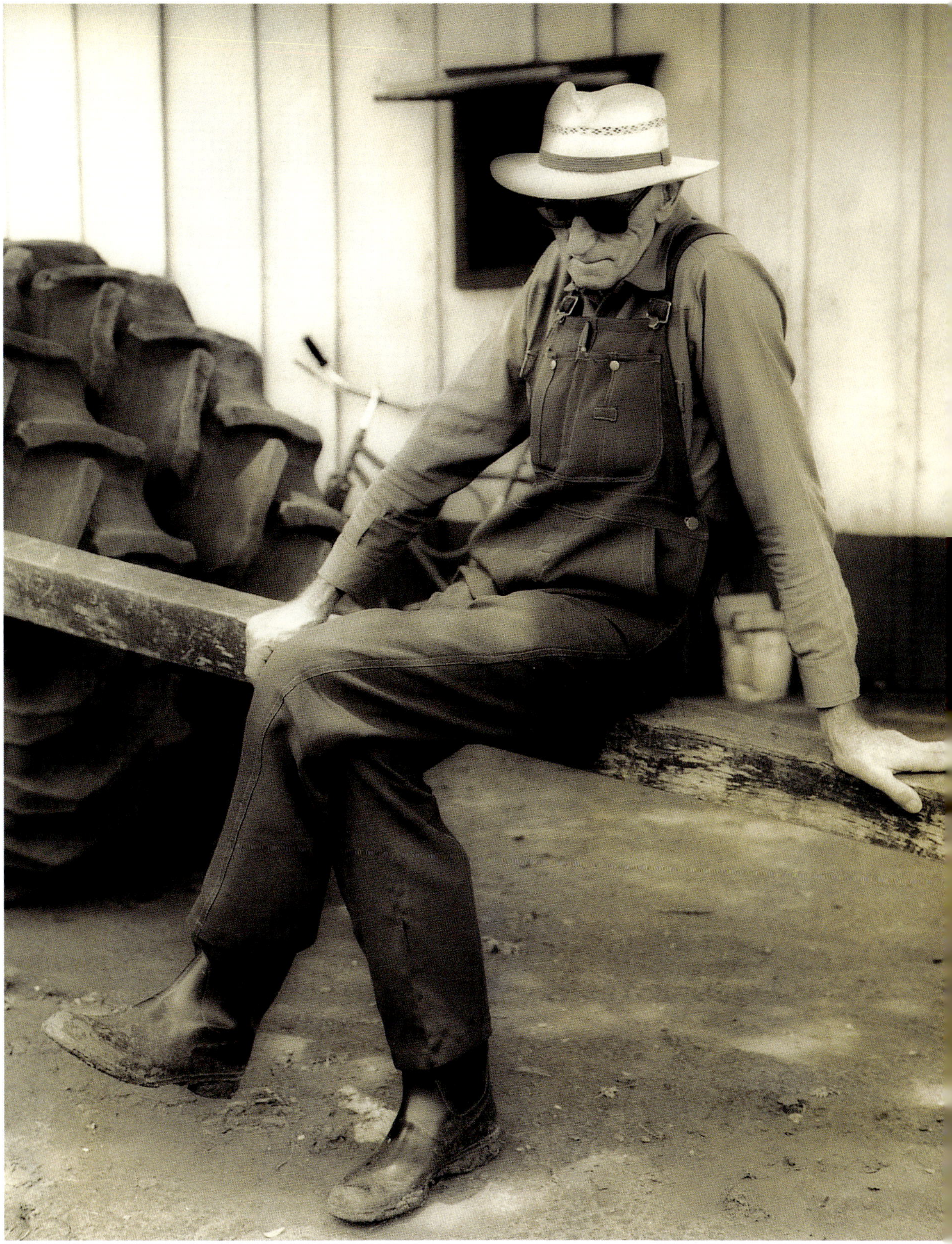

Composition

Rajasthan is one of the most colourful regions of India, both in its architecture and the ornate clothing and jewellery of the women. The annual Jaisalmer Desert festival in Rajasthan, where this picture was taken, is an excellent event for travel portraiture because a large number of people attend, most in their national costume. This young girl was sitting in an enclosed ornate wagon on the fairground and Dennis Cox used a zoom lens to crop in tightly on her face and colourful head-dress.

Technique

Many foreign tourists attend the Jaisalmer festival and so the people are quite accustomed to having their picture taken. It's still best to ask permission first, however, especially if you want a posed portrait such as this. Dennis used a Gitzo tripod here, to allow for an accurate composition and to ensure there was no camera shake. This can otherwise be a problem when using a long telephoto lens.

Lighting

This was taken in bright sunshine but the face of the girl was slightly in the shade of the wagon. Dennis used his Minolta 5400 flash unit, set at one stop underexposed to provide a little fill-in flash through the wagon's window to lift the skin tones.

Technical details

Minolta Dynax 800si camera with 100–300mm zoom. Film was Kodak Ektachrome 100 with automatic exposure.

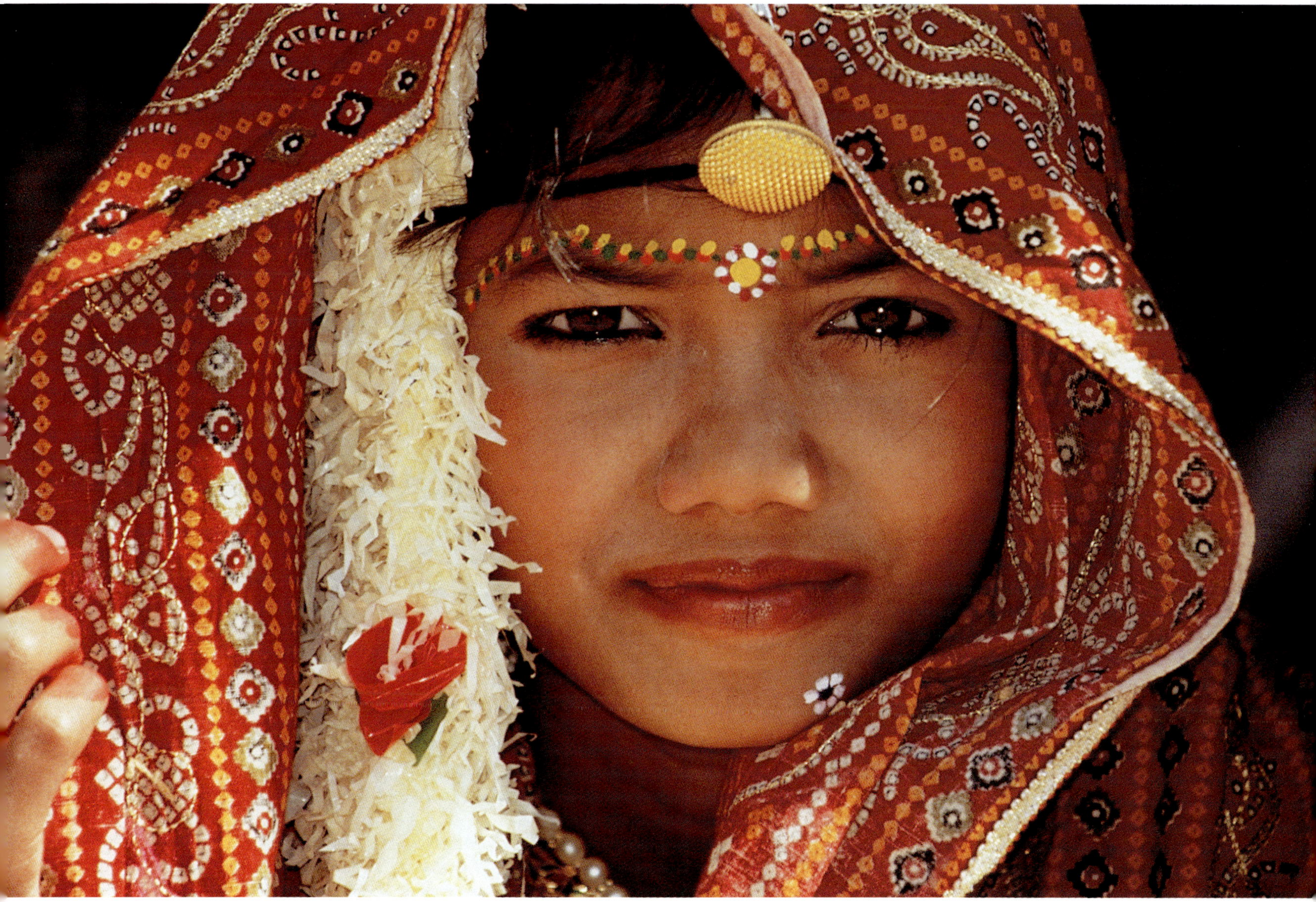

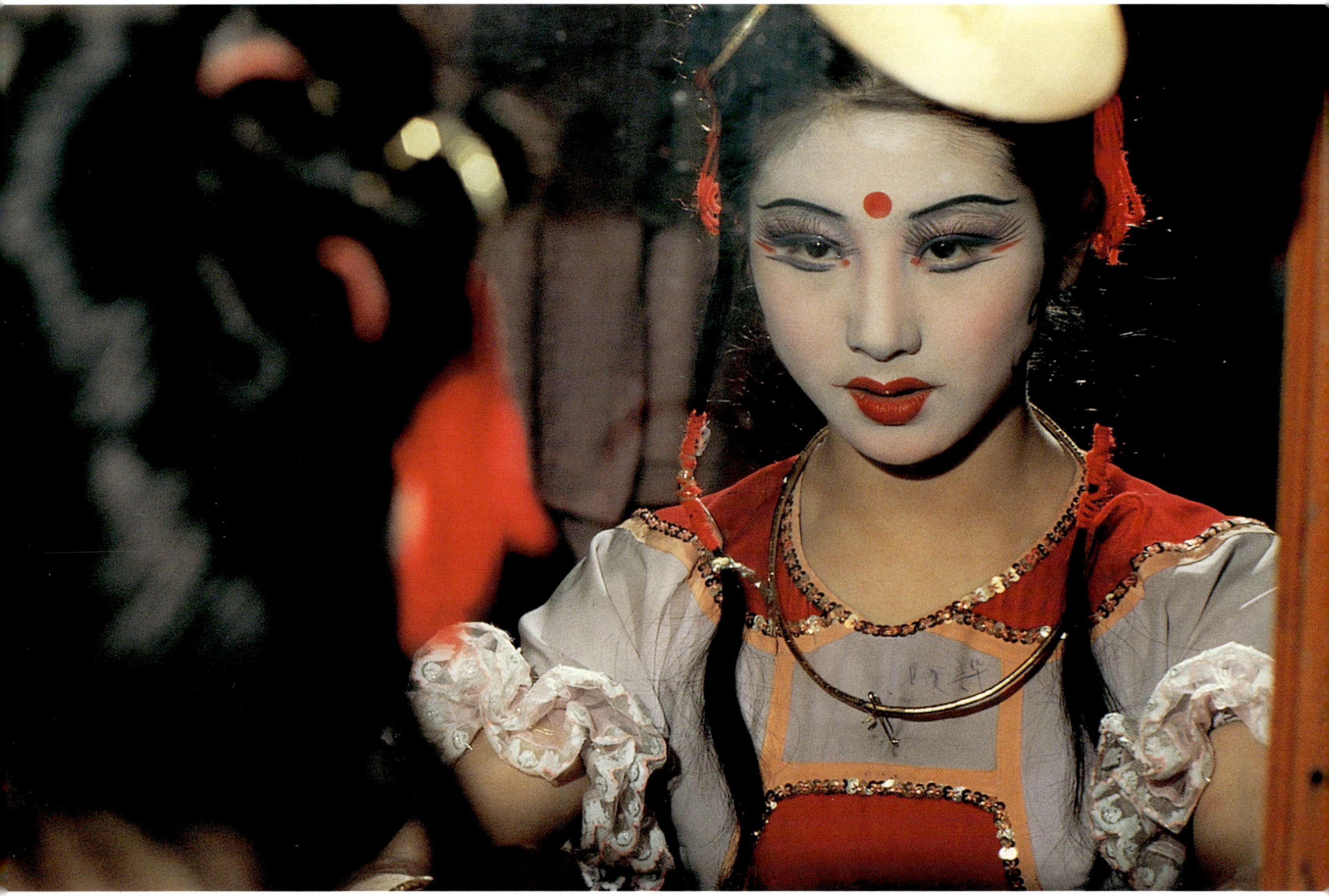

A dancer doing her make-up backstage at a theatre in Beijing, China. Dennis Cox used a Vivitar 283 flash unit, hand-held above the subject and bounced off a white wall above the mirror. A slow shutter speed of 1/15sec recorded some of the warmth from the tungsten lights in the room.

Technical details
Minolta XD-11 camera with 35mm lens. Film was Kodachrome 64 with an exposure of 1/15sec at f/5.6.

Composition

A performer from a touring troupe of traditional Jiangsu opera, shot on stage after a performance in the small town of Qufu, home town of Confucius in Shandong. 'After sitting through an exceedingly long three-hour performance, attended by local farmers wearing their best white undershirts in very warm weather, I was given the chance to take some pictures,' says Dennis. This close-up portrait shows the stunning make-up and costume of the singer, complimented by the floral background.

Lighting

The theatre was fairly dark and so Dennis had come prepared with two Vivitar 283 flash units and light stands. One unit, with a silver umbrella, was supported on a stand in front of the subject with the second one used to light the set in the background.

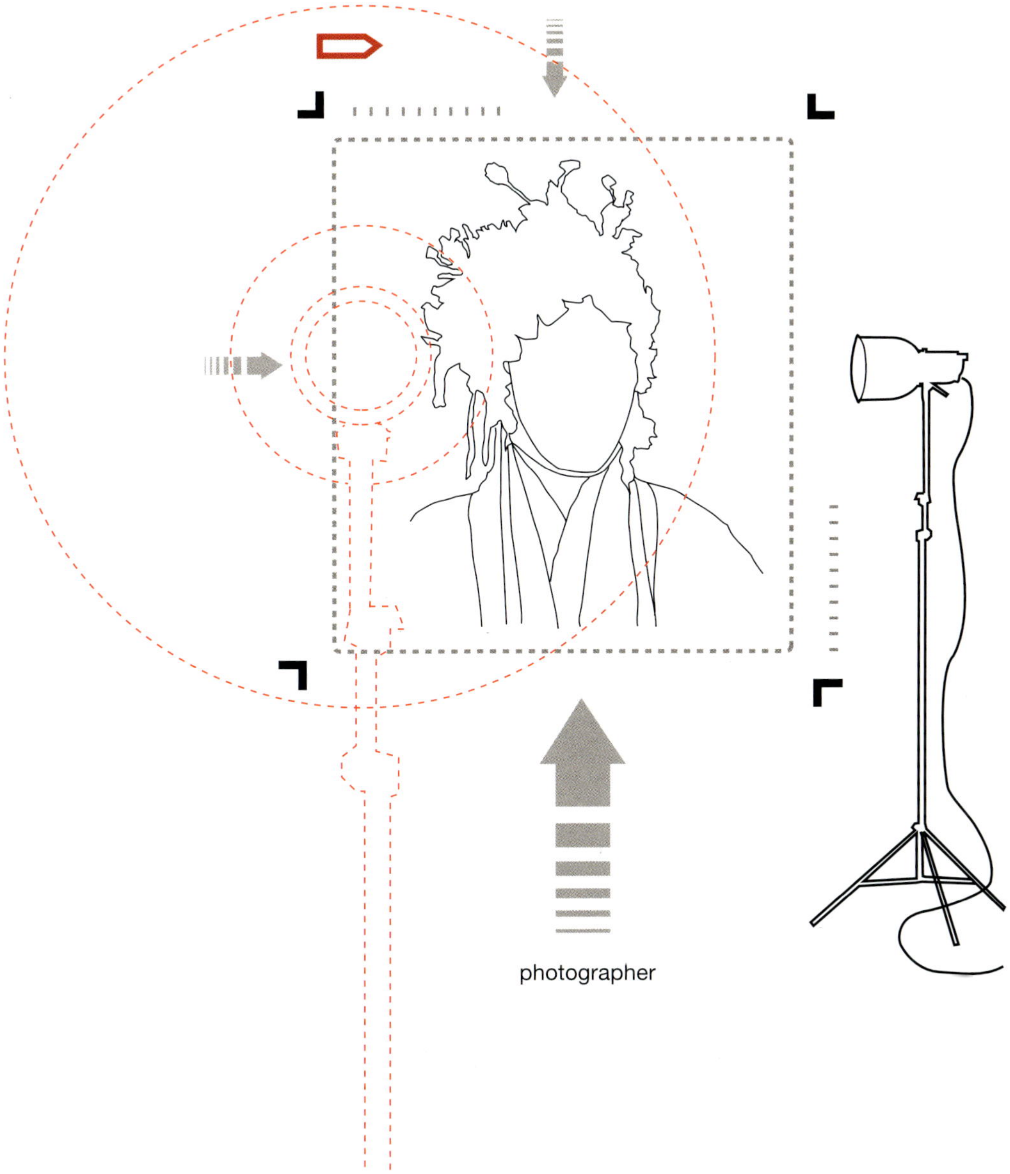

Technical details

Minolta XD-11 with 24–35mm lens. Film was Kodachrome 64 with TTL exposure.

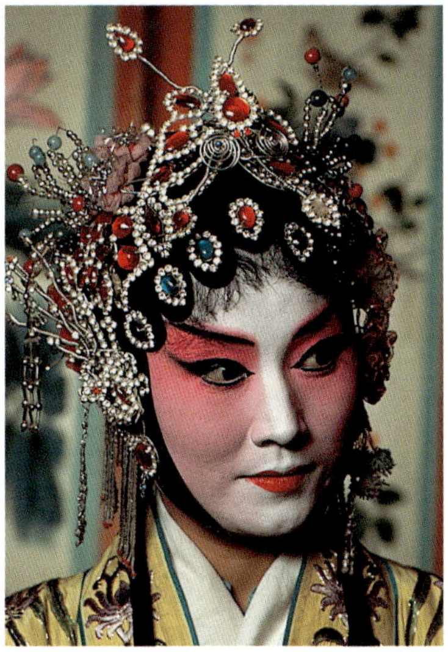

Composition

If you pay close attention to the composition, you can often use the background to provide the viewer with a great deal of information about the life of the subject. Here, the washing on the line, the firewood in the background and the chickens on the ground all give clues about the woman. 'I placed the basket on the woman's arm and positioned her in front of the clothes line,' explains Dennis Cox. 'I believe the lines on her face are mirrored by the years of domestic labour represented by her surroundings.' Notice how the elements in the composition are layered so there are points of interest from the foreground to the background of the picture.

Technique

'This was taken in the early 1980s when foreigners in China were still a curiosity,' says Dennis. 'I was with an interpreter in a small village outside Shanghai when we were invited into a courtyard surrounded by several residents. I knew the old woman in the corner would be reluctant to be photographed, so I systematically photographed all the other residents, while smiling to win them over. Finally, with the crowd's assistance, I asked this woman to pose. How could she refuse as she would be the only one left out?'

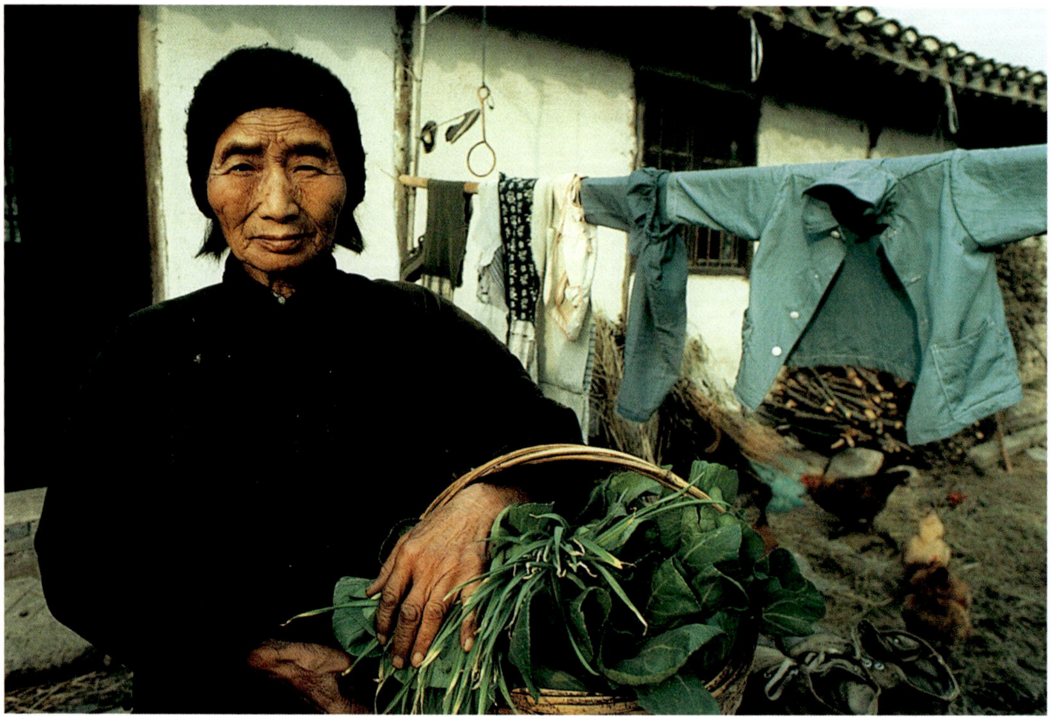

Technical details

Minolta XD-11 camera with 24–35mm lens. Film was Kodachrome 64 with program exposure.

'Taken early in the morning at the Nagaur Cattle Fair in Rajasthan, these men had started the day's business by laying out strands of ropes and bridles,' recalls Dennis. 'A 17–35mm lens was used at the widest angle to emphasise the sweep of the colourful strands and minimise the size of the men.'

Technical details
Minolta Dynax 800si camera with 17–35mm lens. Film was Fujifilm Velvia rated at ISO 40 with program exposure.

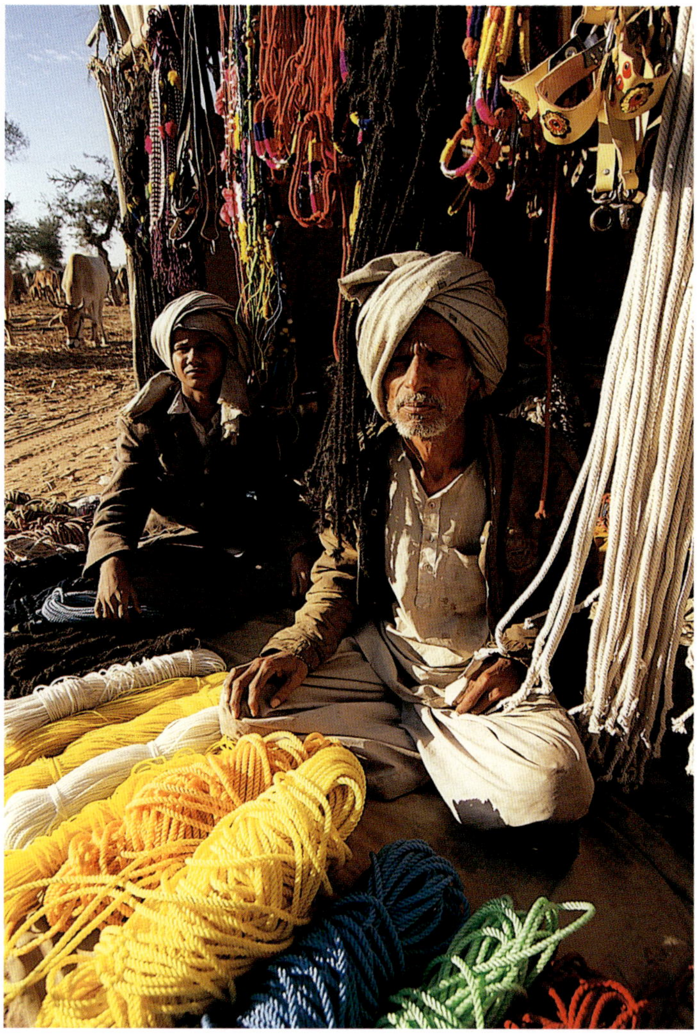

'I was more interested in capturing the colour and dramatic cross light on the merchandise, so I wasn't concerned that the light on the men's faces was very contrasty.'
Dennis Cox

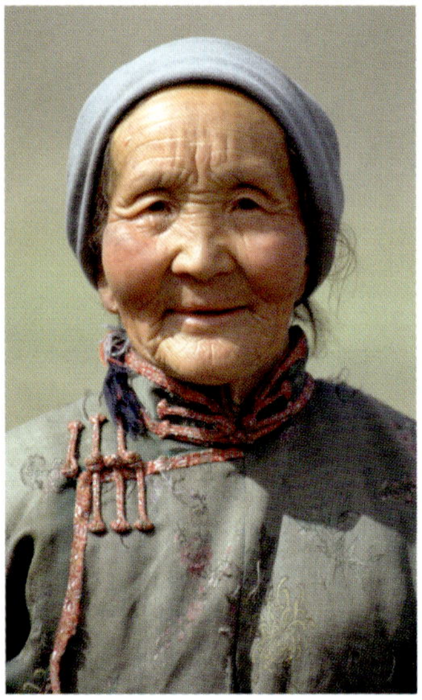

Technical details
Nikon 801s camera with 80–200mm lens. Film was Kodak Ektachrome 100 with an exposure of 1/500sec at f/5.6.

Composition
These two pictures were taken by Dirk Verwoerd when he was in Mongolia on an expedition trekking in the Himalayas. 'The woman in the pictures is a nomad who lived with her husband in a yir, the original nomad tent,' explains Dirk. 'They were very kind, offering us some yak milk and were perfectly willing to pose for the camera. Proud and beautiful people, their faces are etched by the strong winters.' Dirk took the opportunity to take two alternative shots for different potential uses. The close up focuses more on the character of the woman, while the inclusion of the landscape places her in her barren and lonely environment.

Technique
Dirk always carries two 35mm SLR camera bodies with him on location, just in case one should go wrong. It also means he doesn't have to change lenses – a 28–85mm on one camera and an 80–200mm on the other, cover most situations. These shots are good examples of how each lens comes into its own. The shorter zoom was ideal for showing the subject within the landscape where a greater depth of field was required for maximum image sharpness. The 80–200mm allowed him to crop in closely on the woman, from the same position, and select a larger aperture to render the background out of focus.

Lighting
Both these pictures were taken in bright late afternoon sunlight. Dirk dislikes flash and so he always carries a tripod. This allows him to use a long shutter speed if the available light is low.

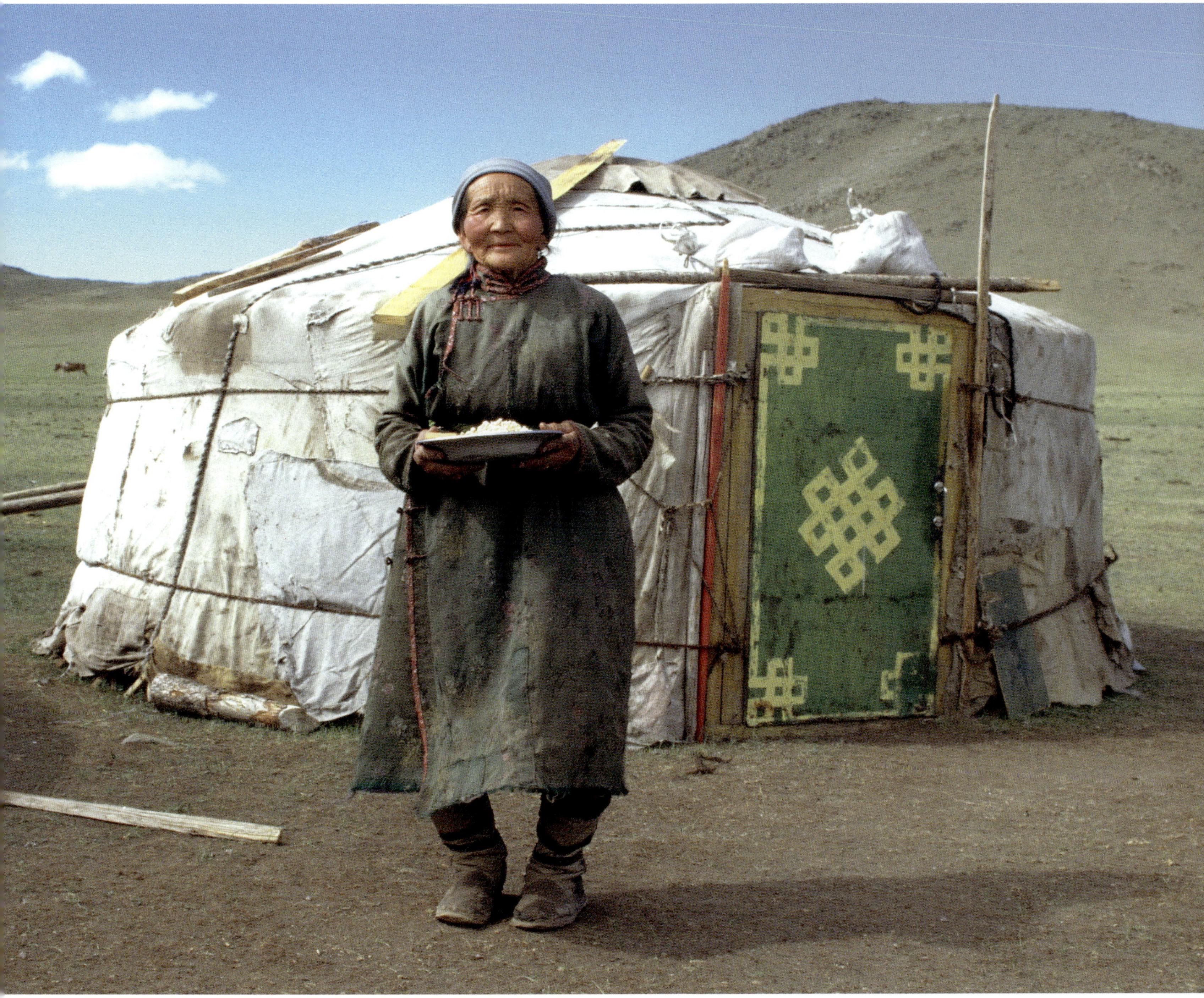

Technical details

Nikon 801s camera with 28–85mm lens. Film was Kodak Ektachrome 100 with an exposure of 1/125sec at f/11.

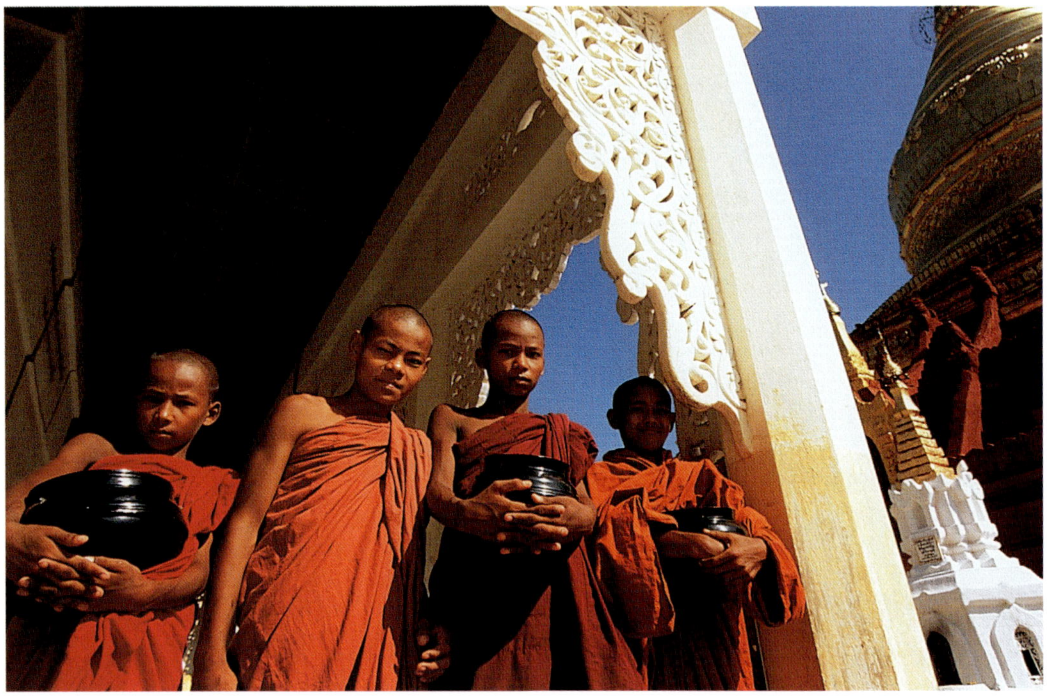

Composition

'The novice monks were following me round the pagoda in Mandalay, Burma,' says Dennis Cox. 'I ducked down low in order to look at them through the ultra wide-angle lens. I love the perspective these lenses give in environmental portraiture because they permit the juxtaposition of subjects against a sweep of background.'

Technique

The combination of the low viewpoint and the wide-angle lens has transformed this image from a fairly standard travel shot to one that really jumps out from the page. It's always worth looking through the viewfinder from different angles and perspectives to see if a more dynamic composition can be found. A low viewpoint – or a very high one – is particularly useful when you want to include architectural details.

Lighting

The sun was directly behind Dennis as he was taking the photograph and it was unavoidable that the boys were looking into it. Strong direct sunshine is not always beloved by photographers because of potential problems with high contrast and unwelcome shadows. In this case, however, the vibrant colours have become wonderfully saturated and this was emphasised by using a slow transparency film.

Technical details

Minolta Dynax 800si with 17–35mm lens. Film was Fujifilm Velvia rated at ISO 40.

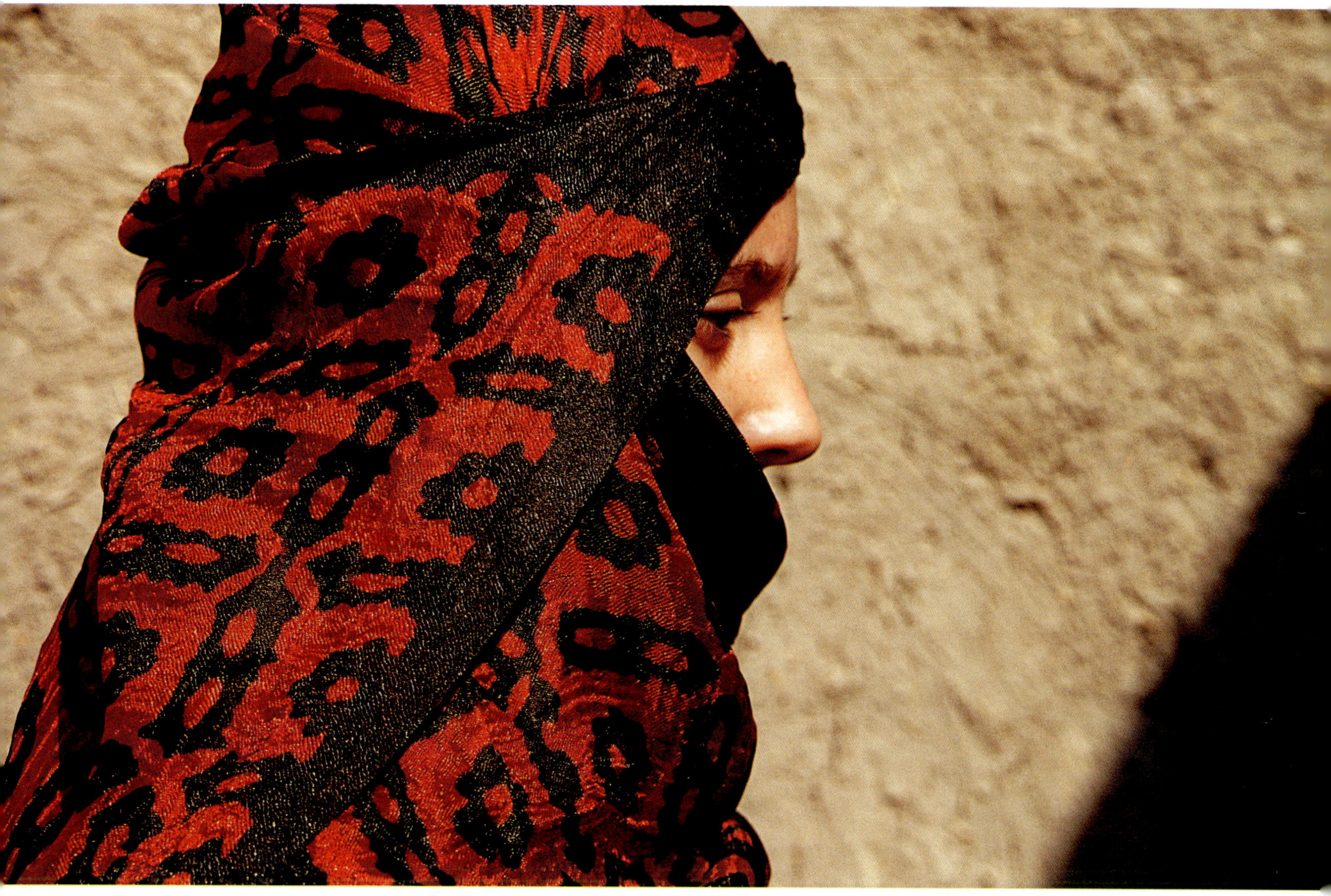

A Kurdish woman in a village in southeast Turkey. 'I asked her to pose by the wall in the midday sun in order to contrast the saturated colour of her headscarf against the washed out detail of the wall,' says Dennis. 'Noticing that the line of shadow on the wall paralleled the line of her scarf, I moved her to get this particular composition.'

Technical details
Minolta Dynax 9 camera with 24–85mm lens. Film was Kodachrome 100 with program exposure.

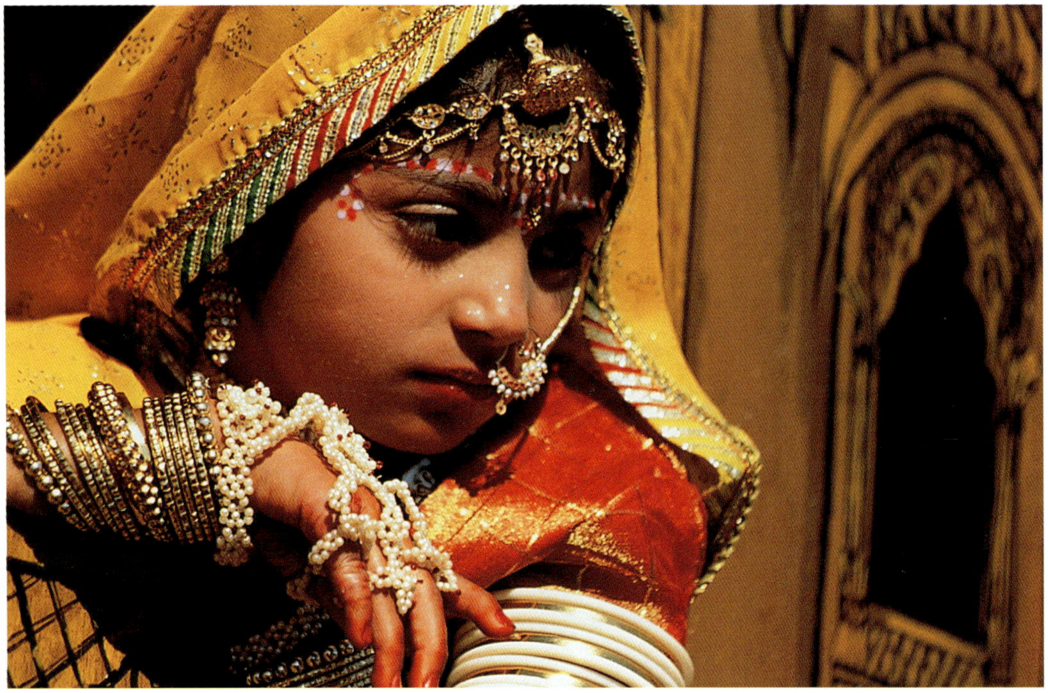

Composition

This young girl was one of many people attending the Jaisalmer Desert Festival which takes place every year in Rajasthan, India. She was sitting inside an ornate enclosed wagon, but leaning out of the window. The pose was quite natural, but she was aware of Dennis Cox taking her photograph and so he had time to concentrate on the composition, with the camera supported on a tripod. He used a long telephoto zoom lens to crop in quite tightly on the girl in her beautiful costume, placing her off centre in order to include the decoration of the wagon in the background.

Technique

At large, colourful events such as festivals, there can be so much going on it's hard to know where to begin to take pictures. While a wide-angle lens is useful for a broader view of the spectacle, it's always worth picking out photogenic individuals with a telephoto zoom.

Lighting

The bright, direct sunshine has saturated the colours here and Dennis has emphasised these by using a slow, ISO 50 colour slide film, which he slightly underexposed by rating it at ISO 40. Because she was leaning out of the window, she was out of the shadow cast by the wagon and so no fill-in flash was needed.

Technical details

Minolta Dynax 800si camera with 100–300mm lens. Film was Fuji Velvia with program exposure.

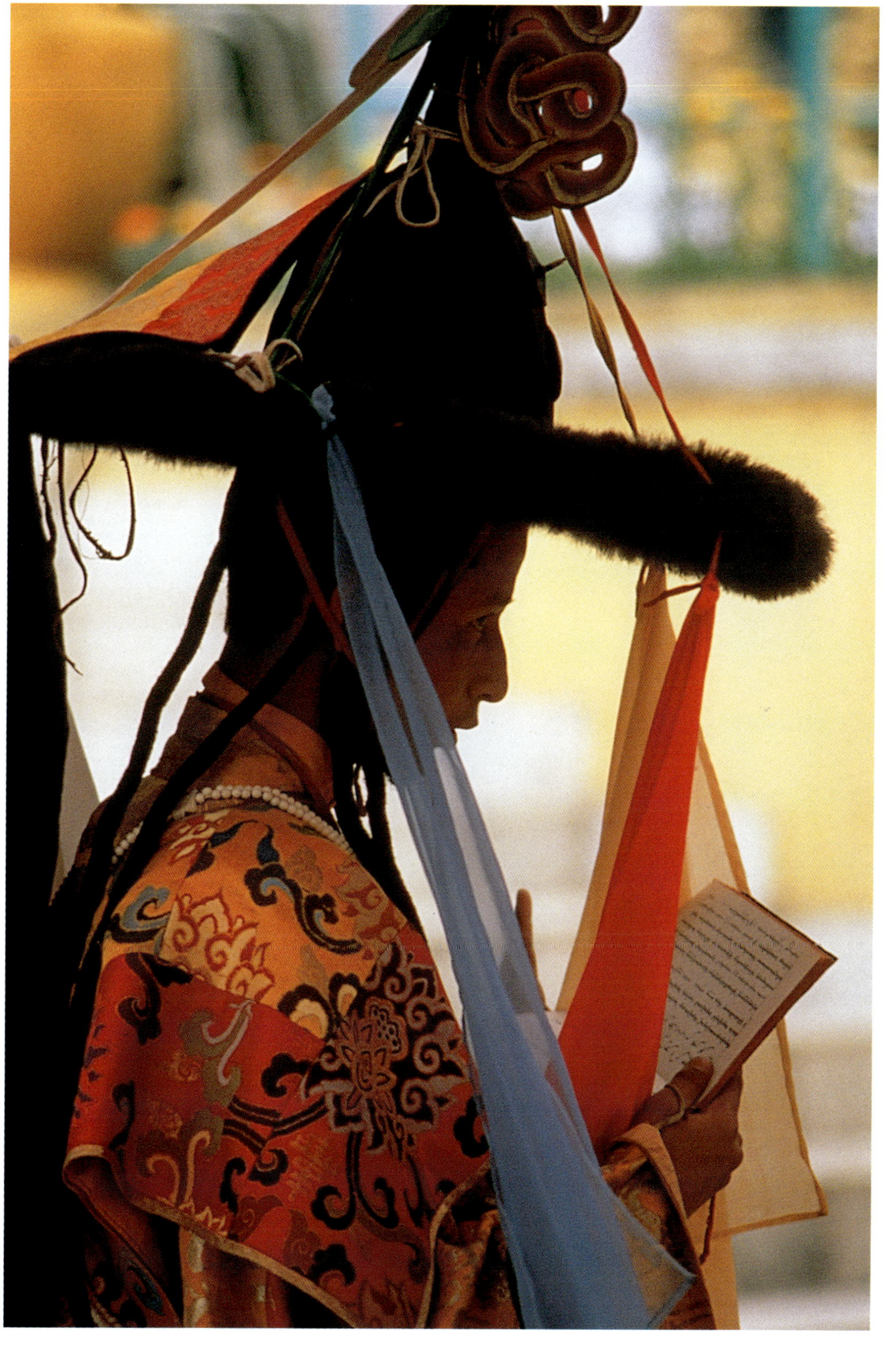

A Cham dancer at the Tash Jong Tibetan community in India. On a bright day Diane Barker took a meter reading from the subject to ensure he was correctly exposed. A wide aperture blurred the background to make him stand out.

Technical details

Nikon FM camera with 70–210mm lens. Film was Fujifilm Provia with an exposure of 1/60sec at shutter priority.

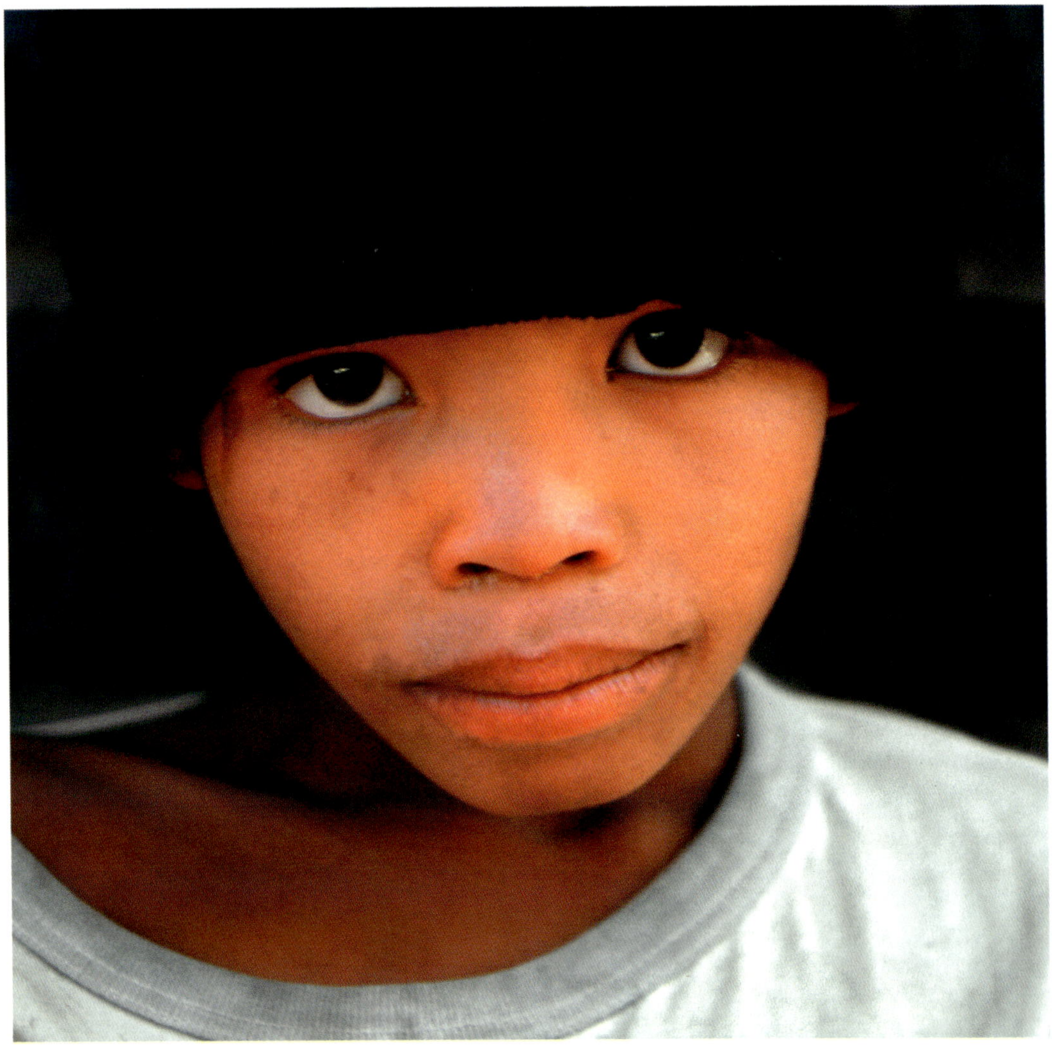

Composition
This was taken on a trip to Namibia, as Philip Sprague stopped in a small town for provisions. 'There were two lads standing against a wall, watching our every move,' he recalls. 'We started talking to them and I was drawn to this little lad's soulful, sad eyes.' Philip used his 80–200mm lens to focus in close on the boy's face to concentrate on this feature. The original slide included more of the boy's hat, but Philip felt the colourful band around it was a distraction and so he cropped it out on the computer.

Technique
Philip always uses slide film for colour photography because the quality has the edge over print film and he also undertakes slide shows and lectures frequently. 'You know what you are getting with slides,' he adds. 'If you use a warm-up filter on a negative, for instance, you can't always tell the difference when it comes back from the printers because the machines can compensate for the filter – you're in the lap of the gods. The disadvantage of slides is that you can't crop them conventionally, but that's the beauty of the computer. You can scan the slide in and do what you want.'

Lighting
Taken in bright sunshine, the boy was standing under a canopy which softened the light but left an all-important catchlight in the eyes to give them life and sparkle. If necessary, Philip will move his subject to an area of light shade to avoid the harsh effect of direct light. He used a wide aperture of f/4 to blur the background, focusing on the eyes to ensure these were sharp.

Technical details
Canon T90 camera with 80–200mm lens. Film was Fujifilm Sensia 100 with an exposure of f/4.

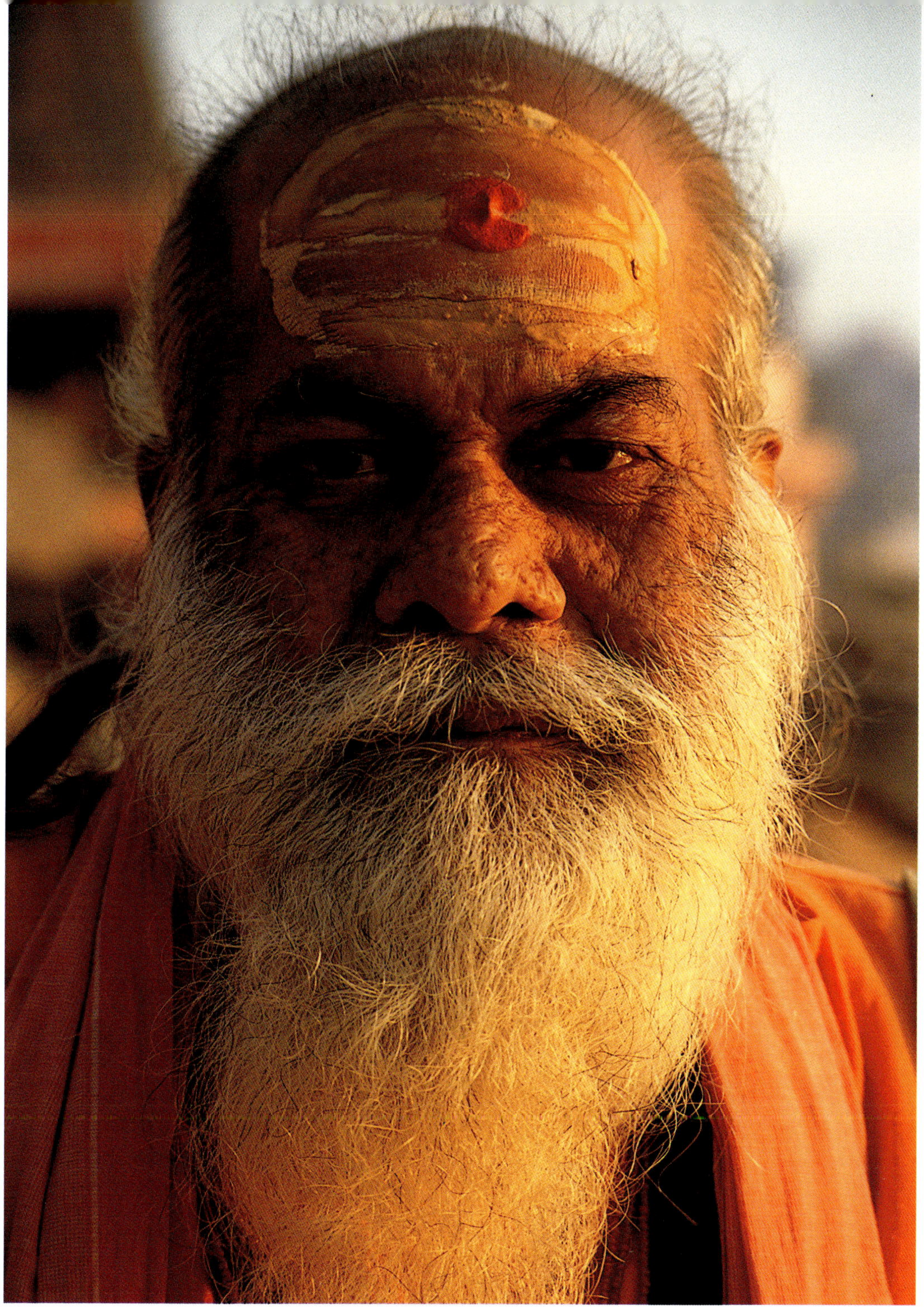

Jon Hicks photographed this man at the Golden Temple, Armritsar, India in the warm light of late afternoon. 'I thought he had a really interesting face so, after asking his permission, I used the long end of the zoom to go in really close and fill the frame,' he says.

Technical details
Nikon FA camera with 70–210mm lens. Film was Fujichrome 100 with an exposure of 1/125sec at f/5.6

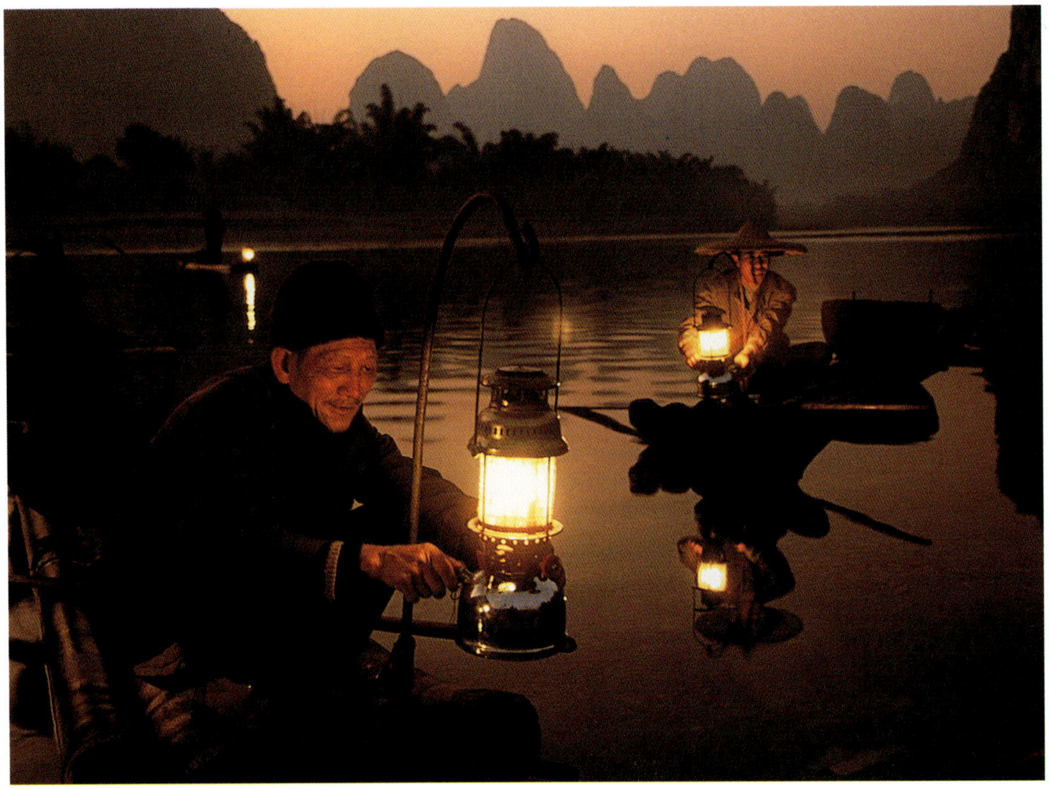

Composition
The best shots don't always come your way by chance and there's nothing wrong with setting up a picture to increase your likelihood of success. These fishermen, near Guilin in China, were hired to pose with their cormorants. They use these birds to catch fish at night from their bamboo rafts on the Li River. The lanterns are used to attract fish close enough to the rafts for the cormorants, tied by cords around their legs, to dive down to catch. Dennis Cox took the picture from the shore, with one raft close enough to provide foreground interest. The raft on the right fills the middle distance, while the pointed hills provide a stunning background.

Technique
It's very difficult to judge the precise exposure for shots at dusk. Dennis took several shots, bracketed at 1/2 stop intervals up to a full stop over and under the camera's suggested exposure. The shutter speed here was around 1/2sec and the camera was supported on a tripod to prevent camera shake. Dennis used a Tiffen 812 warming filter to enhance the sky and the warm glow of the lamps.

Lighting
Timing is crucial for night shots and the best results are achieved at dusk, before the light disappears completely and while the sky still has some atmospheric colour. At this time, details of the surrounding famous Karst hills were recorded in the background, while the lanterns illuminated the faces of the fishermen.

Technical details
Minolta Dynax 700si camera with 24–85mm lens. Film was Fujifilm Velvia with an exposure of 1/2sec at f/5.6.

Dawn is another favourite time for photographers because, like dusk, the light is magical. The tea-picker in Sri Lanka appears almost in silhouette against the bright background but Joan Wakelin took an average meter reading from a grey card to ensure just enough detail of the subject was recorded to make it clear what she's doing.

Technical details
Canon AE1 with 200mm lens.
Film was Kodachrome 64 with an unknown exposure.

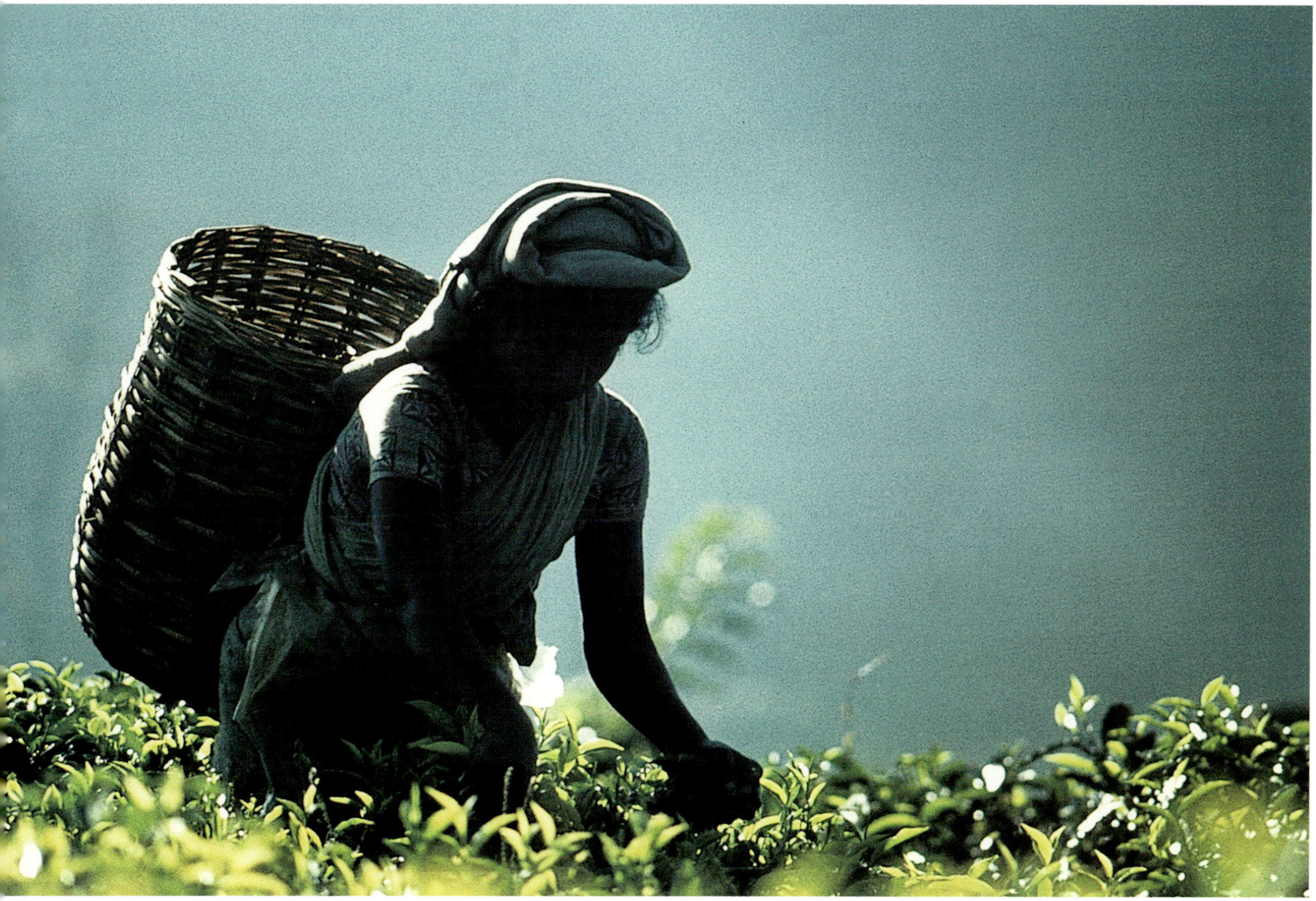

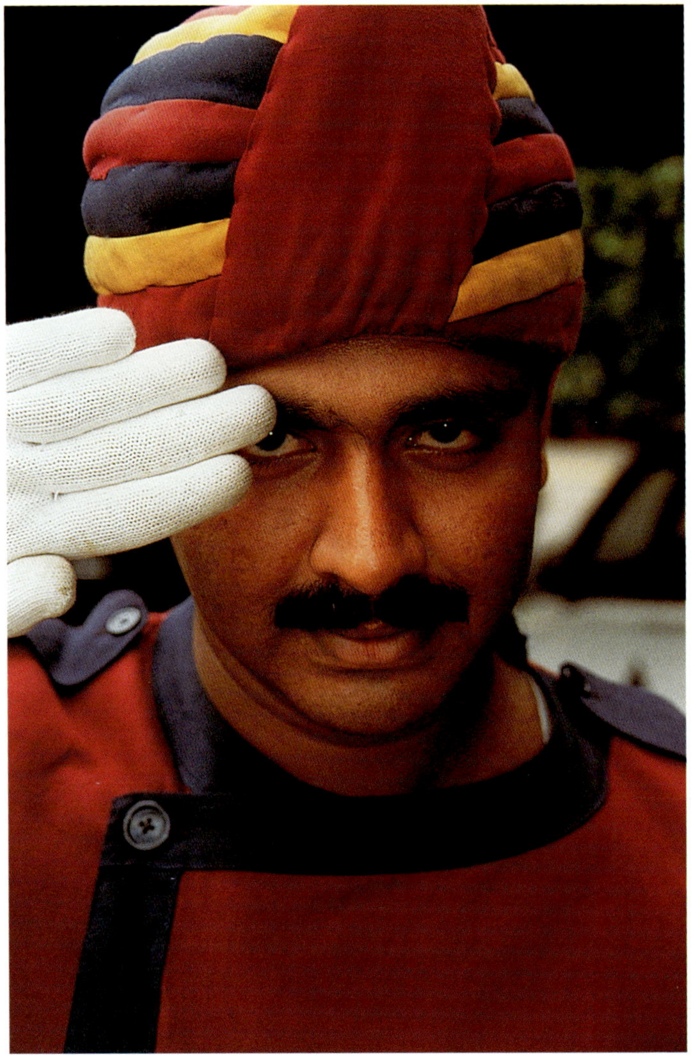

Composition
Dennis Cox always keeps an eye out for punchy, bright colour which will catch the viewer's attention. This is a doorman at a hotel in Cochin, southern India. Dennis asked him to pose with the salute he routinely gives to guests as they enter the hotel and used his 24–85mm lens at its longest end to fill the frame with head and shoulders for added impact.

Lighting
Realising the doorman was facing away from the light, Dennis popped up the camera's in-built flash, set at -1 compensation. Fill-in flash should compliment the ambient light rather than overpower it so that its use doesn't look too obvious.

Technique
This was a quick, spur of the moment shot, but nevertheless a saleable one. If you're relying on colour to give a shot its impact, use a long lens, or move in close to fill the frame and lose a distracting background. If you can't avoid the background, select a wide aperture to put it out of focus.

Technical details
Minolta Dynax 800si camera with 24–85mm lens. Film was Fujifilm Velvia with aperture priority exposure.

Technical details
Nikon FM camera with 50mm lens. Film was Fujifilm Provia with an exposure of 1/600sec at shutter priority.

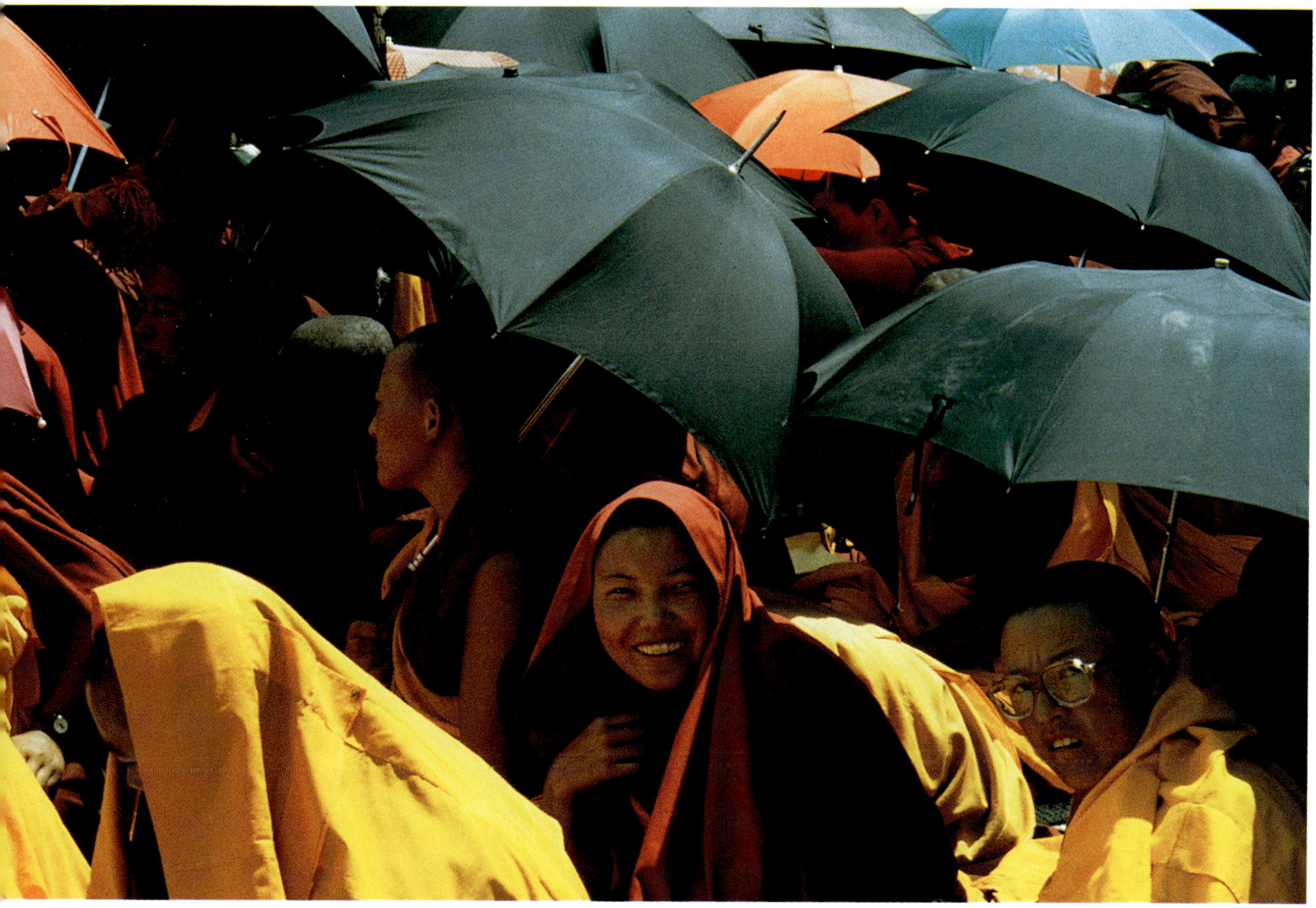

Nuns and monks protected against wet weather provided Diane Barker with a colourful shot. The nun in the middle, smiling at the camera, was a lucky addition because it's her eye contact that makes the picture.

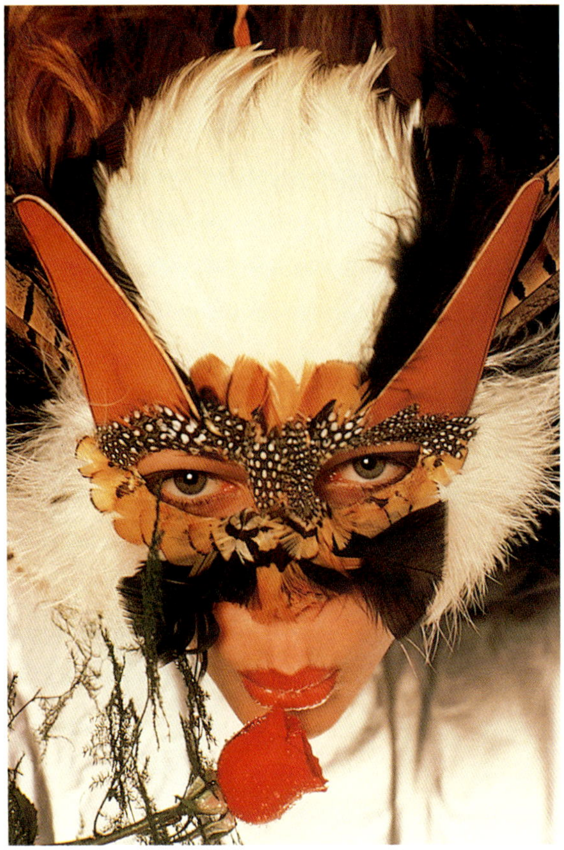

Louis Jawitz wanted a close-up to maximise the impact of this unusual mask. The model was leaning back, with Louis shooting from a ladder above her. It was lit from a skylight and a flash with softbox and there was a reflector on the floor behind her, tilted upwards.

Technical details
Nikon F3 camera with 55mm macro lens. Film was Kodachrome 25 with an exposure of 1/80sec at f/11.

Composition
Louis took this at an Easter Sunday parade in New York City. 'I came across this group of people and I was struck by their bizarre outfits,' he says. Colour has most impact in an image when you fill the frame with it, as Louis has done here. The dark background of the building has helped to make the man's silver face stand out, while the strip of blue sky in the middle works equally well to highlight the woman.

Technique
Louis used a 15mm ultra-wide rectar linear lens made by Sigma which doesn't distort the verticals of buildings. When it's used so close to people, it does produce a strange perspective, which Louis felt was appropriate for the costume of his subjects.

Lighting
The normal daylight exposure for this picture would have been 1/80sec at f/16 but Louis underexposed by half a stop in order to retain detail in the silver face, which would otherwise have appeared washed out.

Technical details
Nikon F3 camera with 15mm lens. Film was Kodachrome 64 with an exposure of 1/125sec at f/11.5.

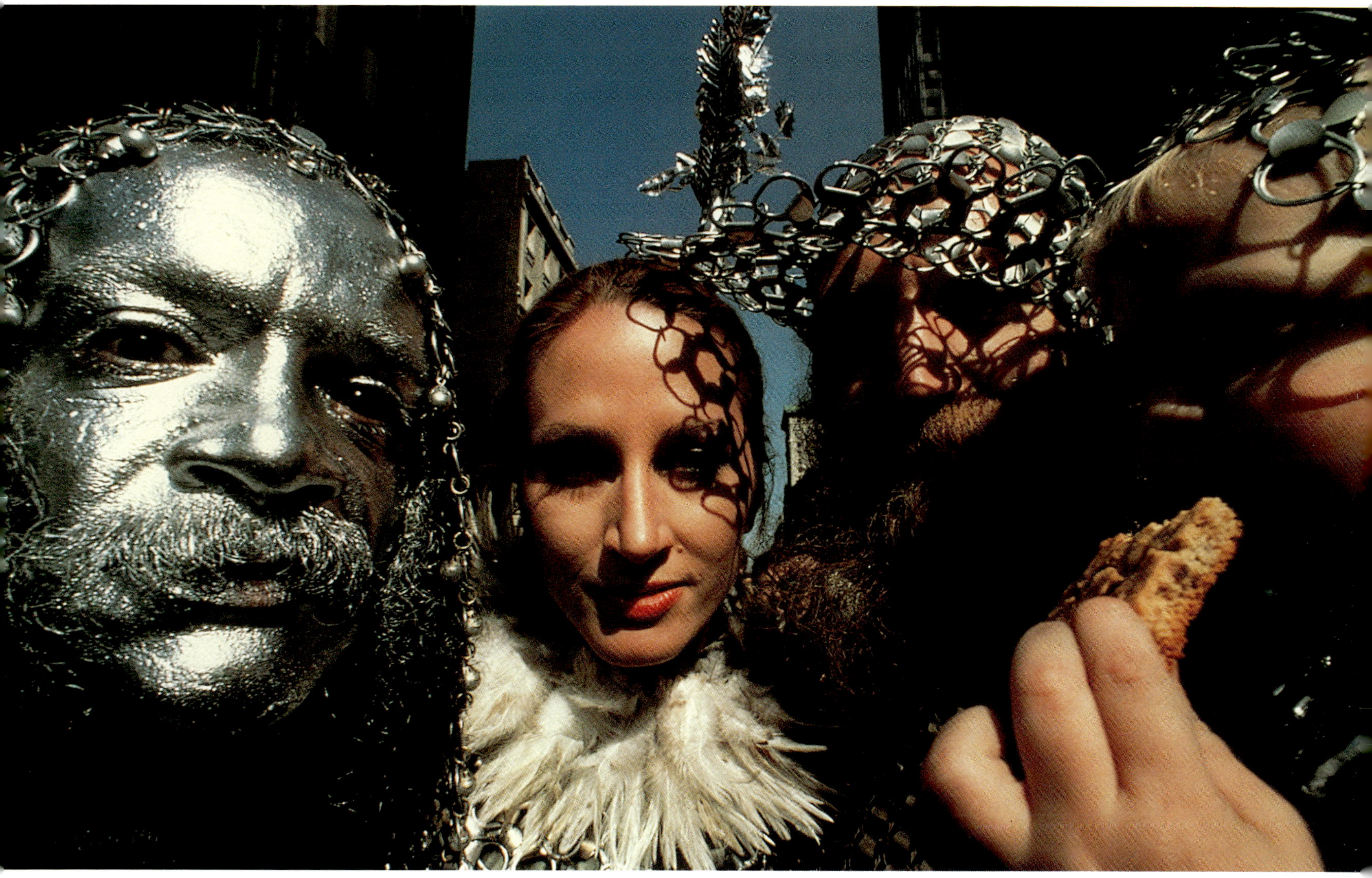

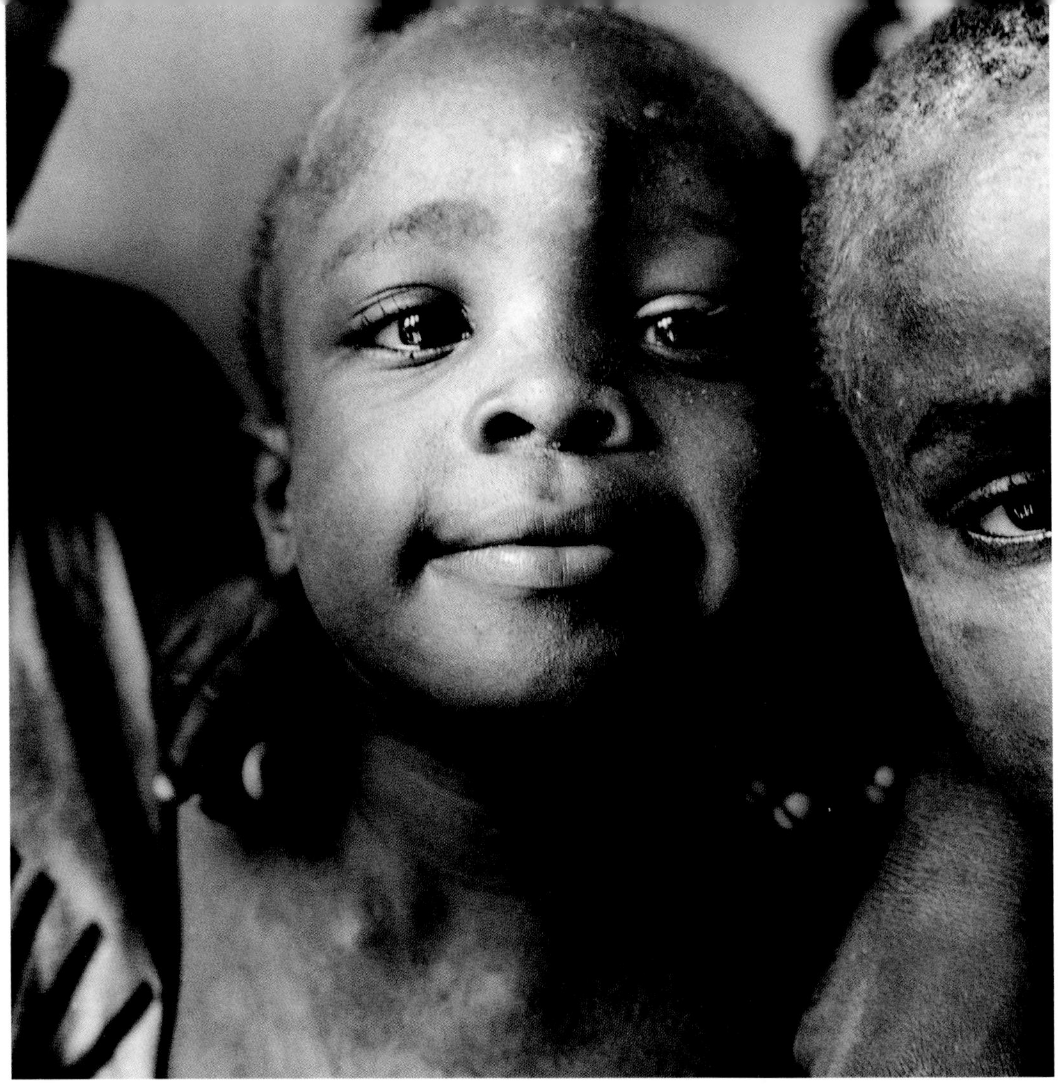

'This photo defines my impression of Haiti in that the people have a very positive, spiritual outlook on life, despite horrible poverty,' says Sandy Huffaker. 'It was taken in natural light and the shadows serve to provide contrast and enhance the intimate mood.'

Technical details
Mamiya C330 camera with 80mm lens. Film was Kodak Tri-X Pan with an exposure of 1/125sec at f/5.6.

'The beauty of black and white is that it allows a clearer understanding of the subject without the distraction of colour. I always carry two camera bodies, one loaded with colour and the other with black and white film.'
Philip Sprague

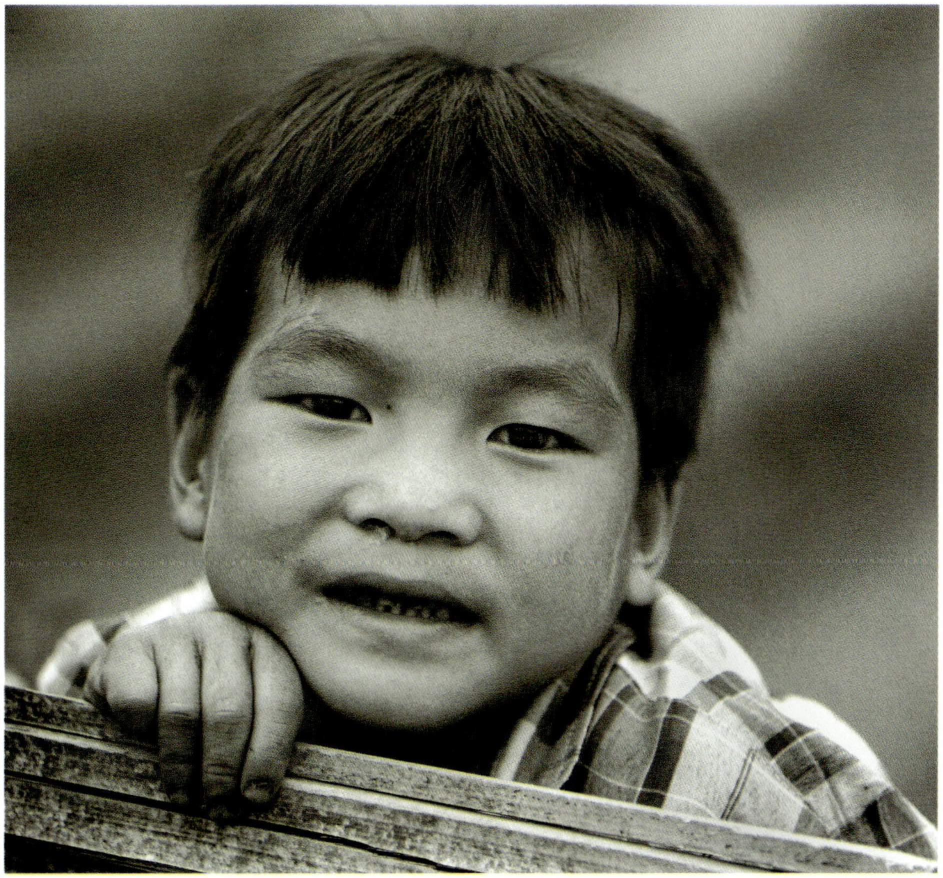

Composition

Philip Sprague went with a small party on a six-day trek to the remote hill tribes of northern Vietnam where the people had only seen westerners since 1996 and still found them a curiosity. 'This was taken in one of the villages where we stopped for the night. The little boy, like the other village children, was interested in us and our cameras. I took a series of portraits of him and particularly liked the composition with the broken fence in this one. The background, of paddy fields, was less interesting to me than his face, so I used a wide aperture to blur it and focused on his eyes.'

Technique

Where there is no common language between you and the subject, it isn't easy to explain what you want. Philip had to rely on his patience and used plenty of film, hoping that a pleasing shot would eventually happen, as it did here. The children in this village were happy to be photographed, but the women were not. 'In that case you have to remember that you're a visitor in their country, and put the camera away,' says Philip.

Lighting

The soft, overcast lighting here is flattering to the skin tones and doesn't produce any harsh, unwanted shadows which can mask the detail of a face. Philip chose to use black and white film because the boy was wearing a colourful top and he didn't want that to become the centre of attention.

Technical details

Canon T90 camera with 80–200mm lens. Film was Ilford Delta 400 with an exposure of 1/125sec at f/4.

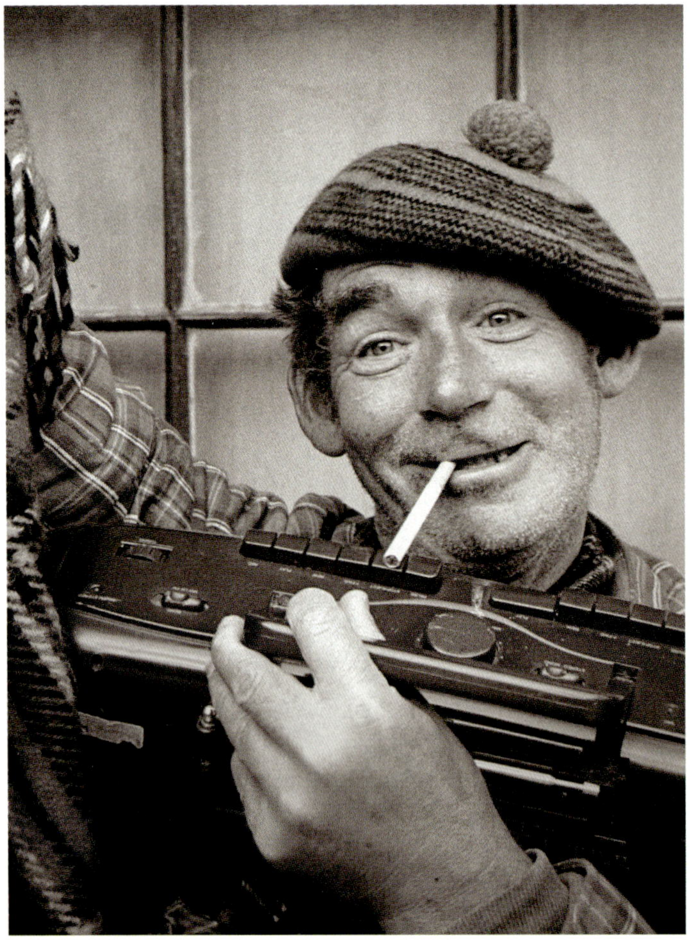

Composition

On holiday in Edinburgh, Philip Sprague started chatting to this man called Monty who had been living rough on the streets near the castle for 17 years. Philip photographed him holding his prize possession, a cassette player, and waving his tartan blanket like a flag. You can also make out the reflections of Edinburgh buildings in the background window. By including these details, Philip has taken a character portrait which also reveals more about the man's situation.

Technique

Philip could have used colour film here but there is a danger that the colour of the rug would have dominated the image. Black and white, by contrast, allows the facial expression of the subject to become the main focus of attention.

Lighting

On a dull, rainy day in a fairly dark corner, the ISO 400 speed of the black and white film allowed Philip a faster exposure and thus, more clarity. This was especially important because the camera was hand held.

Technical details

Canon T90 camera with 80–200mm lens. Film was Ilford HP5 with an exposure of 1/125sec at f/5.6.

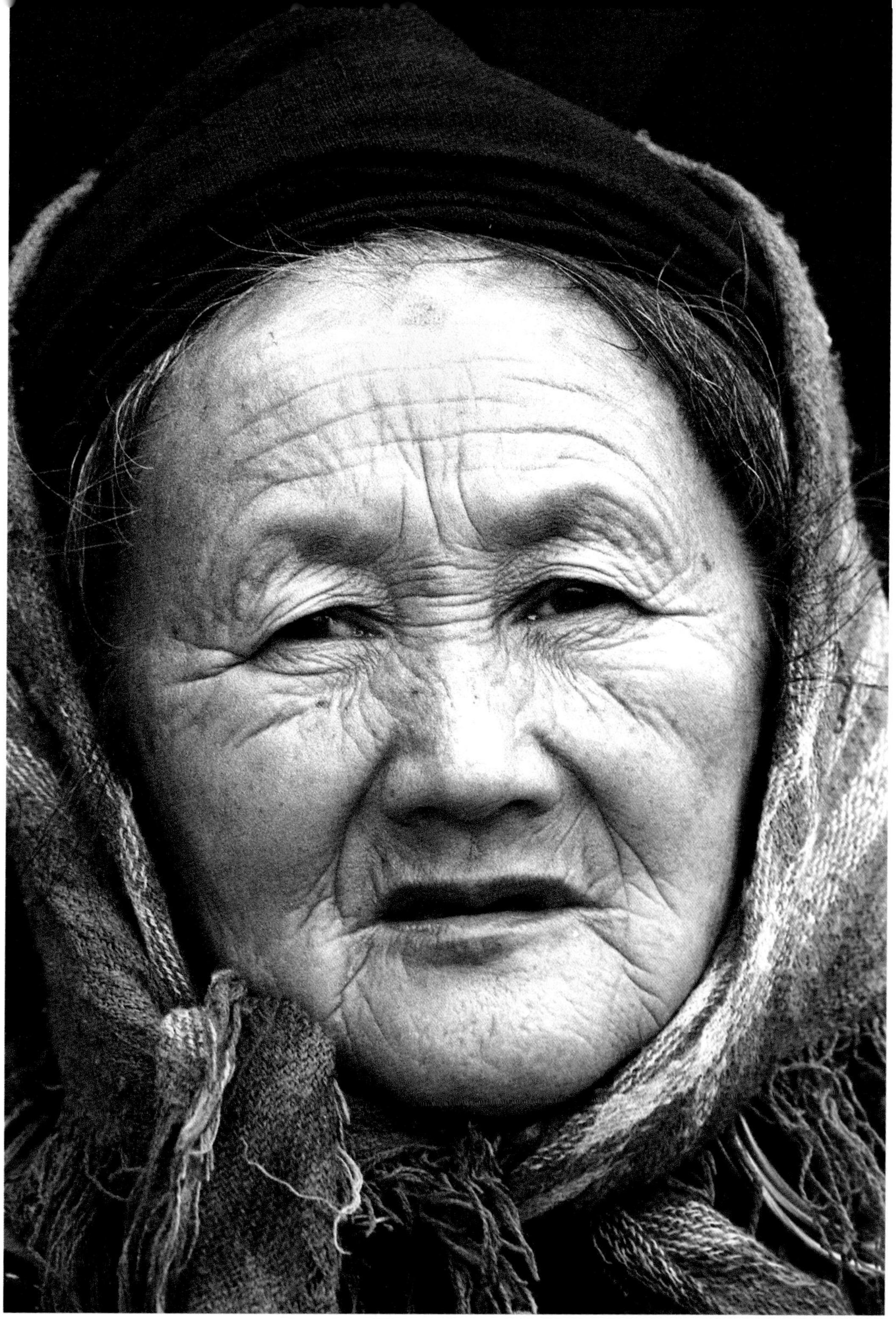

Philip liked the way the scarf framed the face of this member of the Hmong tribe in the high altitude village of SaPa in North Vietnam. 'It was raining at the time and she was holding an umbrella which, conveniently, produced the dark background,' he says.

Technical details
Canon T90 camera with 80–200mm lens. Film was Ilford Delta 400 with an exposure of f/4.

Composition

This was taken at a temple in Xishuangbanna, near the Burmese border in Yunnan. 'I used a 17–35mm lens set at 17mm which made it possible to balance the details of the three monks sitting in the lotus position on the temple wall, with the novice monks,' says Dennis Cox. Links like this between the subject and the background can really benefit a composition. If necessary, move your subject to make the most of them, although you should never spoil the moment if the shot isn't posed.

Technique

An ultra wide-angle lens may seem a strange choice for portraiture because of its distorting effect. It may not be very flattering for close-ups but can produce unusual and dynamic results when you want to show a person or people in their environment. Dennis had emphasised the wide perspective of the lens by shooting from a low angle and tilting the camera.

Lighting

This area of open shade was ideal. There is plenty of light coming through from the open side of the structure, opposite the wall and yet the boys are shielded from the direct glare of overhead sun.

Technical details

Minolta Dynax 700si with 17–35mm lens. Film was Fujifilm Provia with program exposure.

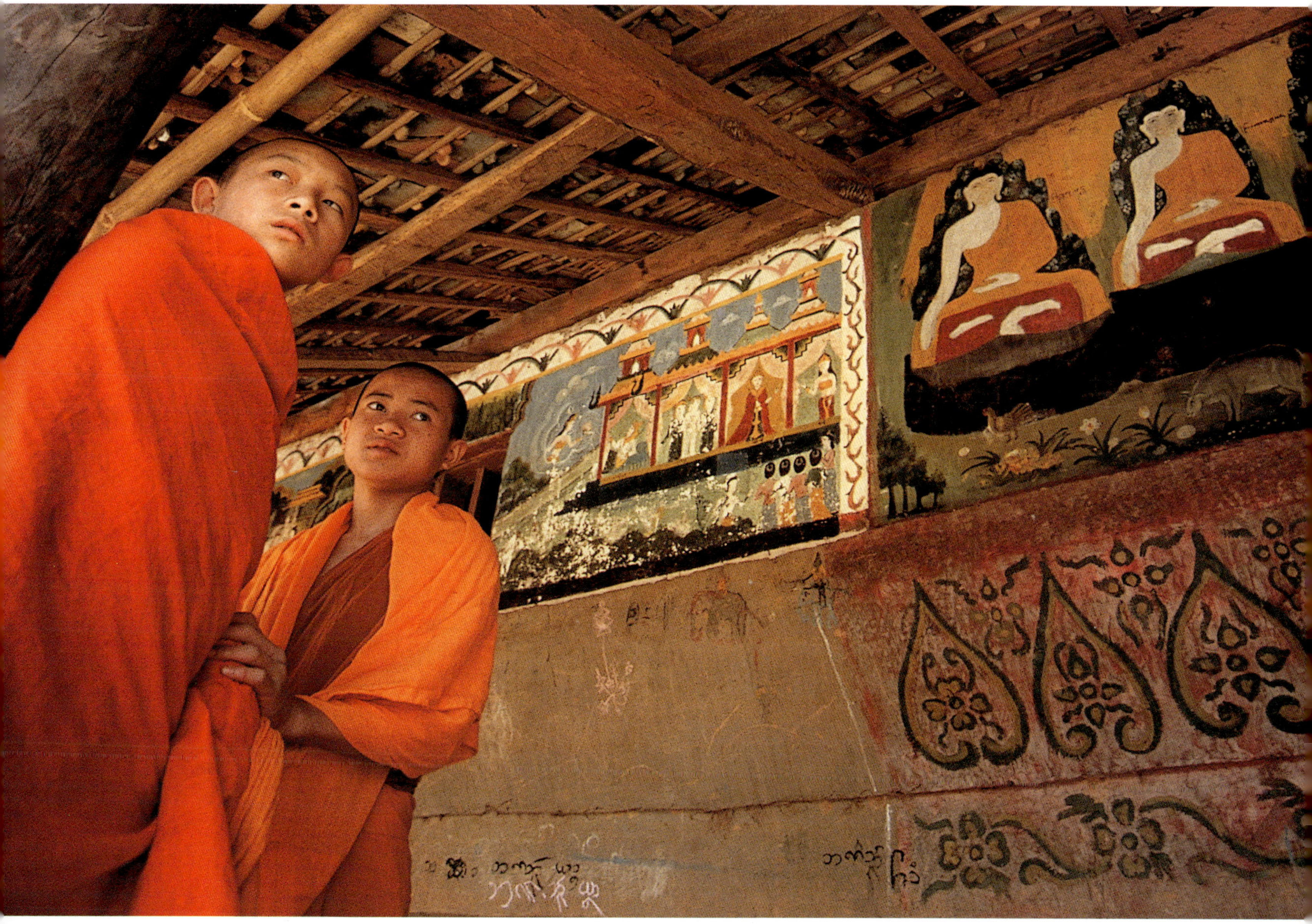

'I tried not to disrupt the naturalness of these young monks by shooting at an oblique angle.'
Dennis Cox

7

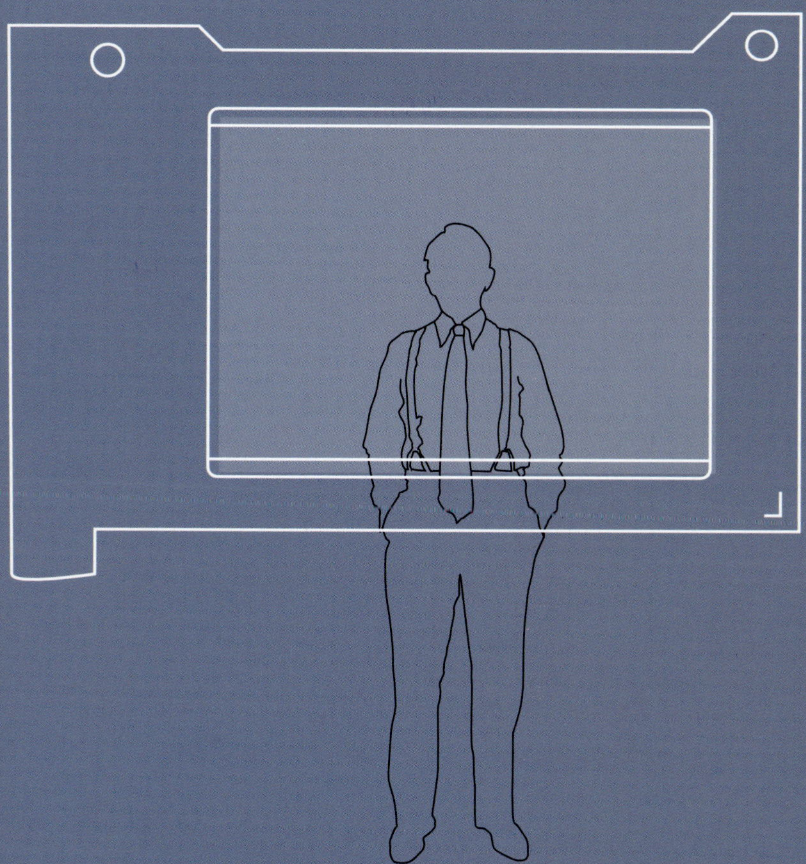

portfolio images

Photographers are often approached by would-be models and actors to take pictures for their portfolios and, while these can be taken in the studio, they usually benefit from a varied range of locations to show the subject's potential in different situations. The same can be said for your own photographic portfolio, particularly if you aim to work in the areas of fashion and advertising.

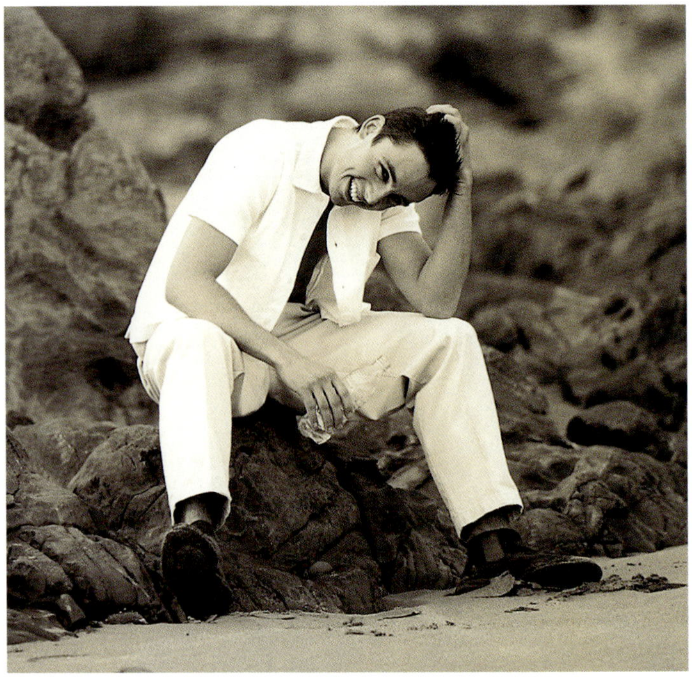

To contrast with the other two shots, Ronald took a longer viewpoint and included the whole figure with space around him. The mood of the shot is also lighter here, with the model in a casual pose and laughing at the photographer's joke.

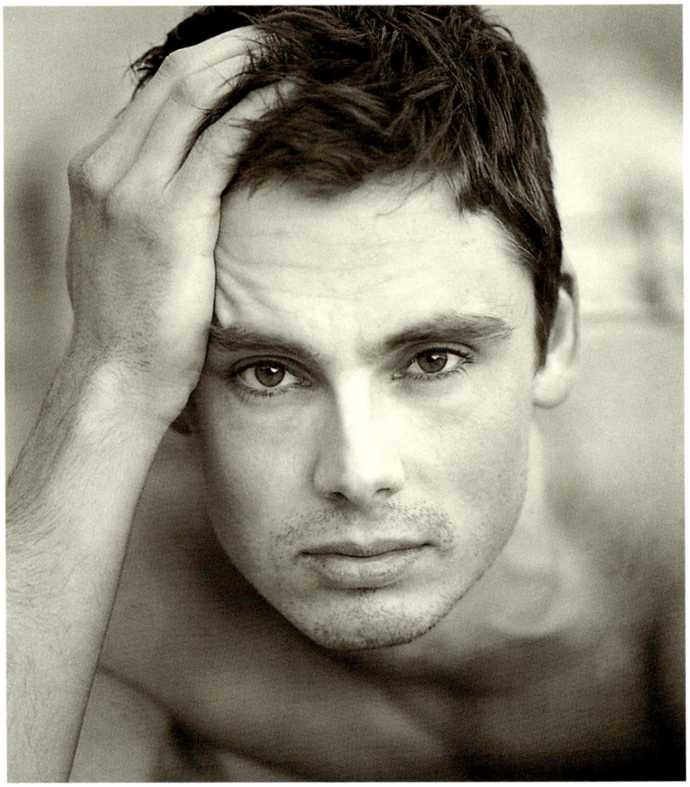

Here the model is lying on his stomach on the beach. In late afternoon, the light was very directional, creating strong shadows which provide good modelling to the face.

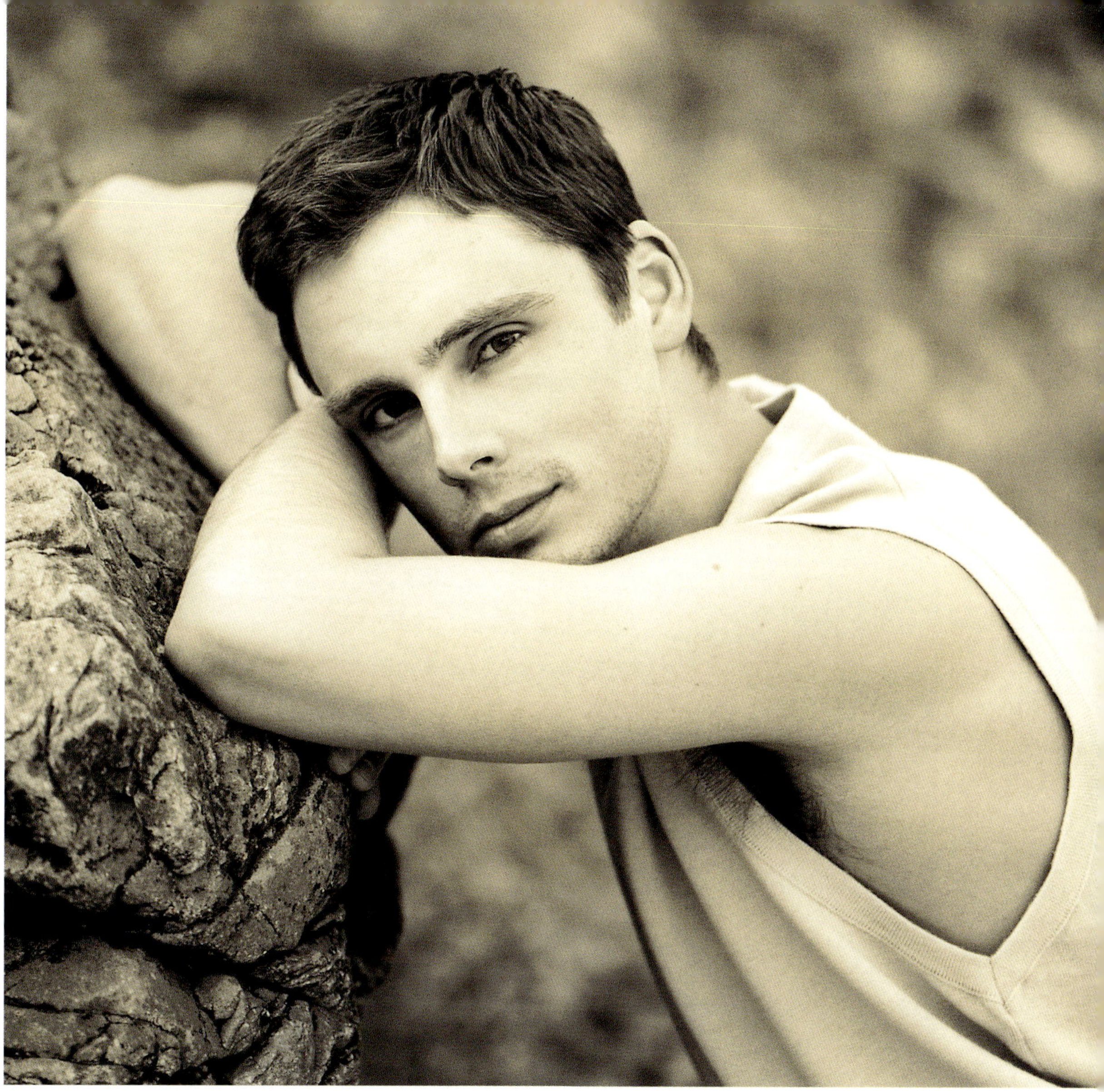

Composition
These three pictures were taken for a model's portfolio during a session on a beach. It's important to show as much variety as possible within the portfolio, but these shots illustrate how different looks can be achieved using the same location but by changing the pose and the direction of the light. For this shot, Ronald Turner directed the model to lean against a rock, making sure that he felt and looked balanced and comfortable. The way the figure is leaning to the left with his head tilted, creates a strong, dynamic shape and this is reinforced by the arm across the centre of the frame.

Technique
Ronald used a 350mm telephoto lens for all these shots. The effect of using a long lens is to put the background out of focus, reducing it to a diffused blur. Ronald focused on the eyes – the most important element in the picture because they immediately engage the viewer's attention.

Lighting
As you're adjusting the pose, you need to be constantly aware of the way the light is falling on the figure and the position of shadows. A reflector is an extremely useful accessory for location portraits in natural light and Ronald used one here to bounce the light from the open sky on to the model's face and arm. A meter reading was taken from the skin tones to ensure that these were correctly exposed.

Technical details
Hasselblad 205 TCC camera with 350mm Tele-Tessar lens. Film was Kodak Tri-X ISO 400 rated at ISO 200.

'It's always a good idea to try out a pose yourself so you can see how balanced and comfortable it feels and adjust it accordingly.'

Ronald Turner

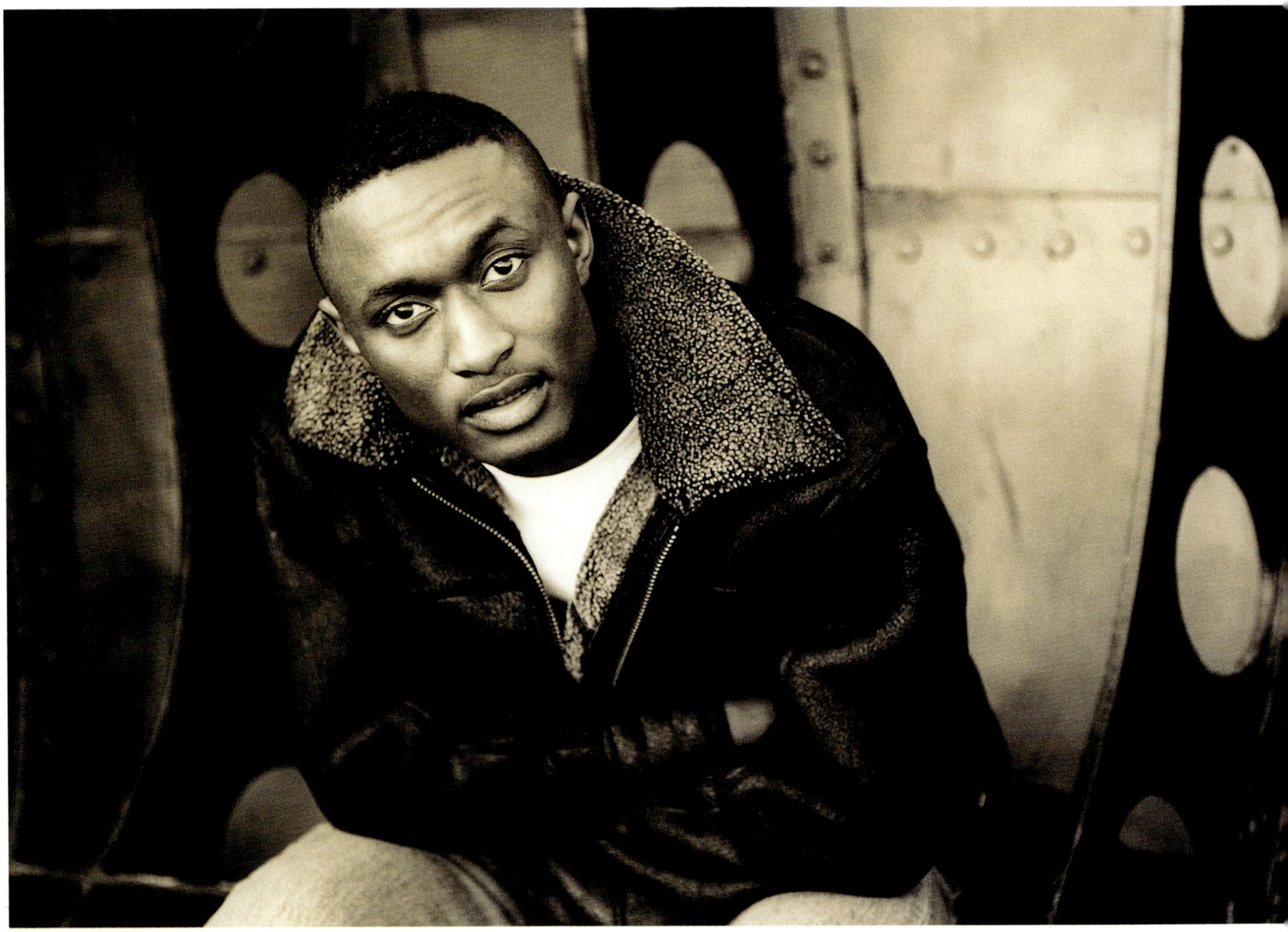

Taken in the hull of a boat, there is an industrial feel to this setting, which provides interest to the background without overpowering the subject. The location also provided good directional light coming from daylight to the right of the subject.

Technical details

Hasselblad 205 TCC camera with 250mm Tele-Tessar lens. Film was Kodak Tri-X rated at 200 ISO with an aperture of f/4.

Composition

Ronald Turner usually uses several different locations for a model's portfolio and this shot was taken at a gym. Ronald saw the potential of a narrow gap between a row of apparatus and a window for the model to appear in a long, thin shape, making maximum use of the contrast between light and shade. Photographed from behind but with strong eye-contact, there's a sense of mystery to this shot, as though we are just catching a glimpse of the figure before he disappears.

Technique

Ronald always looks for the light first, as the direction and quality of this is of paramount importance in a portrait. 'Once you know where the lighting possibilities are you can then consider the background and setting,' he says. An incident light reading was taken with a Minolta IV light meter.

Technical details

Hasselblad 205 TCC camera with 120 Macro-Planar lens. Film was Kodak Tri-X ISO 400 rated at ISO 200.

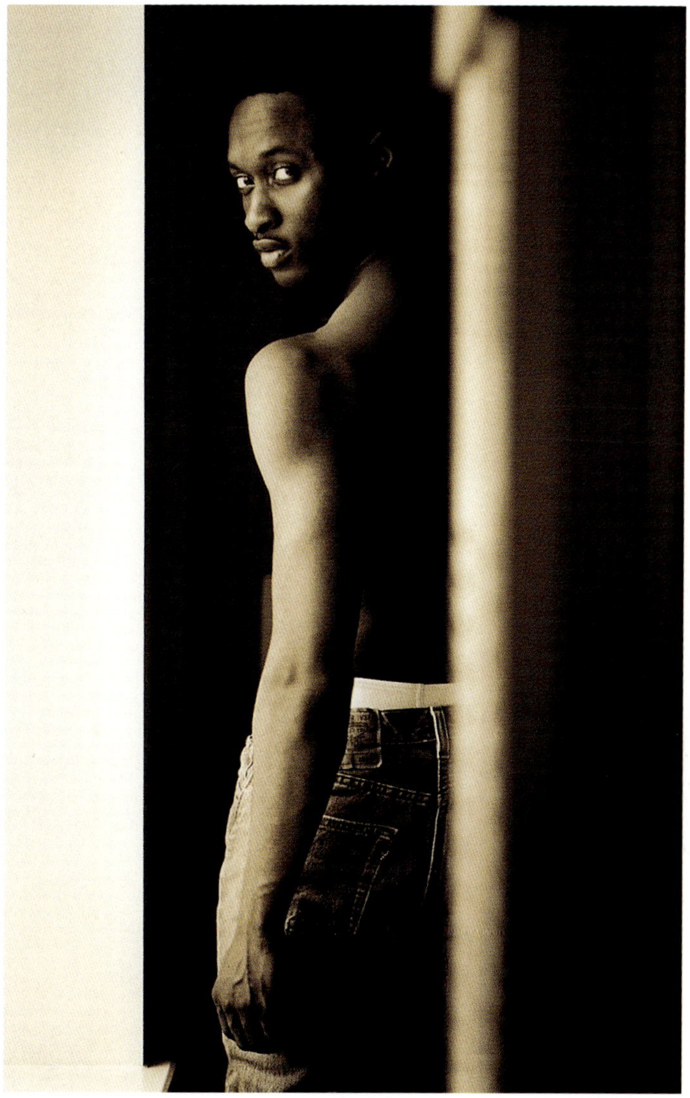

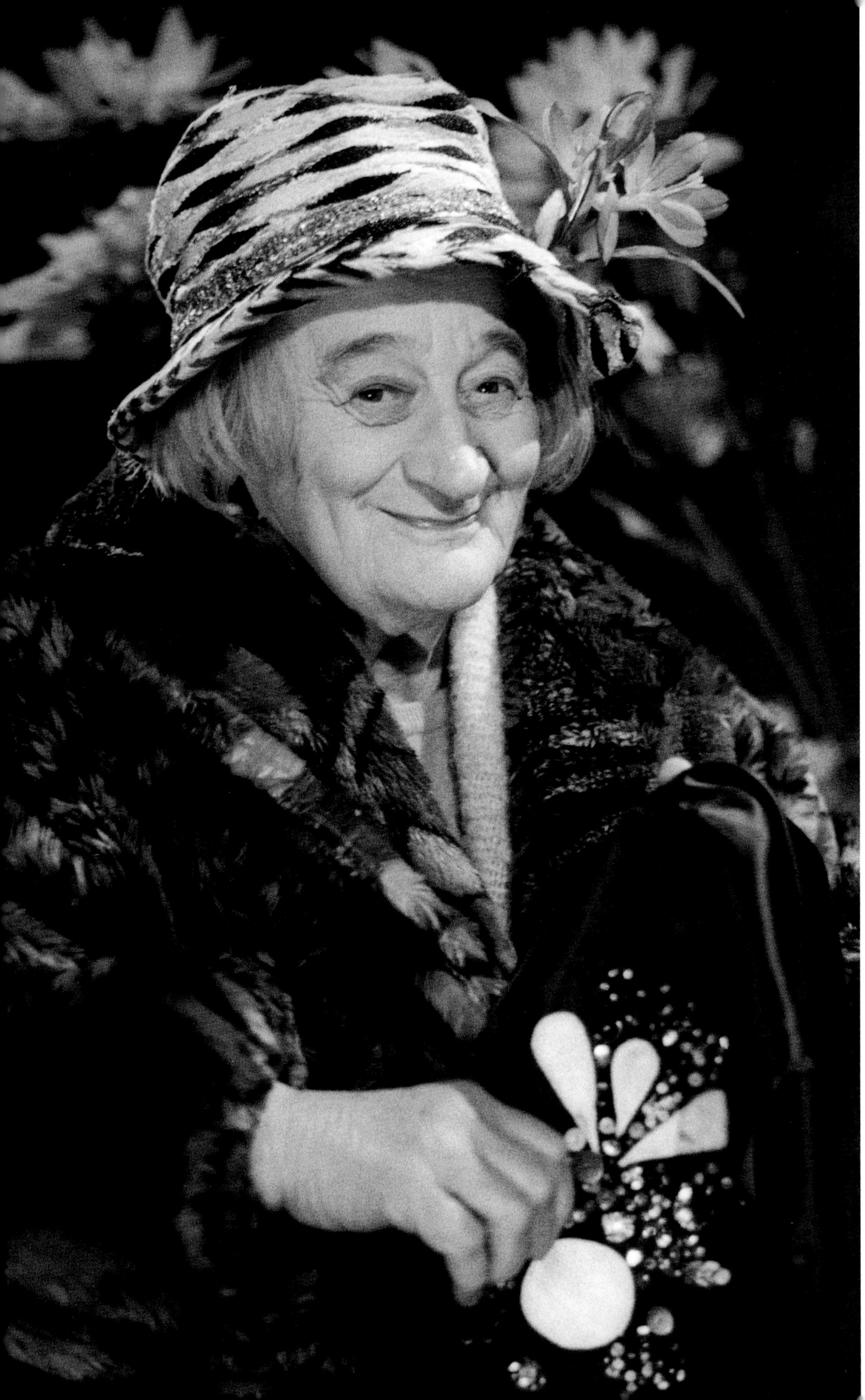

Carlo Chinca frequently works on film productions as the stills photographer and this portrait of the well-known British actress, Liz Smith, was taken on the set of a TV drama. It was taken outdoors, late at night, during a brief break in filming. Carlo made use of the tungsten lights set up for filming and had just a few moments to grab this portrait of the actress, using a wide aperture to put the background out of focus.

Technical details
Nikon F3 camera with 50mm lens. Film was Kodak T-Max 400 with an exposure of 1/125sec at f/2.

Composition
Monica Lewinsky came over to the UK in 1999 to promote her controversial autobiography and Carlo took this portrait when she visited her book publishers in Bath. Sometimes there will be an official photo-call with celebrity events like this. On this occasion, Carlo was one of a handful of photographers present who were allowed to photograph Monica Lewinsky as she was being shown around the premises. She didn't pose formally for the cameras at any time. Instead, it was up to the photographers to seize any opportunities as they arose. As a result, this is a very natural-looking portrait with the subject looking relaxed and happy. Including space around the subject gives picture editors the option of using the picture full-frame, or cropping it to a vertical format for a close-up portrait.

Technique
Carlo always focuses on the eyes of the subject because the shot is often ruined if these are not completely sharp. He also makes sure he can see the catchlight in the pupils of the eyes which can otherwise look flat and dead. The background here was cluttered and distracting so Carlo selected a wide aperture of f/3.5 to reduce it to a blur of black, white and grey tones which helps make the subject stand out.

Lighting
The available light consisted of fluorescent strip lights which would have resulted in an unattractive green cast if Carlo had used colour film. He always prefers to make use of existing light rather than add flash, even if the light is fairly low. Uprating his ISO 400 T-Max film to ISO 800 allows him a valuable extra stop exposure in these situations.

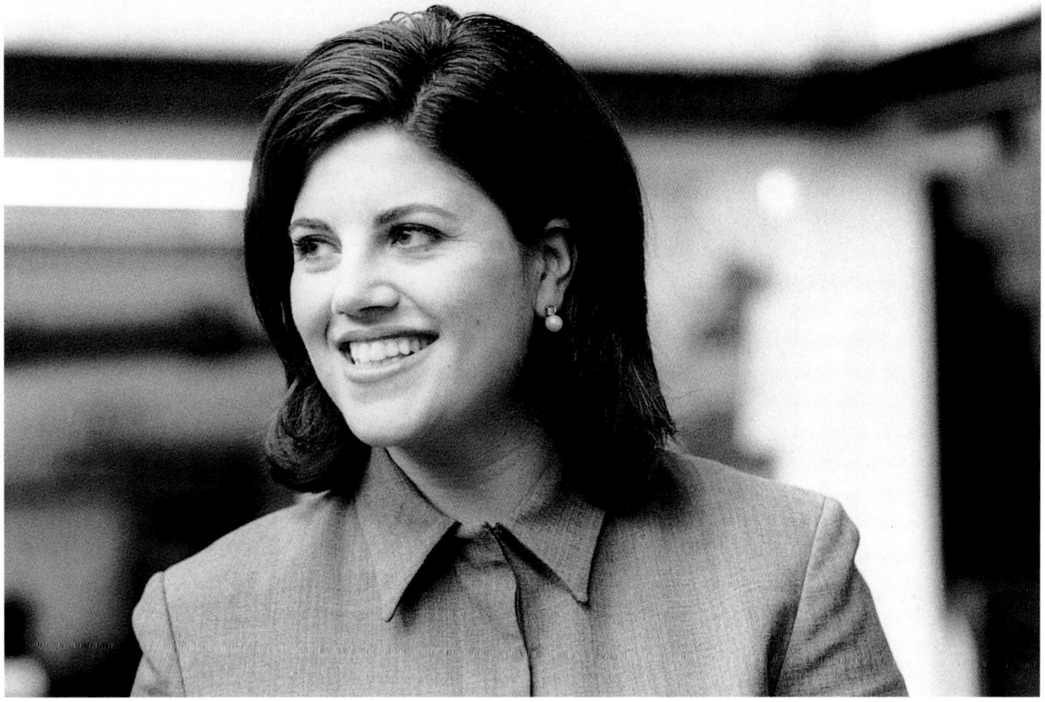

Technical details
Nikon F3 camera with 135mm lens. Film was Kodak T-Max 400 with an exposure of 1/125sec at f/3.5.

Taken at dawn by the River Seine in France, the softness of the morning light is accentuated by the special soft focus Rodenstock Imagon lens. These were originally designed for Hollywood portraits, but are still available today (from Burghard Smachtenburg in Germany) and Ronald Turner had one especially adapted for his Hasselblad camera.

Technical details
Hasselblad 205 TCC camera with 200mm Imagon lens. Film was Kodak GPX Gold 160.

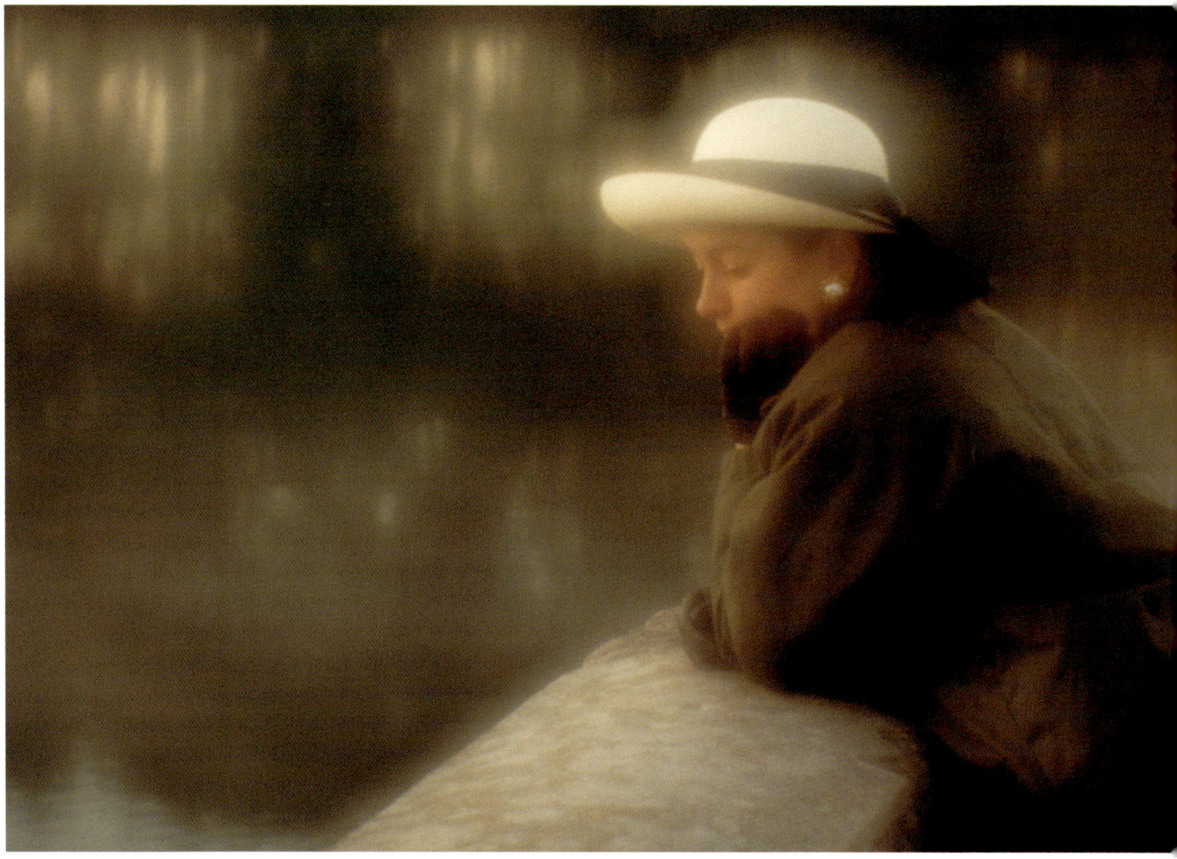

Composition

You don't need to include the whole figure in a portrait to achieve a glamorous-looking result and it's the simplicity of this shot which makes it work so well. Tilting the head upwards is flattering to the subject and the long hair balances the right side of the frame. The mood here is romantic and dreamy which would have been destroyed had the model looked towards the camera.

Technique

This was set up in a room using a sheet as the background and soft light coming from a window. An electric fan was placed beneath the model's hair, at just the right height to achieve the wind-blown look without it looking messy or unrealistic. The photographer, Tracy Turner, used a subtle soft focus filter to diffuse sharp edges and give the skin a smooth, flawless quality.

Technical details

Hasselblad 205 TCC camera with 180mm Sonnar lens. Film was Kodak GPX Gold 160.

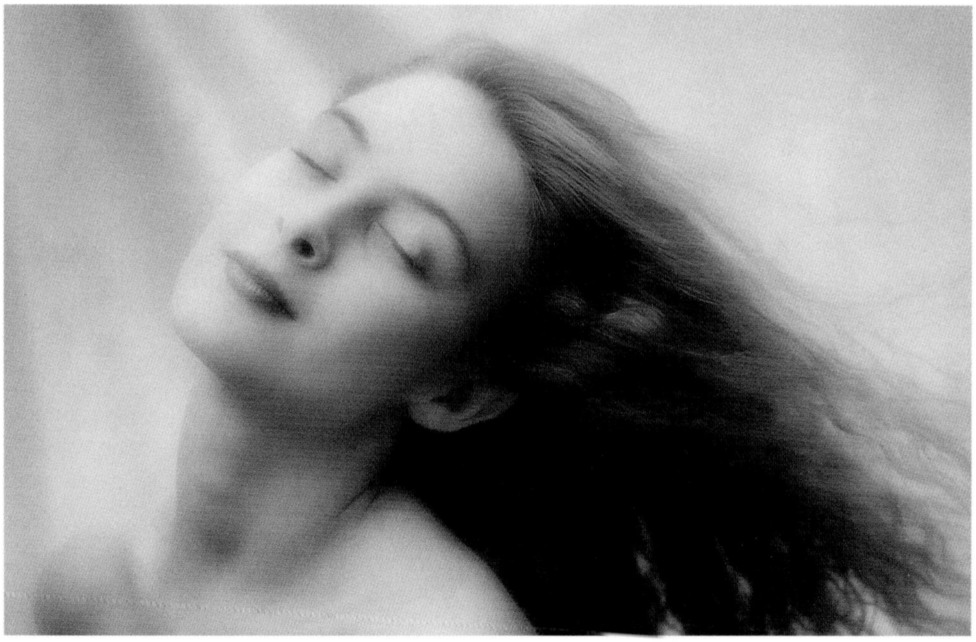

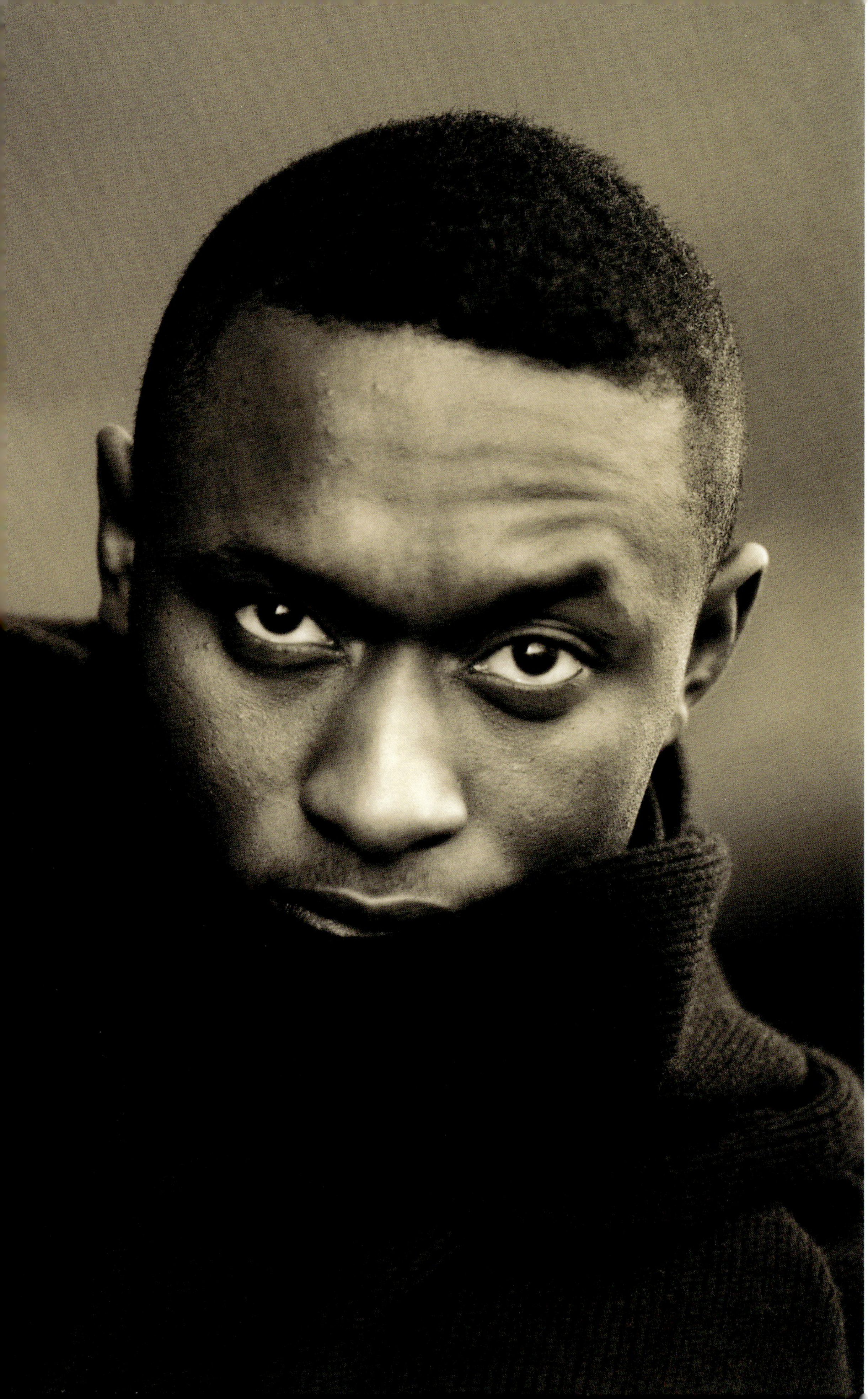

Taken under an overhang of a building which provided overhead shade, there was soft, direct light coming from one side and a break in the clouds behind the subject had a slight backlighting effect on the ears. Ronald Turner focused on the eyes with a 350mm lens and the shallow depth of field rendered the background out of focus. The predominantly dark tones in the image fit with the model's moody facial expression.

Technical details
Hasselblad 205 TCC camera with 350mm Tele-Tessar lens. Film was Kodak Tri-X ISO 400 rated at ISO 200.

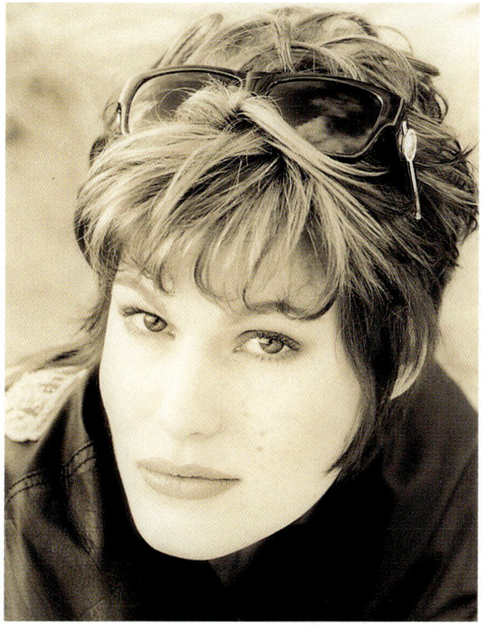

Technical details
Hasselblad 205 TCC camera with 180mm lens. Film was Kodak Tri-X rated at ISO 200.

Composition
Ronald took a series of portraits using different locations and poses for this model's portfolio in order to show her versatility to potential employers. This shot was taken on the beach, with the model crouching on sand dunes. The angle of her face in relation to the camera is very attractive, as is the wide-open look to her eyes.

Technique
Ronald aims for what he calls the 'Indian canoe' effect in the eyes. This is when the whites of the eyes under the pupils form the shape of a canoe, which gives a wide-eyed look. He does this by utilising a slightly high camera angle, directing the model to tilt the head slightly towards the camera and look straight at the camera. The quality and direction of light, the use of a reflector and a subtle soft focus filter create the porcelain look to the skin.

Mood
The style of this portrait reflects the glossy look found in fashion magazines. When shooting for models' portfolios, it's important to keep up-to-date with current trends and magazines are useful reference material. The models themselves will probably have their own ideas about the look that they want to portray, but a successful shoot will depend on the collaboration between the model and photographer.

'We always invite models to bring along some cuttings that reflect the way they see themselves and also show and discuss pictures in our own portfolio. I seldom copy a pose but often use an idea as a springboard to another picture in the same or similar style.'

Ronald Turner

8

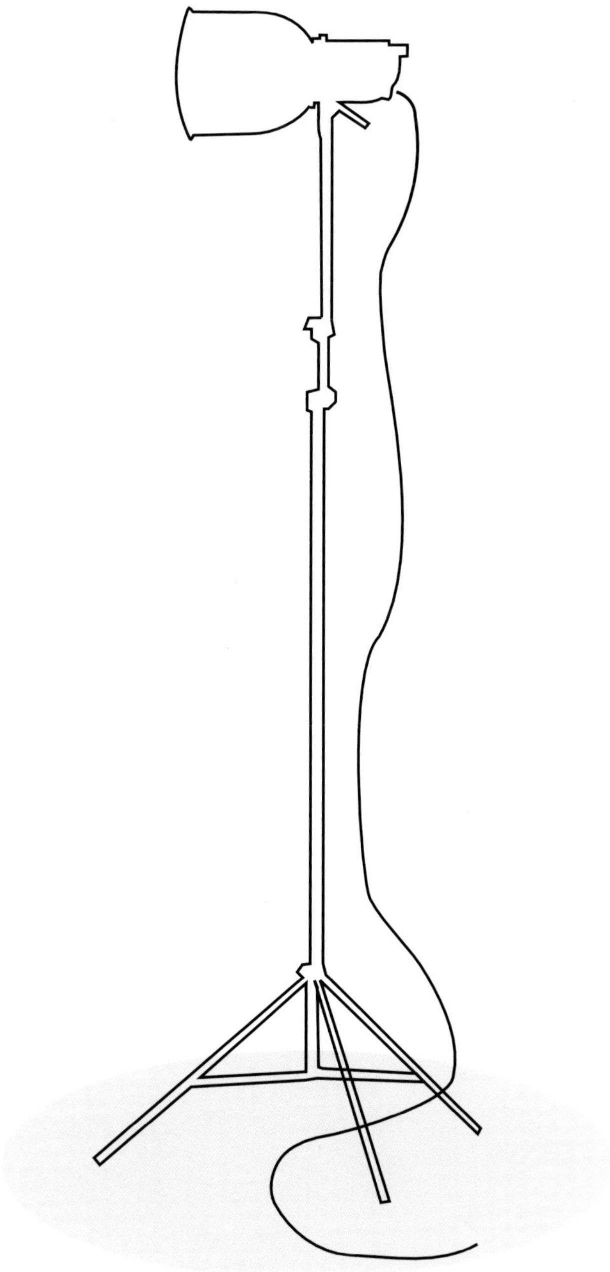

selling your work

You only have to pick up any newspaper, magazine or travel book to realise the enormous commercial potential for location portrait photographs. Some will have been commissioned directly from the photographer, others sourced from picture libraries. Either way, to make sure your pictures are used, you first have to ensure they are seen by the right people. The following pages show you how to do that.

'It may well have been cheaper to get 1000 single-image postcards printed, but this enables me to show a broader range of images,' says Richard Lewisohn. 'I can also update the pictures easily and change them according to the person to whom I am sending it.'

Even if you are just starting out as a professional or only earning part of your income through photography, you'll benefit from some degree of marketing to help your name and your work become more widely known. Depending on your area of interest, this could include advertising in the local press or targeting a particular audience.

If, for example, you take location portraits of families and children, you could advertise in the parenting newsletters that are available in many areas.

You don't need to invest a great deal of money in marketing. A well-presented portfolio is probably your most essential tool. This should include tear-sheets or copies of any publications that your work has appeared in, as well as original images.

As computer ownership is becoming increasingly widespread – and has numerous benefits to the photographer – it's quick, easy and cheap to produce professional-looking personalised cards.

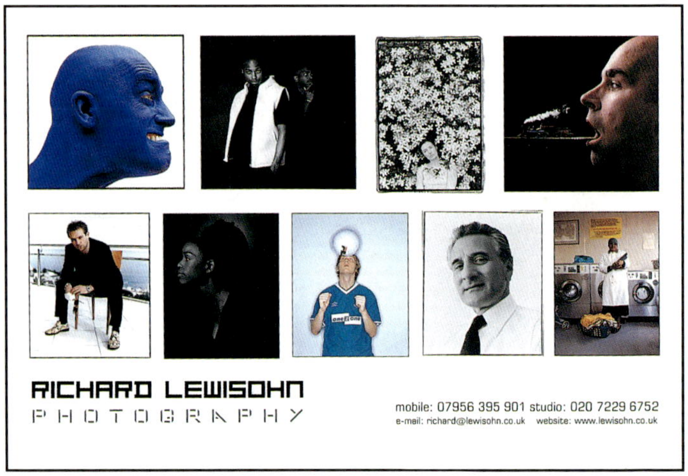

Richard Lewisohn designed his own 8x5in card on the computer, using Corel Draw desktop publishing software, to advertise his work.

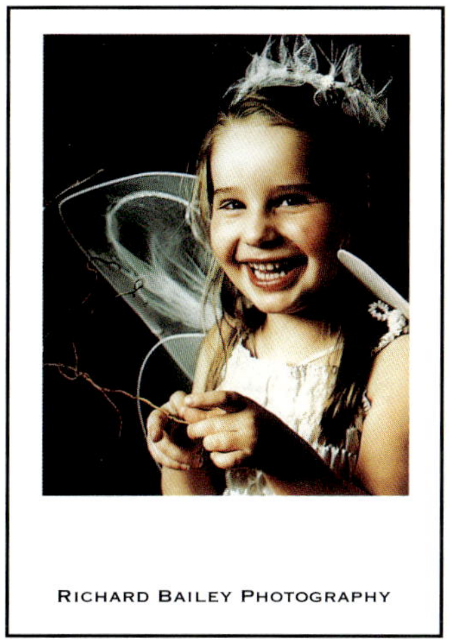

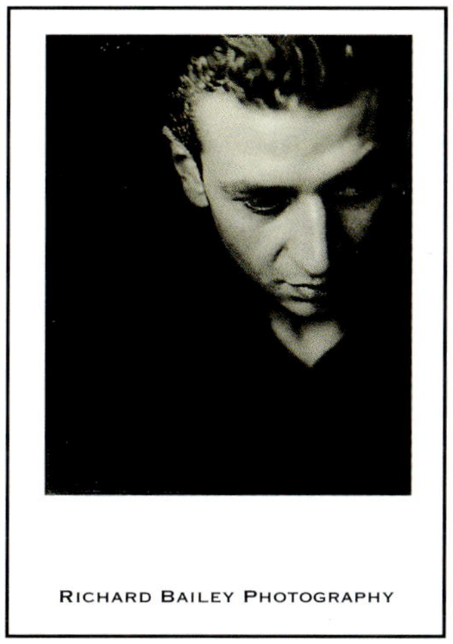

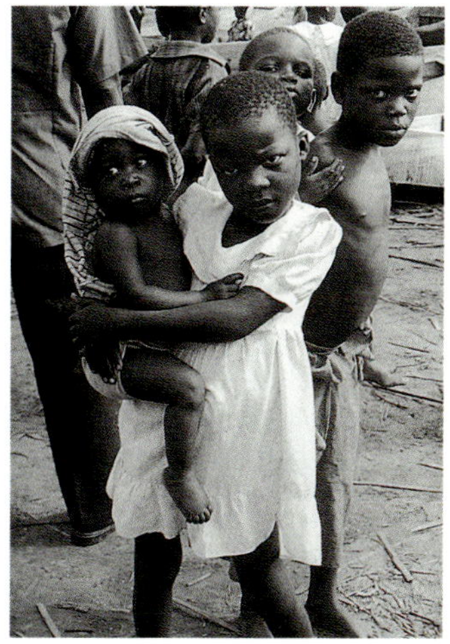
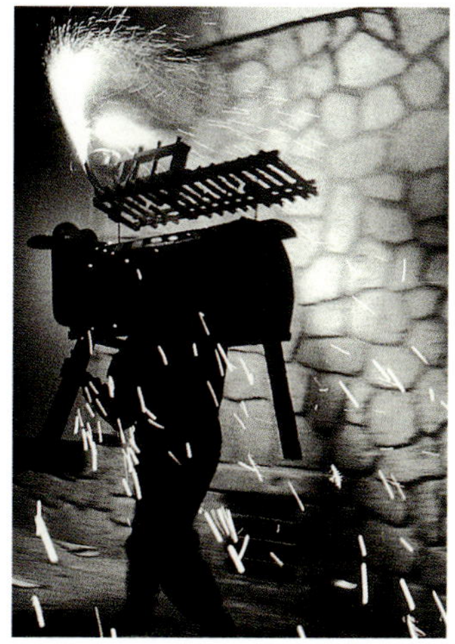
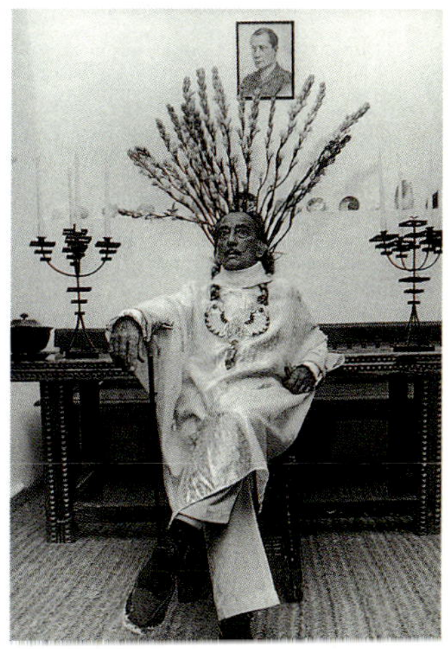
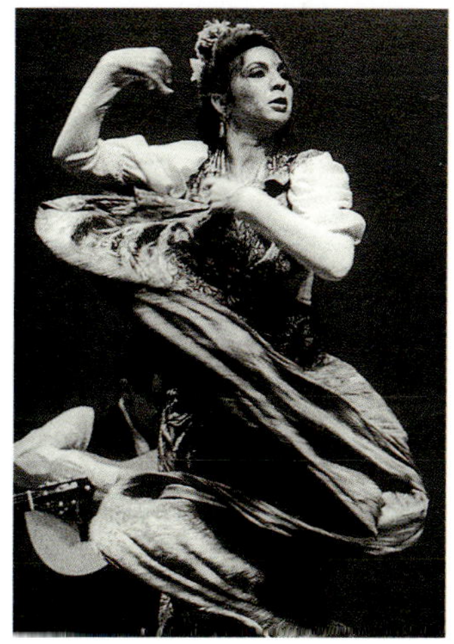
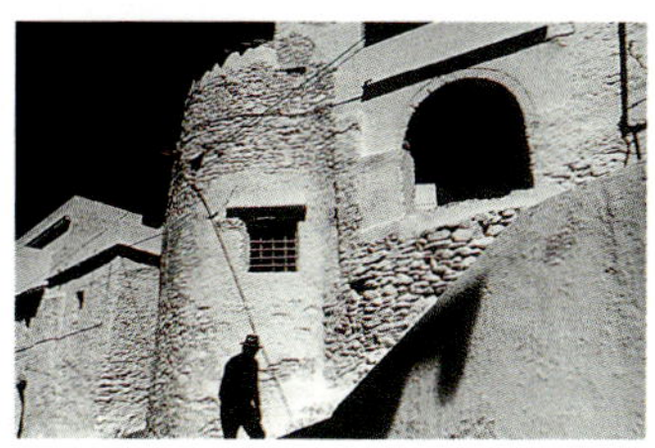
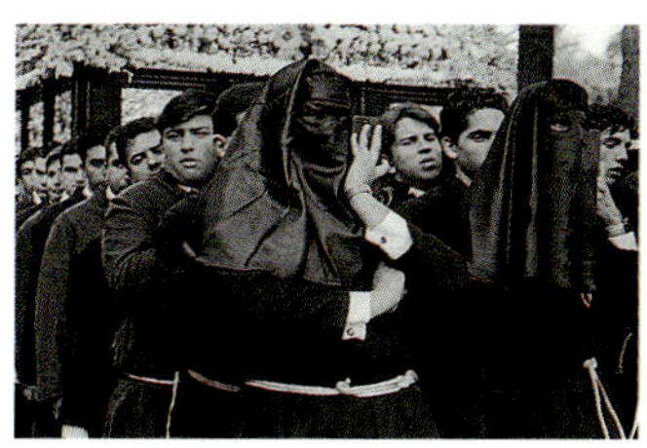

Carlo Chinca and Richard Bailey both use postcards of their pictures to send to new or potential clients and always hand them out when showing their portfolios.

‘I have 12 different postcards representing different areas of my work so I can tailor them to the needs of the client.’

Carlo Chinca

It may be a while, if ever, before digital cameras make conventional film obsolete but many photographers are finding it hard to ignore the digital revolution altogether and there are many positive benefits to be gained. Invest in a computer with a powerful processor, at least 64 Mb of memory (RAM) and a CD ROM drive, as well as a printer and scanner, and you can store your pictures digitally and send them anywhere in the world as JPEG files, without the originals leaving your hands.

There are creative advantages, too. With an imaging program such as Adobe Photoshop, you can crop, tone, retouch and even sharpen your pictures. Elements of different pictures can be merged together to produce extraordinary effects, and unwanted details removed with a few clicks of the mouse.

Philip Sprague taught himself the techniques of digital imaging, but confesses he is still learning through trial and error. This photograph has been very successful for him, winning an award for the best black and white print from the Photographic Alliance of Great Britain.

'It's made up of four negatives, taken at the same spot in Zanzibar, and scanned into the computer,' he explains. 'The lads in the foreground were one negative, the three under the umbrella another, the boy on the right a third and the bodies of the girls in the background came from a fourth. Using Photoshop, I selected areas of each negative and placed them in layers. Some parts were cloned and manipulated until all the gaps were filled and it fitted together. It took a lot of time and experimentation to get to the stage where you can't see the joins.'

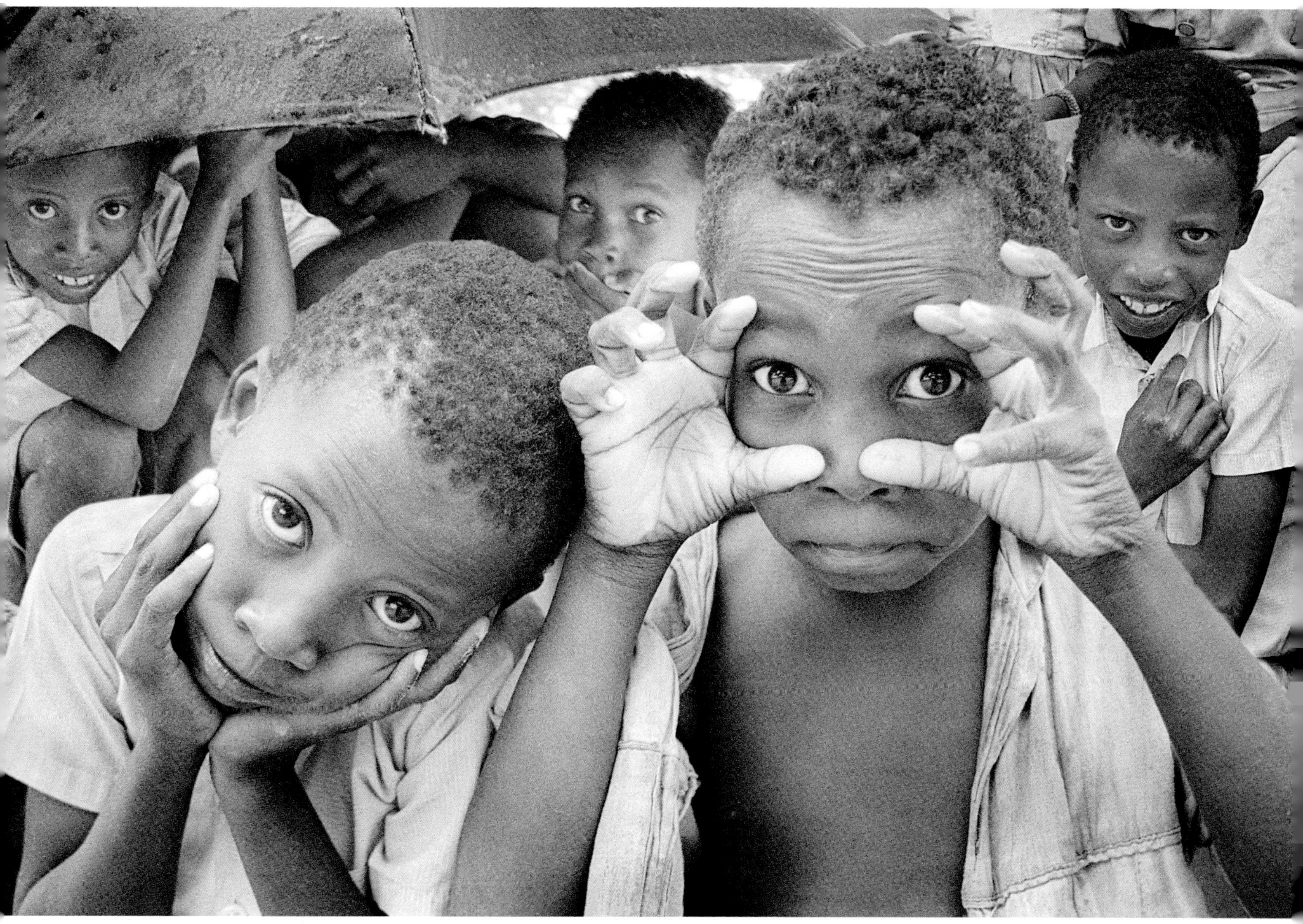

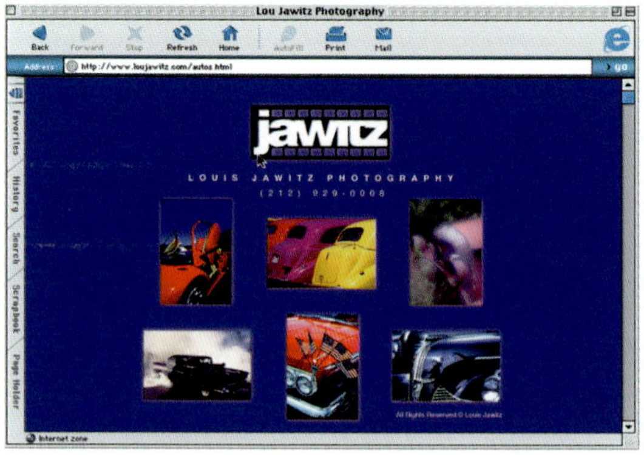

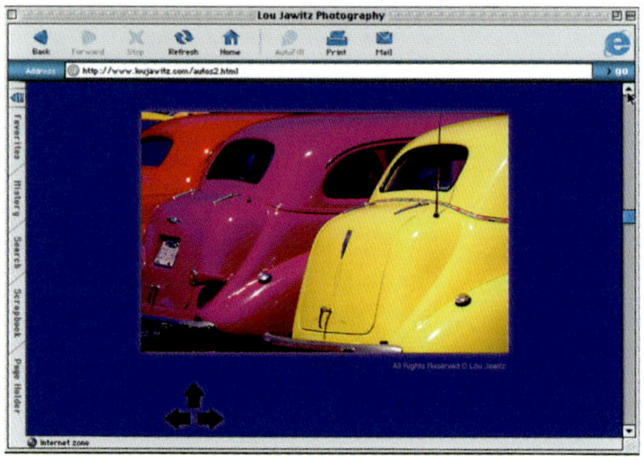

While nothing can replace the impression of a quality print in your hand or a fine transparency on the lightbox, sending out original material to prospective clients can be costly and time consuming. This is where a website can really reap rewards. Set up your own site with a selection of your best images, plus a brief biography and contact details and your work can be viewed immediately, anywhere in the world.

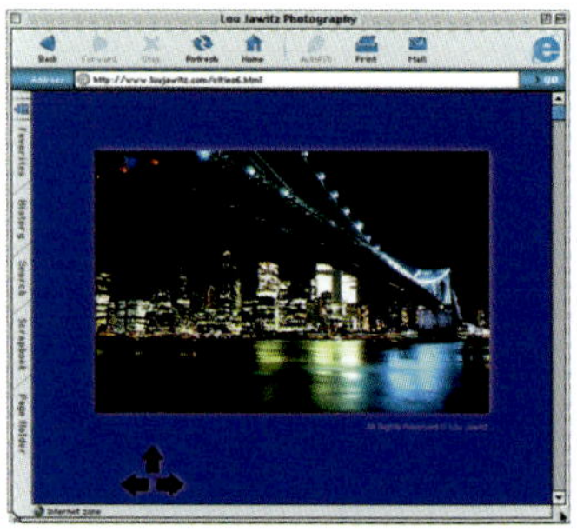

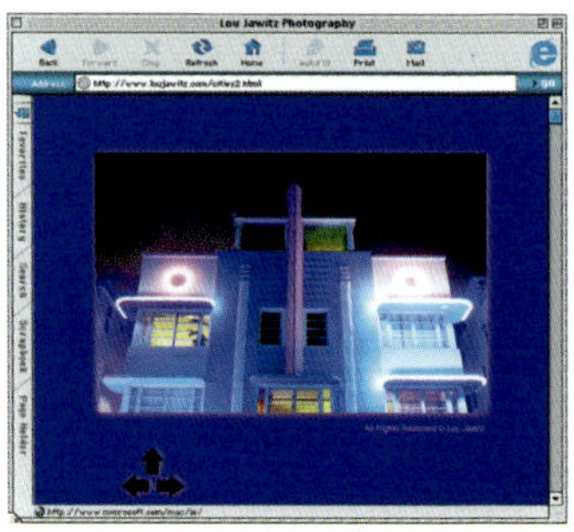

Louis Jawitz, a professional New York-based photographer, made an initial plan for his website and then had it put together by a web designer. As well as his own address, www.loujawitz.com, his site is also accessible via a host site, www.photoserve.com, and he pays them a monthly fee in return. 'I have sold pictures directly from it, but I don't think I have made my money back on the production and service fee,' he says. 'Its real success has been as a way of giving art directors a feel for what I do. As an on-line portfolio it's great.'

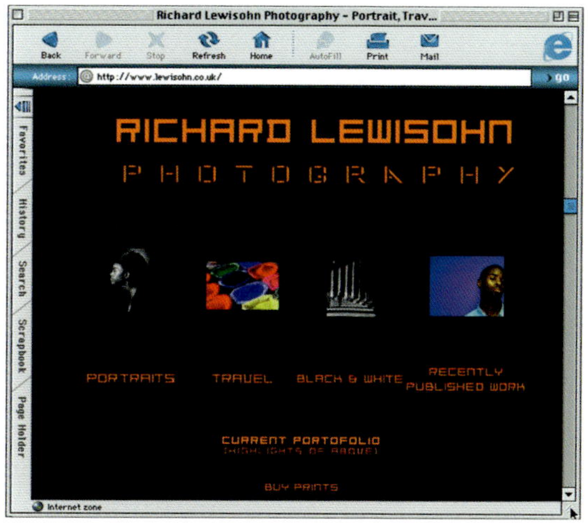

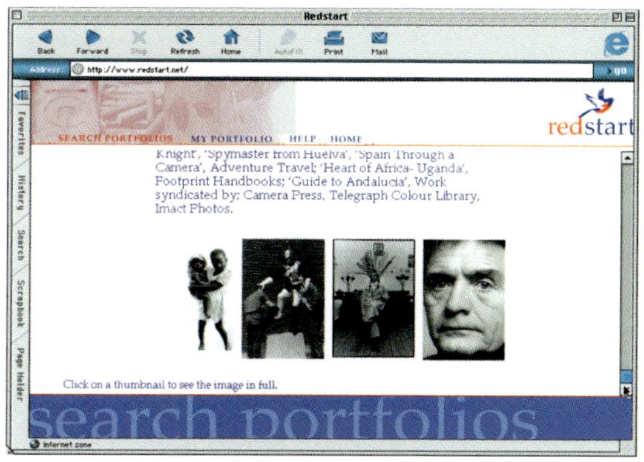

If you can't justify the time or expense of setting up a personal website, why not join a group one? Look in the photographic and computer press for host websites that specialise in photographers' work, like www.redstart.net. These often provide a free service, allowing you to place a small portfolio and contact details on the site which may be accessed by art directors and picture editors.

Freelance photographer Richard Lewisohn designed his own website using web editing software that came free on the cover of a magazine. 'It was quite straightforward really, you just use the template and follow instructions,' he says. Richard's site is divided into five sections – travel, portraits, black and white, recently published work and current portfolio. 'I may have included too many pictures but I couldn't resist having them up. The current portfolio section is useful, though, because people can click on that to get an idea of the range of work without having to look at each section.'

If you're designing your own site, remember to include your e-mail address. Anyone interested can click on it to contact you directly. Keep the website updated with fresh images to ensure it reflects your recent work, but don't be too ambitious in the number of pictures per page or it can take a long time to download.

One of the best ways of marketing your pictures is through picture libraries and agencies as these are regularly used by publishers of books, magazines, newspapers and electronic media, as well as advertising agencies. The library makes the sale and takes a percentage of the reproduction fee while you, in theory, sit back and wait for your share of the money.

There are hundreds of different libraries and most will specialise in specific areas. It's important to do some thorough research before you make an approach, to make sure your photographs suit the library's requirements. Virtually all of them will have websites where you can view some of their current images to get an idea of the style and content.

Impact Photos

This London-based agency, whose pictures you can see on the following pages, represents the work of 150 photographers. It specialises in worldwide reportage, with subjects including education, travel, work, religion and environment.

'We are not a mainstream travel library and we don't simply want pretty pictures of destinations,' says Impact's Darren Wisdom. 'We look for images involving real people rather than posed models and our photographers generally have an eye for the unusual.'

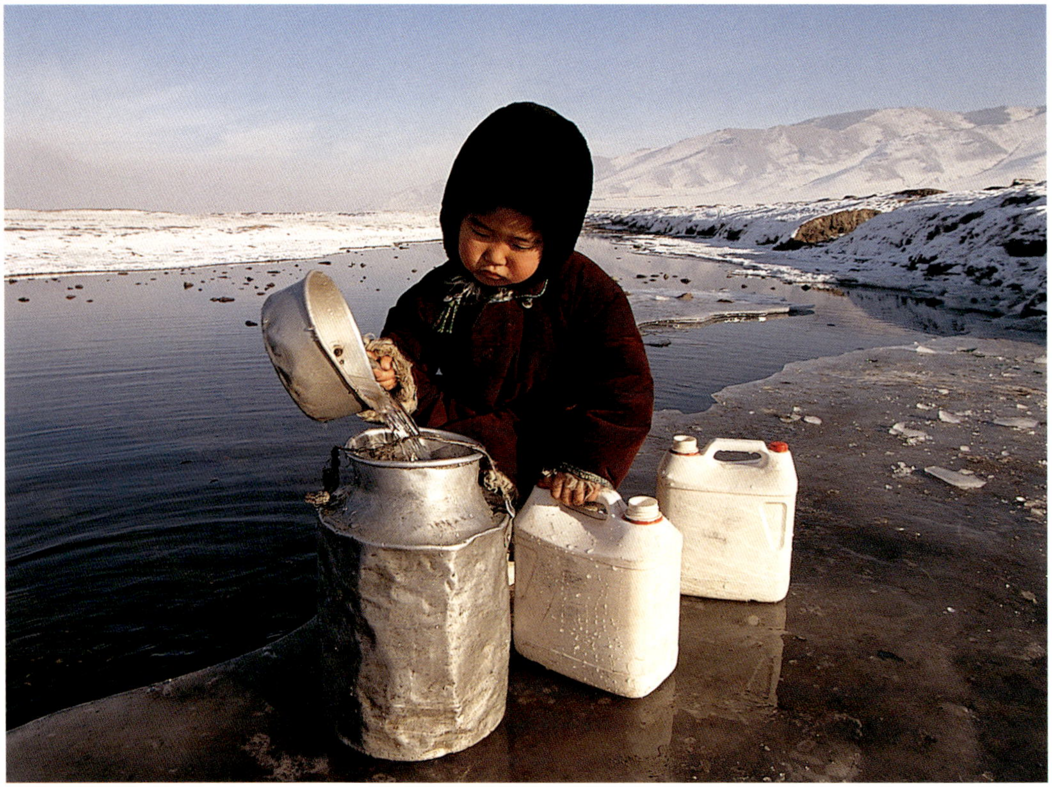

Mark Henley's photograph of a young girl fetching water from the river in Mongolia has sold well through Impact, including to a national newspaper colour supplement. 'It's quite a timeless image, as you can imagine the girl would have been doing exactly the same thing 100 years ago,' says Darren. There's fantastic perspective, with the lines converging behind her and the lovely grouping of the child and water containers in the middle of the image. Composition is the key element in successful pictures.'

Try to envisage the impact of a picture on a page. Look for striking compositions, perhaps with repetitive patterns, and pay close attention to lighting and image sharpness. For reasons of quality and ease of storage, most libraries prefer 35mm transparencies. They may scan these into a computer so they can be transmitted to the client electronically.

This picture by Robin Laurance shows Sikh schoolboys in Calcutta. It falls into the category of education, but could also be used in a travel context.

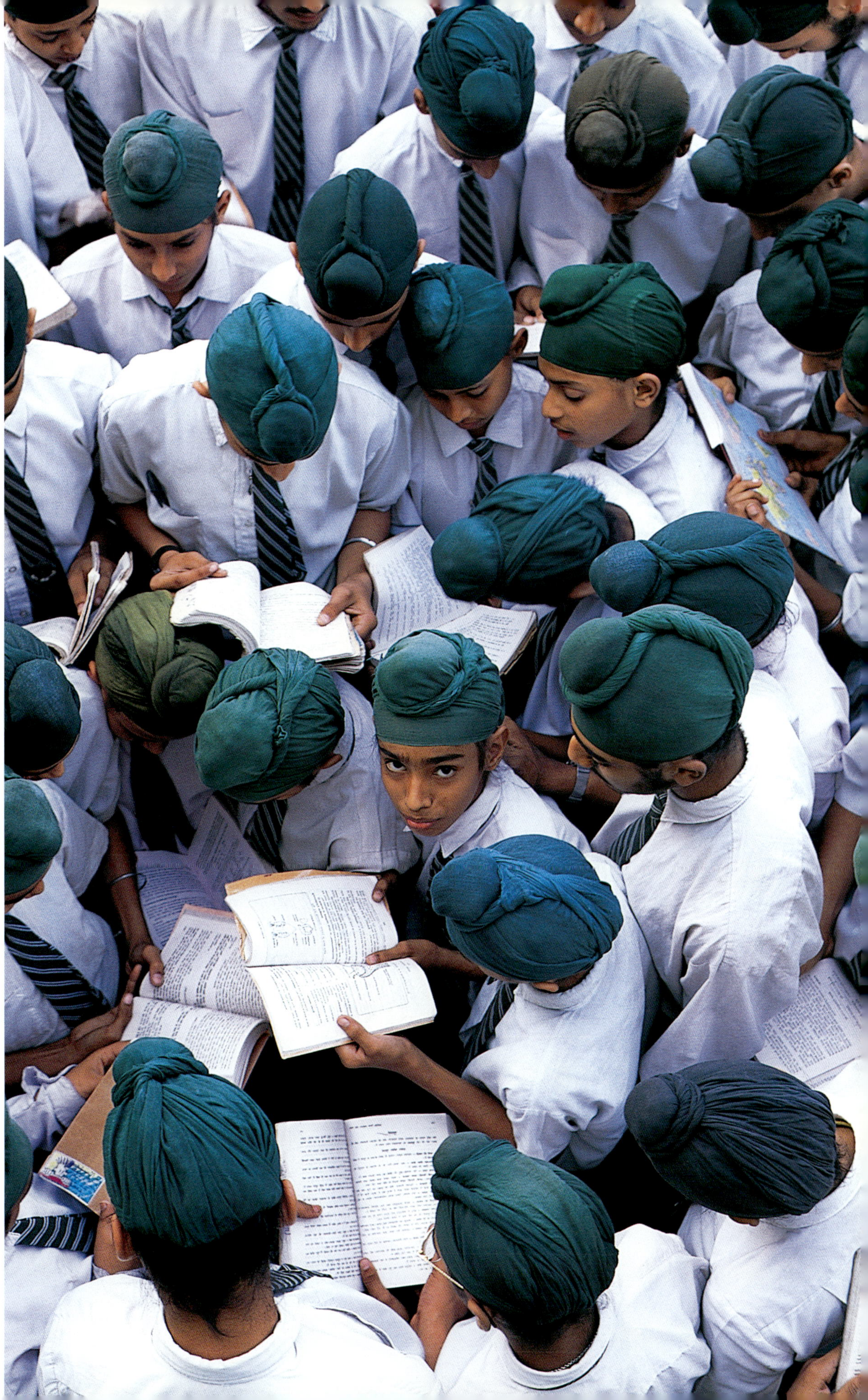

If you're after quick sales and a fast return on your images, think again about submitting to picture libraries. Most will need to hold on to your pictures for a minimum period, which may be three to five years, to give them a chance to sell. They also deal with large quantities of images and may require you to submit several hundred, all of which must be of a high quality. Once on the books, you will usually be kept informed of the library's 'wants' so you can bear this in mind if you're planning a trip.

When shooting for stock, i.e. a picture library, bear in mind the possible sales potential of a shot. This Impact Photos picture by Peter Ginier shows an early morning washing ceremony in the river Ganges, India. It has been used in a multitude of ways for different publications, including the illustration for a feature on the health benefits of water.

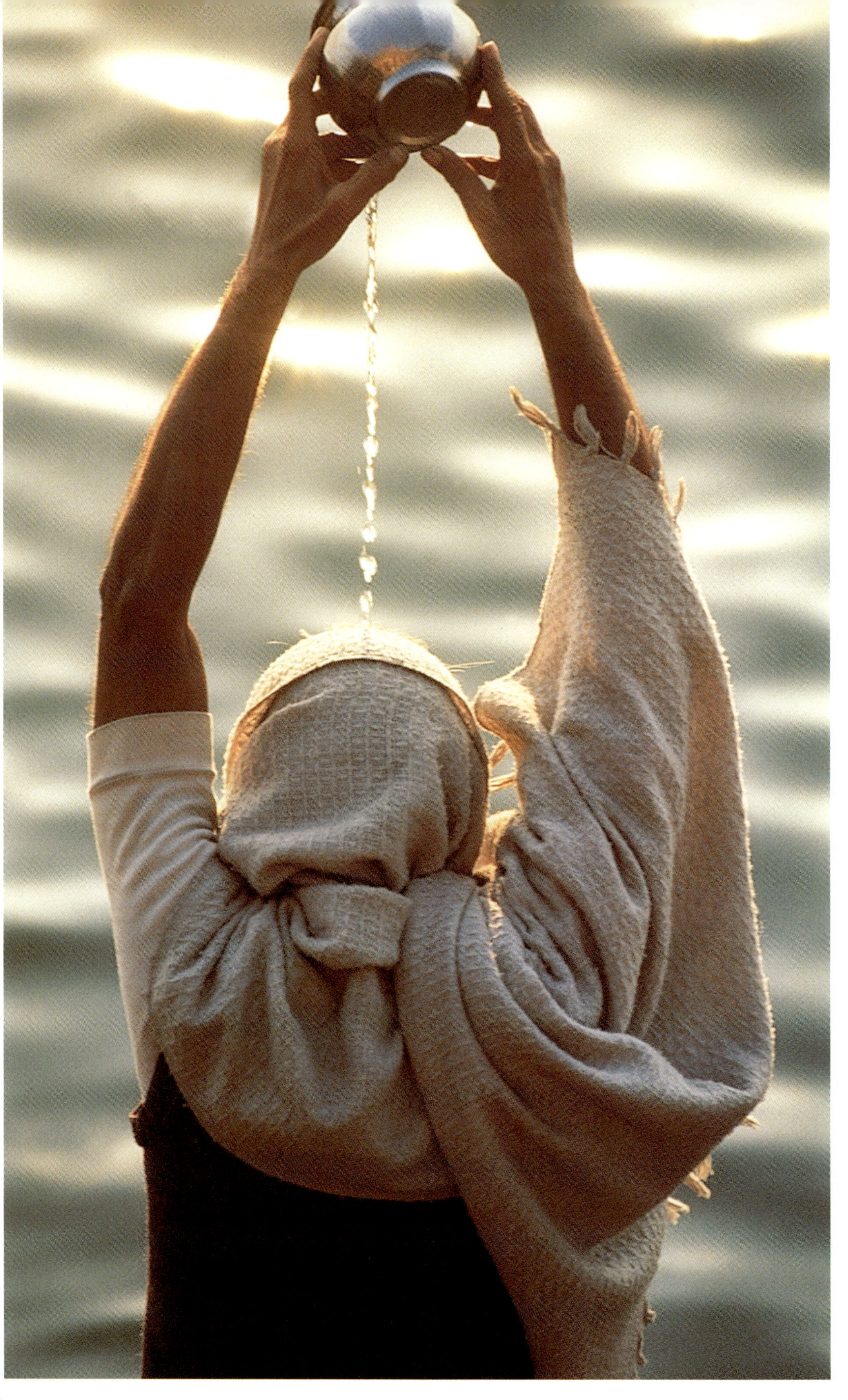

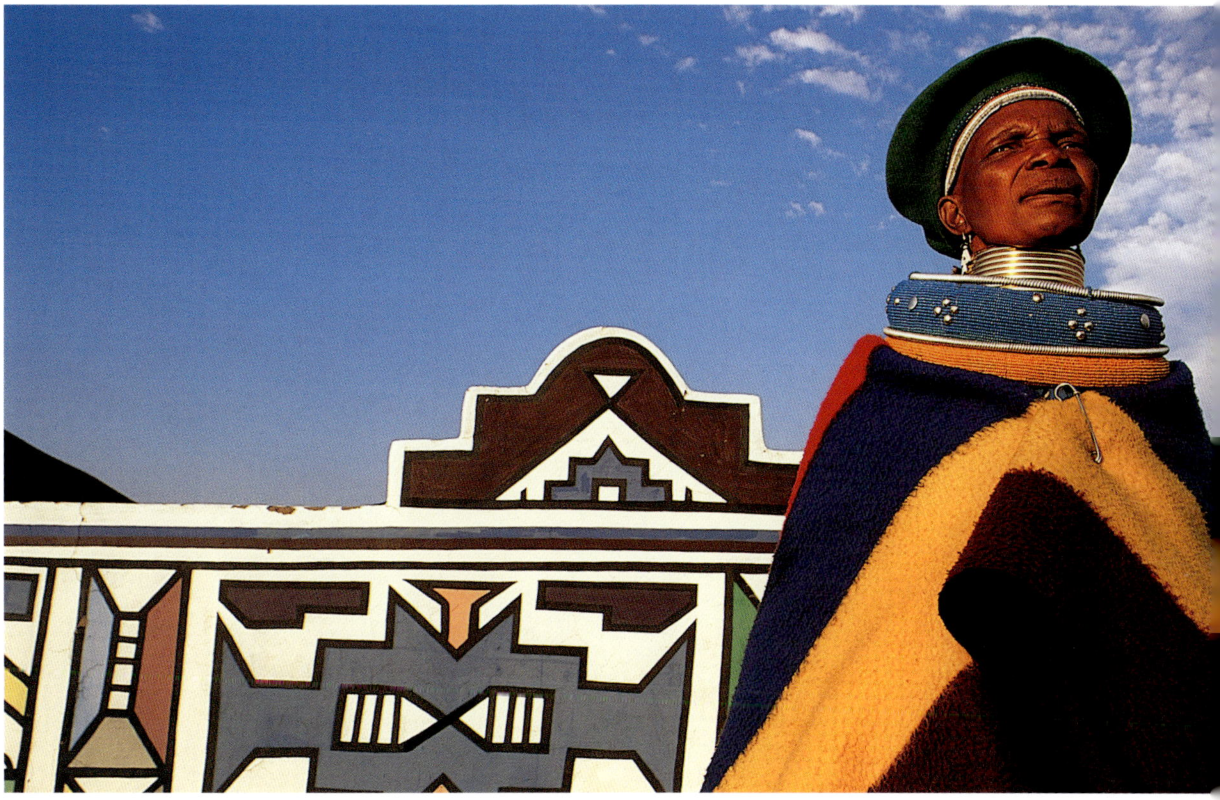

A Ndebele woman in Kwamabhoko, South Africa by Robin Laurance. 'This is one of those stand-out images that tweak your eye and make you stop if you're flicking through a book or magazine,' says Darren Wisdom from Impact. 'The bold colours are wonderful and there's a good juxtaposition of the figure with the painted building and the sky.'

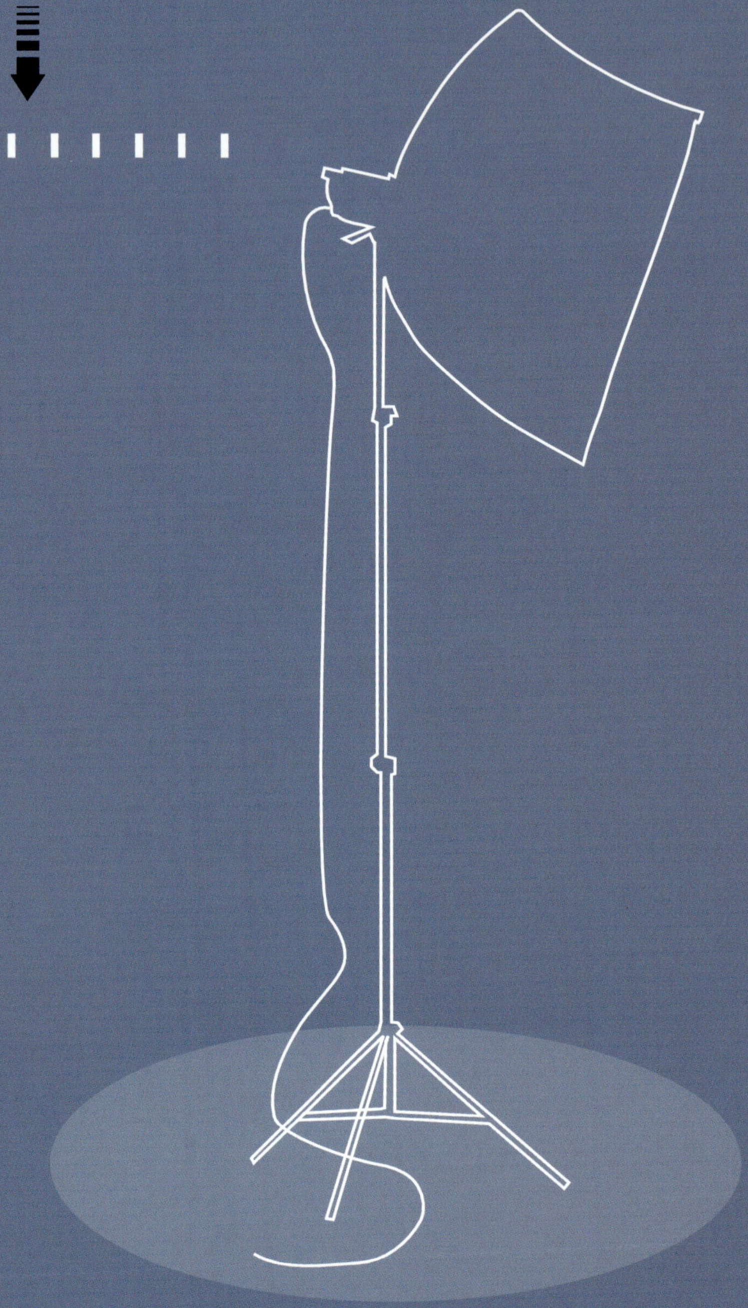

glossary

Backlighting – Natural or artificial illumination that is in the background or directly behind a subject. Unwanted backlighting can be compensated for by an adjustment in exposure. Backlighting can be used to deliberately create a halo- or glow-effect behind a subject.
Ball and socket head – A moveable joint on top of a tripod that provides an infinite number of adjustable positions for an attached camera.
Barn doors – Moveable flaps situated near the front of a studio light that can be adjusted to control light direction.
Bounce flash – A technique that 'bounces' flash illumination off a reflector on a flash unit, or a nearby surface such as a wall or ceiling, on to the subject. The effect is to spread and soften the light.
Brolly diffuser – A special brolly or umbrella covered with semi-transparent material and attached directly to the flash unit. The flash is fired through the brolly to create a soft or diffused lighting effect.
Burning in – A darkroom term for giving part of a print more exposure than other areas to produce a darker result.

Cable release – Cable which screws into the camera's shutter release and allows the shutter to be fired without touching the camera. Mainly used to prevent camera shake.

Dedicated flash – Flash unit which integrates with the camera's settings.
Dedicated flashgun – A flashgun that is totally compatible with, or dedicated to, the exposure metering system of a specific camera.
Depth of field – The area of acceptably sharp focus extending in front of and behind the point which is focused on.
Depth of field preview – A control that shows the amount of the area in front of and behind a subject that is in focus, depending on the aperture that's been selected.
Diffuser – A device that softens or diffuses illumination or creates a diffused effect. A diffuser can be semi-transparent material covering a light-source or a filter that is placed over a camera lens to produce a diffused effect.
Digital read out – Information shown in digital form in an LCD or LED panel, such as on a camera, light or flash meter or on a flash unit.

Exposure compensation – Manually adjusting the exposure to compensate for false readings made by the camera's metering system. Used when photographing predominantly light or dark subjects.
Exposure Value (EV) – A particular exposure setting using any chosen aperture and shutter speed combination that will produce a correctly exposed result, depending on the existing lighting conditions. An EV range provides several aperture and shutter speed options to choose from. Camera exposure systems and external light and flash meters have specific EV ranges.

Fill-flash – A blast of flash that provides just enough illumination to light or fill any areas of shadow.
Flag or French flag – A variation on the barn doors. It's a single flap of opaque material attached on to or near a studio flash so as to partially or completely block illumination.
Flash meter – A special type of light meter that's used to measure flash illumination. The appropriate exposure required for a given amount of flash illumination is shown on a digital read out.
Flash sync lead – A cable that connects a camera to an external flash unit, so that when the shutter button is pressed the external flash unit is automatically triggered.
Flat – A free-standing card or similar material that is used as a reflector. A flat can be large and used as a background or smaller and positioned behind, above, below or to either side of the subject.

Gel or Acetate – A piece of special coloured plastic that can be used like a filter, placed over a camera lens or over a lamp or studio flash.
Grain – The name given to the cluster of silver halides in the light-sensitive emulsion. Faster film has bigger clusters and a more obvious grain structure which can be used for pictorial effect.
Guide Number – The Guide Number or GN of a flashgun is an indicator of its maximum power output. The higher the GN the more powerful the flashgun. If you use a flashgun which has a GN of 25 and if your chosen aperture is, say, f/5.6, there will be sufficient illumination to light a subject that is 4m away. Flashguns built into cameras usually have a GN of around 12, while externally attachable flashguns usually start from 25 and go as high as 90. (GN figures for flashguns are based on ISO 100.)

Halo effect – See Backlighting.
Honeycomb – A grid designed to look like a honeycomb pattern and placed over a light source to provide more controlled, directional lighting.

Large format – Cameras which take pictures larger than 6x9cm.
Light meter – Device for measuring light and providing exposure readings.
Lighting stand – A free-standing support for a studio flash unit.

Matt surface – A non-shiny surface, such as felt or stone, that has little or no reflections on it.

Needle-and-dial read out – A system used to display the read out from a light meter, usually found in older light meters.
Ni-Cad batteries – Special rechargeable batteries that use Nickel Cadmium.

Polariser – A special filter that is used to reduce reflections in shiny objects. It is also helpful for increasing the intensity of blue skies. Can be in the form of a screw-on lens filter or as a large sheet that can be cut to size.
Programme exposure – The camera controls the aperture and shutter speed automatically.

Reflector – An object, such as a piece of card, a mirror or other reflective material, that is used to direct light on to a subject.
Rim light – A light, usually placed behind or to the side, that illuminates the edge of a subject. It is a technique that is sometimes used to light hair.

Scanner – Electronic device for converting photography images into digital images. Flatbed scanners are used for prints and film scanners for negatives and transparencies.
Scrim – A cloth-like material that is placed over the light source to provide diffused lighting.
Sepia toner – Adds a brown tone to prints, of varying density according to the level of dilution. Often used to recreate the effects of old photographs.
Slave unit – A tiny stand-alone receptor that is used to trigger flash units that are not physically connected to the camera. Several flash units can be triggered in this way. Slave units are handy for selectively illuminating large interiors.
Snoot – A tube used for directing illumination in the shape of a narrow beam.
Soft-focus filter – Fits over the lens to gently add diffusion to the image. Also called a diffuser by some manufacturers.
Softbox – A large box diffuser that is placed over a light source, producing a large area of soft, even lighting.
Spot – A device fitted over a light source or built into a light source, that provides a very narrow directional light beam.
Spot-metering – A feature that measures a very narrow area of light on a subject. This is to ensure accurate exposure for one part of a subject, or to take several light readings to obtain an average exposure.
Stroboscopic flash unit – A special flash unit that emits several small, high-intensity flashes in quick succession. It can be used to freeze fast action, resulting in images that show sequences of a fast-moving event. N.B. Not to be confused with a strobe, which is sometimes used as an alternative term for a conventional flashgun.

Thiocarbamide toning – A two-bath process that can give a variety of tones ranging from dark brown to a subtle yellow brown. Often used to increase the archival properties of the print.

Uprating – Exposing the film at a higher speed than its nominal rating, for example setting an ISO 100 film to ISO 200, usually to suit difficult lighting conditions. This is done via the camera's film speed dial. Often followed by increased film development.

Warm-up filter – Available in different strengths to add tonal richness to an image when fitted over the lens.

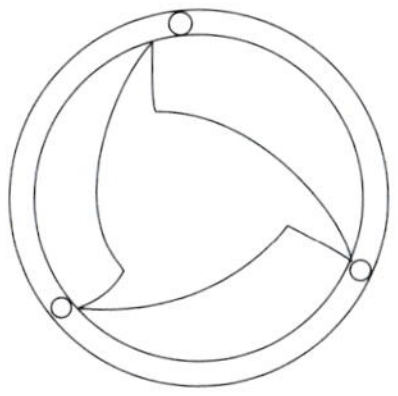

Gary Auerbach lives in Tucson, Arizona, where for 20 years he practiced chiropractic until a wrist injury compelled him to make a career transition. A serious amateur photographer all his life, Auerbach turned his attention to professional photography. He began searching for photographic methods that offered archival permanence and rediscovered the world of platinum photography. Specialising in large format cameras, and printing with hand-coated platinum papers, Auerbach's work in platinum photography has received acclaim for images of Native Americans and portraits of celebrities. His work is in the collections of the U.S. Library of Congress, the Ville de Geneve Musee d'Ethnographie, and other museums around the world. He has had exhibitions in the United States, Switzerland and Russia
Website: www.azstarnet.com/platinum
pages 34,35,74,75,77

Richard Bailey has been working as a freelance photographer since 1992, mainly in the fields of corporate and portrait photography. His book, The Road to Glory – Portraits of British Paralympians was published in 1996. A selection of the photographs were part of an exhibition at the National Portrait Gallery called Britain's Sporting Heroes.
E-mail: Richard@richardbaileyphotography.co.uk
Website: www.richardbaileyphotography.co.uk
pages 65,66,67,84,85,86,87,128

Diana Barker has been exhibiting widely as a painter since 1982 in London and around the UK. She began photographing Tibetan exile communities in 1992 and recently received funding for a new project on the nomads of Tibet. Her pictures have appeared in many magazines and books and have been used by many charities and campaigning organisations.
E-mail: dianebarker@hotmail.com
Website: www.spirit-of-tibet.co.uk
pages 99,105

Ronnie Bennett became a portrait photographer as a second career after completing a City and Guilds Professional Photography course. Since then she has won over 40 awards, including a fellowship of the Royal Photographic Society and an Associateship with the British Institute of professional Photographers. During the past five years she has worked mainly for private clients but is planning to diversify into advertising and editorial portraiture as well.
Tel: 01962 773 140.
E-mail: tim@tba.u/net.com
page 28

Angelo Cavalli
page 15

Carlo Chinca is a freelance photographer and writer. Between 1975 and 1986 he lived and worked in London, then moved to Spain, working as a freelance for five years. He is now based in Bath, UK. His work has been published in many newspapers and magazines, including the Telegraph Magazine, The Independent, The Sunday Times and Country Life. Exhibitions include Heart of Africa – Royal Commonwealth Society, London 2000 and Peace in Our Time – UNESCO, Paris 1998.
Tel: 01761 470 258
Website: www.redstart.net
pages 46,47,120,121,128

Dennis Cox is a Michigan-based award-winning travel and location photographer for magazines, books and corporate publications. As the founder and director of Photo Explorer Tours, he has been leading photo tours to China since 1981 and to other world destinations since 1996. His stock photography is marketed worldwide through Tony Stone Images and other libraries, as well as his own stock photo agencies, China Stock and DE Cox Photo Library, which contain the work of over a dozen other travel photographers worldwide.
Website: www.denniscox.com
pages 27,29,30,31,33,89,90,91,92,93,96,97,98,102,104,113

EJ Haas studied and then taught photography at the State University of New York at Fredonia before a spell as a staff photographer on a New York newspaper. He moved to Thailand in 1990 and currently lives in Chiang Mai. He works as a freelance travel, editorial, commercial and nature photographer and his pictures have appeared in publications around the world.
E-mail: ejhaas@cm.ksc.co.th
page 83

Jon Hicks has been a professional photographer since 1988. He specialises in travel and architecture photography, mainly for stock, and supplies 11 agents around the world. He is a Fellow of the British Institute

contacts

of Professional Photography.
Tel: 01566 773 305
E-mail: Jonhicks@altavista.net
pages 18,19,20,21,22,23,101

Sandy Huffaker Jr. is currently the features photographer for the San Diego Reader and has been published in numerous books, magazines and newspapers around the world, including People Magazine, USA Today, LA Times and Mother Jones Magazine.
He lives in San Diego with his wife Michelle and two daughters.
E-mail: huffaker@ad.znet.com
Website:http;//ad.znet.com/~huffaker/
pages 37,40,41,42,44,45,48,49,68,69,70,71,72,73,108

Impact Photos can be contacted at 18–20 St John Street, London EC1M 4NX, UK
Tel: 020 7251 5091
E-mail: library@impactphotos.demon.co.uk
Website: www.impactphotlibrary.com
pages 134,135,136,137

Louis Jawitz has been a professional photographer for 30 years, specialising in advertising, travel and editorial work for major clients in New York City, for which he has won many awards. He also produces stock photography, marketed throughout the world by himself and agencies such as The Image Bank and Age agency in Spain. Over the past years he has added digital skills to his photographic techniques. Most recently he has begun to specialise in car photography.
Website: www.loujawitz.com
pages 106,107,132

Richard Lewisohn
pages 128,133

Philip Sprague has 20 years experience as a photographer, taking landscapes, travel and sports. He travels extensively, especially to the Far East which he favours for portraiture. He has taken part in many regional, national and international exhibitions and won several gold medals for his work.
pages 12,13,80,81,100,109,110,111,130

Ronald Turner F.B.I.P.P., M.Photog., C.P.P. and daughter **Tracy Turner** F.B.I.P.P., together with Barbara (Ronald's wife) run a busy portrait studio in Cardiff, Wales. Their main specialisation is location portraiture for which they have won international acclaim and taught seminars and masterclasses worldwide. Ronald Turner has twice won Kodak Portrait Photographer of the Year, twice B.I.P.P. Portrait photographer of the Year, three times B.I.P.P. Wedding Photographer of the Year and The Grand Award of Wedding Photographers International. Tracy Turner was a joint winner of the B.I.P.P. Peter Grugeon Award for best Fellowship entry, the Gold and Silver Cups of the British Guild of Portrait Photographers. Between them the Turners have won a world studio record of 30 Kodak Gold Awards.
E-mail: rt@ronaldturner.com
pages 52,53,54,56,57,59,60,61,116,117,118,119,122,123,124,125

Pete Turner was born in Albany, New York and currently works from a studio in New York City. A seven month expedition to Africa for National Geographic magazine was an early turning point in his career and Africa has been a constant source of inspiration for him. His editorial photo essays have been published worldwide and he has worked on advertising commissions for many major clients, while pursuing personal work. His photographs are in the permanent collections of major museums and he has received over 300 awards from various design groups and photographic associations.
Website: www.peteturner.com
pages 10,11

Dick Verwoerd lives in Amersfoot, Holland and has been working as a photographer since 1978. He mainly works in the fields of advertising, architecture and travel photography. His company, Lighthouse Productions, also specialises in web design and multimedia.
Website: www.euronet.nl/~verwoerd
E-mail: verwoerd@euronet.nl
pages 94,95

Joan Wakelin has travelled widely during her 30 years as a photojournalist and has had a lifelong fascination with the Far East. She has had many individual and joint exhibitions and her awards include an Honorary Fellowship of the Royal Photographic Society in 1992.
pages 82,103

Acknowledgements

Many thanks to all the photographers who contributed their pictures and their time to this book. Thanks also to Angie Patchell at RotoVision and to Brenda Dermody and Austin Carey for the design.